The Education Invasion

The Education Invasion

HOW COMMON CORE FIGHTS PARENTS FOR CONTROL OF AMERICA'S KIDS

Joy Pullmann

ENCOUNTER BOOKS

New York · London

First American edition published in 2017 by Encounter Books, an activity of Encounter for Culture and Education, Inc., a nonprofit, tax exempt corporation.
Encounter Books website address: www.encounterbooks.com

Manufactured in the United States and printed on acid-free paper. The paper used in this publication meets the minimum requirements of ANSI/NISO Z39.48-1992 (R 1997) (*Permanence of Paper*).

FIRST AMERICAN EDITION

LIBRARY OF CONGRESS CATALOGING-IN-PUBLICATION DATA

Names: Pullmann, Joy, 1986-
Title: The education invasion : how Common Core fights parents for control of American kids / by Joy Pullmann.
Description: New York : Encounter Books, [2017] | Includes bibliographical references and index.
Identifiers: LCCN 2016011694 (print) | LCCN 2016024531 (ebook) |
ISBN 9781594038815 (hardcover : alk. paper) | ISBN 9781594038822 (Ebook)
Subjects: LCSH: Common Core State Standards (Education) | Education—Standards—United States. | Education—Parent participation—United States.
Classification: LCC LB3060.83 .P85 2017 (print) | LCC LB3060.83 (ebook) |
DDC 379.1/58—dc23
LC record available at https://lccn.loc.gov/2016011694

CONTENTS

What Happened to My Children's School?

MICHELLE FURTADO'S SON and twin daughters attended the same schools in Fairhaven, Massachusetts. When the girls started middle school, three years after their brother, Furtado began noticing a marked difference in their school experience. Her son's education had been "very disciplined and structured" since kindergarten, she told me over the phone, but with her daughters, "now we hold hands instead of doing our work."

There was worry in Furtado's Boston-accented voice. Her daughters were spending a lot of time in assemblies talking about feelings and playground altercations, leaving less time for class. Teachers had stopped assigning homework. To learn about medieval history in middle school, the students watched *Monty Python and the Holy Grail*, a campy British spoof film. At Christmastime, they saw the movie *Elf*. Furtado considered such things a huge waste of time her kids could otherwise spend actually learning.

"Had I not noticed what my son had, I would not have known what my daughters were not getting," she said. "My daughters are getting far less than I got." She thought the instruction had lost rigor and expectations had become too lax. "I don't want my kids to have a pretty close answer. I want them to have the right answer." Declining academic quality in American schools has been a subject of concern for nearly a century, but the recently launched Common Core State Standards Initiative, touted as a remedy, has hastened the intellectual and cultural descent.]

Furtado views the loosening academic standards as a breach of contract. She has done her part for her children's education, volunteering at school about twenty hours a week through the years, attending school board meetings or watching them on local television, and refusing to let her kids watch TV or play video games until their homework is finished. But her local schools are no longer doing *their* part.

"What I see just aches me," she said. "I tell teachers, 'I send my sponges to you.' My kids have been read to and read to and read to.... When I see the school trying to destroy what I tried to build, it bothers me. If kids' parents are not paying attention, they're not going to see this."

The biggest change Furtado noticed was in her daughters' math classes. Like their brother, the girls had earned a place in advanced math when they entered middle school, which would have put them on track to complete algebra in the eighth grade. This in turn would have meant they could finish calculus in high school, giving them a high chance of success in any college pursuits involving math and science.

Massachusetts was one of only two states (along with California) that had rearranged its elementary curriculum in 2001 so more students could take algebra in eighth grade, which is standard in high-achieving countries. In 2010, more than half of Massachusetts students were completing algebra on that timetable. The state's restructuring of its curriculum requirements, combined with tougher exams for teachers, was key to propelling Massachusetts from mediocre K-12 achievement to international distinction. In 2005, it became the first state to attain the top ranking in both math and reading at both of the tested grade levels on the National Assessment of Educational Progress, a set of tests the U.S. Department of Education administers to random samplings of children in every state at least every two years. Massachusetts repeated that feat in 2007 and 2009. It wasn't only rich, white kids who benefited from high academic expectations, either. [In fact, poor and minority children made the greatest gains.] The state's high expectations gave any child who happened to live in Massachusetts an edge over kids everywhere else in the country.

Furtado had been looking forward to seeing her girls achieve the same success in math that got their older brother into one of the state's prestigious, competitive-entrance technical high schools. But when her daughters started attending Hastings Middle School in Fairhaven in fall 2011, she found that advanced math classes had suddenly disappeared. All the students in a grade were placed in the same math class. High achievers like the Furtado girls could take an additional "enrichment period" every other day, but would not receive advanced instruction in the new, mandatory math class.

Alarmed at the loss of high-quality math instruction for her daughters, Furtado emailed a math teacher to ask what happened. The teacher explained that a consultant had ended the advanced math classes and recommended a new curriculum called the Connected Math Program (CMP). Over protests from the math department, administrators insisted that teachers use the program, which is notorious for promoting "fuzzy math" in which kids spend more time discussing hypothetical scenarios that involve math than learning to do math procedures. "Many students struggled with the program," the teacher wrote to Furtado, "but we were told by [the consultant and the principal] that we were not getting rid of CMP and that the students would get better with it as time went on."

After a few months of talking with other parents and quizzing teachers and administrators to find out why her daughters were getting less rigorous math instruction than her son had received, Furtado stumbled onto something much larger than the Connected Math Program. She learned that Massachusetts had recently joined most of the other states in replacing their curriculum requirements with a new set of national standards. "I finally came across Common Core," she said, "and all the puzzle pieces fell into place."

What Is Common Core?

The Common Core State Standards are a 640-page set of blueprints for K-12 math and English curriculum and tests. This initiative is the biggest education overhaul in the United States since No Child Left Behind, which in 2001 mandated that schools focus on standardized tests in math and reading in exchange for a gush of federal funds, and established penalties for low-performing schools such as forced restructuring, mass staff layoffs, open enrollment in nearby districts, and loss of funds. But NCLB left it to the states to formulate their own standards and tests. Common Core goes further: it specifies what a set of unelected committees thought every child should "know and be able to do" at each grade level. The introduction to the curriculum requirements says the document lays out "a vision of what it means to be a literate person in the twenty-first century." That vision somewhat resembles the way we think of our electronic devices: "The Standards are intended to be a living work," the introduction explains, so "as new and better evidence emerges, the Standards will be revised accordingly."[2]

The Common Core idea of "a literate person in the twenty-first century" differs fundamentally from the conception of the human person that inspires classical education, a more timeless and transcendent view of human nature. In the classical vision, the human person has a soul that needs to be nourished on what is enduringly good, true, and beautiful, as expressed in civilized man's greatest achievements – in literature and art, in politics and science. Classical education also equips children with time-tested intellectual tools to navigate the world, including efficient ways of doing math.

Common Core falls short in both respects – in building a solid foundation of cultural knowledge and in teaching practical skills. Instead, it serves up cumbersome process requirements wrapped in obscure jargon. Here's the kindergarten English standard labeled RF.K.3.b (which is code for Reading: Foundational Skills, Kindergarten, standard 3.b): "Associate the long and short sounds with the common spellings (graphemes) for the five major vowels." This might sound sophisticated to many adults, but it's almost completely incoherent, as Dr. Terrence Moore demonstrates:

> Presumably the authors of the standard are telling teachers to teach children the long and short sounds of the vowels. But that is not what it says. Rather, students are supposed to associate (know?) the long and short sounds when they see "the common spellings ... for the five major vowels." What?
>
> Now ask yourself: How many ways are there to spell the letter A? I can only think of one, unless you mean to distinguish between capitals and lower case, which is not what is being said. A is always spelled A.... Why learn only the short and long sounds? Every vowel except for *e* has more than a long and a short sound. The letter A, for example, has four sounds: /ă/, /ā/, /ah/, /aw/, as in *at, tape, want, talk*. Consider the word *father*. You do not call your father your făther, nor your fāther. Yet this simple truth about the code that is

the English alphabet is lost on the very people who are in charge of writing "standards" for our children's schools.[3]

This is just one example of the nonsense that "education experts" have determined to be the optimal way to teach language skills. Moore collects many others in *The Story Killers: A Common-Sense Case Against the Common Core*. His book is the place to go for a thorough critique of the standards and the kind of curriculum they spawn.

Common Core kills stories in part by recommending that children read progressively less fiction and more "informational text" as they go through school.[4] It suggests assigning sections of the U.S. Code, for instance, which consumes time that could be better spent on studying classic literature. The emphasis on nonfiction does not mean students will get a solid grounding in a cohesive body of cultural knowledge, as some proponents have claimed. Far from it. An appendix to Common Core does mention elements of cultural knowledge that are central to a classical education, but it mangles them, as Moore points out. For example, it selectively quotes the Bill of Rights and then recommends blatantly biased secondary materials to interpret it as a racist, sexist document. As for the fiction on the recommended reading list, some of it is rather disturbing. The list for high school students includes *The Bluest Eyes*, a Toni Morrison novel featuring graphic descriptions of pedophilia, incest, and child rape.[5] Among the other books on the list are *Black Swan Green* and *Dreaming in Cuban*, which also include graphic descriptions of sex and sexual violence.[6]

While the language standards are deficient in the good and beautiful, the math standards bring counterproductive complication to the enduringly true. Common Core introduces standard mathematical algorithms a year or two later than the world's highest-achieving countries do, and it revives what was mocked as "fuzzy math" not long ago. The document is replete with calls for "visual models" and time-wasting techniques for solving problems, as in this "number system" standard for sixth grade (6.NS.1): "Interpret and compute quotients of fractions, and solve word problems involving division of fractions by fractions, e.g., by using visual fraction models and equations to represent the problem. For example, create a story context for $\frac{2}{3}$ divided by $\frac{3}{4}$ and use a visual fraction model to show the quotient . . . ."[7] This kind of demand drew a vigorous critique from Marina Ratner, an internationally respected professor emerita of mathematics at the University of California at Berkeley. "Who would draw a picture to divide ⅔ by ¾?" she asked. "This requirement of visual models and creating stories is all over the Common Core. The students were constantly told to draw models to answer trivial questions." What's worse, "A student who gives the correct answer right away (as one should) and doesn't draw anything loses points." In Ratner's judgment, the Common Core math standards are inferior not only to those of high-achieving countries but also to the old California state standards.[8]

A mother in Indiana named Heather Crossin learned about the new demands for inefficient methods in fall 2011, around the same time Michelle Furtado began her investigation. Crossin's third-grade daughter brought home an assignment to determine which of two bridges was longer, one that measured 448 feet or another that was 407 feet, and to explain how she arrived at her answer. Simple enough, right? The girl correctly picked the 448-foot bridge, but the teacher marked her answer incorrect because she hadn't returned a scripted response to the question of how she knew, like this: "I compared the addends in the hundreds column, and saw that four and four were equal. Then I compared the addends in the tens column, and saw that four was greater than zero. Then I compared the addends in the ones column, and saw that eight was larger than seven."[9] Crossin objected, saying her daughter could practice ten math problems in the time it would take to answer a single one in that fashion. She thought such a time-wasting exercise deprived her daughter of practical math fluency, and the research backs her up.[10]

Frustrated parents across the nation have been piling up examples of similarly convoluted or incomprehensible math assignments on social media. Young children are taught to add by making hundreds of dots. Traditional ways of doing arithmetic – such as stacking numbers and adding up the columns from right to left – are prohibited. Math problems require many more steps than necessary. Children cry over homework assignments that take them (and their parents) hours to figure out. Parents wonder why the "experts" are making things so complicated and abandoning methods that have worked for generations.

Spreading Tentacles

Common Core starts by dictating what kids must encounter in class, but then it goes much further. Its creators and supporters have linked that one set of documents with myriad other mandates and programs, so its tentacles extend across the whole educational landscape. That wide reach is achieved mainly through the second major component of Common Core: the federally funded tests that influence not just curriculum, but also school funding, teachers' job security, data collection on kids, college acceptance, and much more.

Because the SAT and the ACT (the main national college entrance exams) and the GED (a test that can be taken in place of completing high school) have been aligned with Common Core, these curriculum benchmarks are affecting schools that technically don't have to follow them – charter schools, private schools, even homeschools – and their influence filters into the handful of states that have not signed on. So almost every school in the country has been scrambling to adjust its curriculum to meet what Common Core demands. It's fair, then, to say that the Common Core apparatus touches virtually everything about American education.

Common Core is as big a change in education as Obamacare is in health care, but unlike Obamacare it needed no votes in Congress to become national policy. It garnered practically no notice from the media before the Obama administration, in concert with largely unelected state bureaucrats and a shadow bureaucracy of private organizations, locked it in nationwide. That meant no public debate before the scheme was imposed upon a country supposedly run with the consent of the governed. Reams of substantive criticism have emerged only after the fact, along with data indicating that Common Core has actually set back student achievement.

Let's look again at the National Assessment of Educational Progress, where Massachusetts made impressive gains after its curriculum revision in 2001. NAEP results in 2015 showed a small decline in math scores – a reversal of the upward trend. In the interim, Massachusetts had lowered its math standards to match most other states, instead of remaining an exemplar that motivated them to reach higher. Because Massachusetts still ranked ahead of the other states overall, the outgoing education secretary, Arne Duncan, held it up as a national model for education.[11] A sensible education policy would have expanded on what Massachusetts had been offering its children when the NAEP scores were climbing. Instead, Duncan spent his tenure in the Obama administration pushing America's schools in a different direction. That may explain why nearly every other state showed declining student achievement across subjects, especially math, for the first time in twenty-five years – that is, since the NAEP began measuring achievement in every state.

According to Tom Loveless, an education researcher at the Brookings Institution, many schools have been using the Common Core mandates to justify *reducing* their math expectations. NAEP data showed that the percentage of schools teaching algebra in the eighth grade had dropped in 2015 for the first time in a decade, from 33 percent to 29 percent nationally.[12] Parents throughout the San Francisco Bay Area and elsewhere were complaining because their middle schools had changed algebra from an eighth-grade default to a special class only for advanced students – because of Common Core.

Michelle Furtado and Heather Crossin were far from the only parents spurred to ask questions about what was happening to her children's education. As Common Core has unfurled in schools across the country, public opposition has swelled.[13] Angry citizens have been pressing their elected representatives to reassess their states' commitment to the national standards and associated tests. But instead of backing down, Common Core's advocates are digging in and sneaking their scheme in through the back door whenever it's sent out the front.

At its heart, Common Core is about who controls education. With its bureaucratic enforcement structure and centralized, command-and-control model, it accelerates the nationalization of American education, further eroding our tradition of local school governance. And few Americans – parents or teachers – have been given the chance to participate in deciding whether this is something our country really wants.

CHAPTER 1

Origins — Nationalizing Education under the Radar

J AMIE HIGHFILL ENTERED the classroom in 2002 as an eighth-grade English teacher in Fayetteville, Arkansas. A Gulf War veteran, she had no idea that she was stepping onto another battlefield.

Highfill quickly proved to be an excellent teacher. Her specialty was preparing students for Advanced Placement classes in high school, which can earn students college credit. In 2005, she was selected as codirector of the Northwest Arkansas Writing Project at the University of Arkansas, a local affiliate of an international writing program that attracts some of the world's best teachers. In 2011, the Arkansas Council of Teachers of English Language Arts named her Middle School English Teacher of the Year. In the 2011-12 school year, 77 percent of her students scored "advanced" on state tests.[1] That's an amazing success rate. Typically, no more than one-quarter of students score "advanced" on state English tests, even the less rigorous ones.

Highfill's eighth graders learned about comedy and political satire from James Thurber's "The Secret Life of Walter Mitty" and O. Henry's "The Gift of the Magi." They read Arthurian legends, poems by Robert Frost and Emily Dickinson, and George Orwell's *Animal Farm*. They learned about internal dialogue, quest literature, parody, and symbolism.

15

Highfill's guide for choosing assignments was Henry David Thoreau's maxim, "Read the best books first, or you might not have a chance to read them at all."[2]

When Arkansas signed on to the Common Core curriculum mandates in 2010 – to be followed later by national tests to enforce them – Highfill joined the committee her school convened to decide how to put the mandates into place. Schools across the country created similar committees.

In the era of "education accountability," curriculum mandates spell out the learning requirements that annual tests assess. The national Common Core tests measure only reading and math to fulfill the federal mandates, but Common Core actually asserts authority over the entire curriculum, since its English mandates also apply to "literacy in history/ social studies, science, and technical subjects."[3] A series of grant competitions and executive rewrites of federal education law during the first year of the Obama presidency ensured that Common Core would determine far more than what teachers hand to children in the classroom. The administration required schools to use Common Core test results in evaluating, ranking, hiring, firing, and even redistributing teachers, and required states to use the results to judge and rank schools and even to take them over from local authorities.

Unlike most teachers, Highfill had paid attention to how Common Core became her boss. When she got a look at the mandates, she was dismayed at what they would do to the extraordinarily rich lessons she had been providing her students.

In language arts, Common Core explicitly requires schools to give "much greater attention to a specific category of informational text – literary nonfiction – than has been traditional." A graph included in the standards document shows an increasing nonfiction intake through the school years: 50 percent in fourth grade, 55 percent in eighth grade, 70 percent in twelfth grade.[4] This requirement alarmed Highfill, who had achieved great success with her students by feeding them a diet replete with poetry and short stories and classic novels.

"Where is the research that proves more nonfiction is better for students?" she asked. "What about inferencing skills that you only get with fiction and poetry? That was my whole issue: please, tell me where the research says this is better for kids." Indeed, research indicates that students' experience with high-quality *fiction* is a major predictor of their college success, while it finds nothing of the kind for nonfiction.[5]

Highfill expressed her concerns to some colleagues. When administrators asked teachers what they thought about Common Core, Highfill and others began pointing out its flaws, but the principal said, "You guys are being too negative." The administration, said Highfill, "wanted us to accept the document lock, stock, and barrel."

She had to toss out six weeks' worth of poetry lessons and a favorite unit on Arthurian legends to make way for light nonfiction (but not always scientifically accurate) reading, such as a chapter from Malcolm Gladwell's *The Tipping Point*.[6] And she could no longer select her own reading assignments. The school had hired a curriculum consultant who, like all of Common Core's main authors, had no experience in English teaching or research. This consultant required teachers to reorganize their curriculum around vague nonliterary themes such as "how the world affects our decision to do the right thing."[7]

"We'd all bring our [lesson] ideas, and the consultant would consistently say, 'You can't use that, it's not the Lexile level,'" Highfill recalled. "So eventually people stopped suggesting things" and resigned themselves to following the consultant's "suggestions."

Hold it — what on earth is a "Lexile level"? Well, Common Core requires that students read books at or slightly above their grade level, and it recommends using algorithms to determine those levels. The Lexile Framework is a computer program that runs such algorithms. The Common Core document even shows which Lexile levels correspond to which Common Core grade levels.[8] The problem with these computerized measurements of readability is that they routinely make silly mistakes. The Lexile Framework rates *The Grapes of Wrath*, for instance, as a second-grade book.[9] Computers can judge things like vocabulary and sentence length, but not the more abstract qualities of literature such as irony, syntax, and metaphor.

Highfill began expressing her frustrations on the widely read blog of Diane Ravitch, a historian of education. She also talked to a *Washington Post* reporter, Lyndsey Layton, in December 2012. "With informational text, there isn't that human connection that you get with literature," she told Layton. "And the kids are shutting down. They're getting bored. I'm seeing more behavior problems in my classroom than I've ever seen."[10]

That *Post* article was one of the first in a mainstream publication to include criticism of Common Core. It went viral.

Within weeks, Highfill found herself in the principal's office. The ostensible complaint was that her students' writing on Common Core practice tests was "too good." Yes, really. The testing machines could not rate their essays because the writing was too complex – like the high-quality literature Highfill gave her students. Apparently, eliciting excellent student work was now "professional insubordination." Highfill said the principal told her, "This cannot happen again," then required her to complete an "improvement plan," which included a ban on talking to the media. This plan also brought in a district administrator to sit in the back of her class every week and to review every lesson plan from that point forward.

When I contacted Highfill for an interview soon after her remarks appeared in the *Washington Post*, she wanted first to review with her union representative whether she had any speech protections in her contract that would allow her to give the interview without imperiling her job. After a few weeks, she decided it didn't matter. She was quitting.

"It's not just happening to me, it's happening everywhere," Highfill said, speaking in a rush of heartfelt frustration, "and it's happening to good teachers. They're being given ultimatums to stop talking, stop becoming activists."

She's right. This is happening across the country, and it means that millions of American children are losing out on some world-class instruction, even as pundits once again raise alarms about the nation's academic mediocrity. The teachers who stick it out are being forced to feed their students mental junk food, according to some of the country's top academics and researchers. Since the mandates were published in 2010, scholars in psychology, child development, education, mathematics, and literature have come out with a variety of substantive criticisms, most prominently in dozens of studies published by Boston's Pioneer Institute. Another report, published in 2015, concluded that "Common Core reading requirements for kindergarten are inappropriate and not well-grounded in research," and are likely to set children back academically.[11] It recommended immediately yanking Common Core's kindergarten standards.

A literacy researcher who helped write Common Core, Dr. Louisa Moats, sharply criticized the final product in 2014, saying, "We drafted sections on Language and Writing Foundations that were not incorporated into the document as originally drafted." She continued:

Classroom teachers are confused, lacking in training and skills to implement the standards, overstressed, and the victims of misinformed directives from administrators who are not well grounded in reading research. I'm beginning to get messages from very frustrated educators who threw out what was working in favor of a new "CCSS aligned" program, and now find that they don't have the tools to teach kids how to read and write.[12]

Why didn't the critics speak out earlier, when their input could have improved the final product, or deep-sixed it? Because there *was* no public discussion of Common Core before the education-industrial complex pushed states into this ill-considered scheme. Teachers are now left to deal with the mess that credentialed "experts" with no classroom experience have made — unless they decide that dealing with it is not worth the trouble.

Highfill had an easier out than some: she got married in the summer of 2013 and moved to Virginia. So a top-notch teacher and Navy veteran left the field after eleven years. "I miss being in the classroom," she said a few weeks before her wedding. "I miss watching their eyes glow when they get excited about learning. So I don't think I'm going to be out of the classroom for a long time. But after last year I felt like a break was in order. I'm hoping that by the time I go back all of this Common Core nonsense will be gone. This is a behemoth."

Unfortunately, if Highfill waits until Common Core disappears, she will have to wait a long time. Despite swelling opposition from parents and teachers across the country, it remains embedded in almost every classroom in America. It even affects the four states that didn't adopt the mandates when Common Core steamrolled the country in 2010 — Virginia, Nebraska, Texas, and Alaska. It sounds like a national curriculum, doesn't it? But that's illegal. So how did it come about?

The "State-Led" Façade

In the "Myths and Facts" section of the initiative's website, we read that "Common Core is a state-led effort that is not part of No Child Left Behind or any other federal initiative. The federal government played no role in the development of the Common Core."[13] The U.S. secretary of education,

Arne Duncan, used the "state-led" argument in various public statements, including a major speech defending Common Core before a convention of journalists in 2013.[14] It was crucial for Common Core's creators that it not technically be a federal project, although the federal government has been funding curriculum models and overseeing state tests for decades.[15] Yes, it has, even though the U.S. Constitution gives no powers over education to the federal government, and even though the three major federal education laws that define the currently existing, extraconstitutional federal role in education explicitly prohibit federal meddling in curriculum or test content.[16]

The laws are this way because Americans have consistently objected to federal control over what children learn. According to the 2014 PDK/Gallup poll on public attitudes about education, 84 percent of Americans say that states or local school boards, not the federal government, "should have the greatest influence in deciding what is taught" in local schools.[17] The poll questions changed slightly in a 2015 follow-up, which still showed that "Only one in five Americans believe the federal government should play a role" in K-12 testing, curriculum, accountability, or funding.[18] Common Core effectively means the opposite, which is a reason the 2015 poll found twice as many Americans against it as in favor. Opposition included majorities of whites, Hispanics, public-school parents, Republicans, and independents.[19]

Aware of Americans' strong preference for local control of education, Common Core's originators ran it through a series of private nonprofit organizations, trying at the same time to make the project appear "state-led." In so doing, they followed the nationalization strategy a Brookings Institution paper recommended in 2000.[20] The paper describes attempts by big government and big business to nationalize and standardize American education during the 1980s and 1990s, particularly with the Goals 2000: Educate America Act of 1994. The law provided for a national council to review and approve state curriculum guidelines in all grades and subjects, but the specter of a "national school board" became a political issue in the 1994 election season. A set of federally sponsored history standards drew widespread public criticism, leading to a 99-1 Senate resolution opposing their certification. Consequently, the council to approve state standards never materialized.

To get around those pesky American rubes and their antiquated ideas about individual liberty and local authority, the Brookings paper suggested a backdoor approach: nonprofit organizations could "assert a national interest in education without having to defend themselves against the charge of wanting to become a national school board."[21] Accordingly, the Common Core project was led by a collection of private lobbying groups, with a handful of public officials adding their names, including a few former governors: James Hunt (North Carolina), Richard Riley (South Carolina), and Bob Wise (West Virginia).[22] At most, only a minuscule fraction of the nation's elected state officials had a part in developing this "state-led" initiative.

Common Core grew under the radar, then, making almost no news until it was a done deal. While media outlets of all sizes and audiences were giving copious attention to the Obamacare debate that raged in summer 2010, they published close to nothing about the education mandates that came out around the same time. The backlash took a few years to swell because people can't protest what they don't know is coming.

I first heard about Common Core in fall 2012 from Heather Crossin, the Indianapolis mother we met in the prologue who objected to the convoluted math her daughter was being taught. Then I started trying to figure out who exactly made it, and by what process. I contacted every major organization that was openly named as having a hand in it, as well as several dozen of the individuals listed as contributors on Common Core documents. Nearly all refused an interview; others simply ignored my repeated emails and phone calls.

A Gates-Led Scheme

Once Common Core had actually become news, and four years after it gained control of American education, three top Core-pushers sought a *Washington Post* interview.[23] This is a common public relations technique for trying to contain negative press, which at that point was increasing rapidly: Reach out to a friendly reporter and offer an exclusive interview where you "reveal" your side of the story. The interviewees carefully prep their tale. It's called "staying on message" and "controlling the narrative."

The *Post* article that appeared in June 2014 featured Bill Gates, whose foundation funded almost the entire project; David Coleman, one of Common Core's five "lead writers," dubbed "the architect of Common Core" by media outlets; and Gene Wilhoit, who served as president of the

Council of Chief State School Officers while it midwifed Common Core. CCSSO is a private networking and lobbying organization that has pushed national curriculum mandates for decades and was explicitly named as a potential vehicle for national standards in the Brookings paper cited above.

"One summer day in 2008," the *Post* reported, Coleman and Wilhoit visited the Gates Foundation's massive Seattle compound of glass-encased, V-shaped offices. It's only logical they went to Gates. The three biggest education grant makers are the Bill and Melinda Gates Foundation, the Eli and Edythe Broad Foundation, and the Walton Family Foundation. Gates is by far the largest. In total assets, Walton has $1.7 billion,[24] Broad, $2.2 billion,[25] and Gates, $37 billion,[26] according to public tax documents.

Coleman and Wilhoit pushed Gates to bankroll Common Core, citing the high remediation rates for U.S. college freshmen and the need for nationally interchangeable K-12 curriculum. A poor K-12 system drags down the economy, they noted. A few weeks later, Wilhoit told the *Post*, Gates called and said he was in.

And how. Gates's foundation, the richest in the world, gave CCSSO an initial $10 million grant to have people write Common Core, and began sending millions of dollars to every conceivable organization in the United States to grease the skids. Gates paid to have lobbyists prod lawmakers to adopt Common Core, to help teachers unions write curriculum and coordinate public relations campaigns, to have researchers compare Common Core with existing state curriculum standards (and, unsurprisingly, pronounce the former superior) – you name a Common Core component, Gates paid for it.

The Gates Foundation has given millions to state and federal departments of education, and to national teachers unions. It has spent hundreds of thousands to "assist state education agencies in tying teacher evaluations to Common Core." It has spent millions to sponsor forums where advocacy groups have lobbied governors, state school board members, state lawmakers, local school board members, business leaders, teachers, military representatives, and other key groups to accept and promote Common Core. It has given millions toward developing "parent advocacy training modules."

From 2009 to June 2016, the Gates Foundation dished out $384,605,464 in Common Core-related grants. The greater part of it, some $269 million, went to public relations efforts, such as training teachers to go on camera for TV ads, and gathering lawmakers in posh locales to explain how wonderful Common Core will be for the nation.[27] Two years after that 2008 meeting in Seattle between Gates, Coleman, and Wilhoit, forty-five states and the District of Columbia had accepted Common Core, to nearly no public fanfare. Wyoming signed on the following year, bringing the total to forty-six states.

"Without the Gates money, we wouldn't have been able to do this," said Kentucky's education commissioner, Terry Holliday, to the *Post*. Holliday was on CCSSO's board of directors while it facilitated Common Core, and subsequently became its president. And he wasn't kidding about the Gates money. But throwing money at everything labeled "Common Core" was only a part of Gates's influence peddling, which has since sparked debate among wonks and watchdogs over whether some of its activities served as a cloak for government actions and amounted to tax-free, disclosure-free lobbying.

Over the years, the Gates Foundation has steadily increased its grants for education, particularly for advocacy, said Sarah Reckhow, a political science professor at Michigan State University who has studied education philanthropists. She calculated that 20 percent of its education grants went to advocacy in 2010, while its grants to schools had dropped from 50 percent in 2005 to 25 percent.[28] A quarter of education spending by the Gates and Broad foundations in 2010 went to nationwide advocacy of Common Core, Reckhow later found.[29] The same trend has been noted in education philanthropy generally: large education foundations such as Gates, Broad, and Walton have moved from sponsoring local charity to sponsoring political activism.[30] The reason is that in a centralized system it's easier to influence the few people who have power than to convince the public at large to go along with one group's agenda.

Philanthropists "don't have an obvious constituency," Reckhow observed. "Teachers unions represent teachers. Who does the Gates Foundation represent?"

Manufacturing Consensus

The Gates Foundation confirmed but did not return my repeated calls and emails requesting comment on their role in developing and promoting

Common Core, but employees have granted other interviews. After all, "systemic changes" require advocacy, as Allan Golston, president of Gates's U.S. program, told the *New York Times* in 2011. Gates funds myriad seemingly grassroots education groups, the *Times* article noted.[31] An academic study Reckhow coauthored with Megan Tompkins-Stange in 2014 that includes anonymous interviews with Gates employees found this was a deliberate strategy to build an ersatz grassroots movement. "All of these organizations suddenly singing from the same hymnbook are all getting money from the same organization," one Gates official said, adding, "we fund almost everyone who does advocacy."[32]

Gates funds advocacy not just to influence lawmakers directly, but also to influence the groups that influence lawmakers, thereby creating a kind of echo chamber, a Gates employee explained. An organization with the size and resources of Gates "can make grants to lots of organizations to promote a certain message not just ... with government but also with business and with the public."[33]

This kind of manufactured "consensus," disguised as a grassroots movement, muddied the waters for local elected officials when they deliberated over education policy. Take, for example, a January 2013 legislative hearing in Indiana, which would become the first state to repeal Common Core. Among the thirty-two people who testified against the repeal, twenty-six were members of organizations that received money from the Gates Foundation. That's more than three-quarters of the anti-repeal voices. Gates also funded Common Core proponents who came out in force to oppose a repeal bill in Georgia in 2014.[34] I witnessed the same pattern myself when testifying against Common Core in 2014 hearings on similar bills in Wisconsin and Tennessee.

"Gates has a sort of magnetic force" to attract media attention, as well as other donors and politicians, said Reckhow in an interview, noting also "the single-mindedness with which they pursue an agenda." Gates can "crowd out" other interests with its vast resources and elevate its priorities over those of the public at large, in part by creating echo chambers and by hosting fancy events with big-name attendees to buy favor with public officials.

Gates knows it. Buying political influence is a deliberate strategy. "Starting with the governors," one foundation official explained, "we've got to build support at the state level, and once we build support at the state level, then when the dynamics are right, which would have been

2008, and we get an administration – more importantly, an education secretary whose school district benefited from our support – then you've got the ability to drive forward and push it off-balance at the federal level."[35] (We'll return to the point about the education secretary later on.)

The effectiveness of this strategy actually surprised foundation leaders, an insider told Reckhow: "We have this enormous power to sway the public conversations about things like effective teaching or standards and mobilizing lots of resources in their favor without real robust debate.... I mean, it's striking to me, really."[36]

In her book *Follow the Money* (2012), Reckhow suggests that foundation grants are most effective when they support existing local activity, rather than impose outside agendas. The Gates Foundation has instead worked hand in glove with the U.S. Department of Education to "push down into states and localities the consensus they have already arrived at" on policies entangled with Common Core, said Jay Greene, a libertarian-leaning researcher who runs the Department of Education Reform at the University of Arkansas.

Another critic, Kevin Welner, who directs the left-leaning National Education Policy Center at the University of Colorado Boulder, doesn't mind Gates's efforts to influence education policy, but he is concerned about balancing its influence. "I'd like others – particularly [in] the communities that are impacted by the most high-profile school policies – to have at least an equal voice to those from the outside," he said in an email.

Concern over nonprofit activity in politics is bipartisan and has grown considerably since Common Core became national policy. Of the four most prominent education foundations, Gates has taken the most criticism, according to a study by Michael McShane and Jenn Hatfield for the American Enterprise Institute. They note that criticism of education philanthropy has been coming from the left for many years, but "it was really the Common Core that brought the right flank of journalists and activists into the fight against education philanthropy and helped the pushback swell to its current levels."[37]

McShane and Hatfield also found that news coverage of education philanthropy has remained mostly positive. In this connection, it's important to point out that the Gates Foundation gives millions of dollars to major news outlets to cover education. Beneficiaries include the industry flagship *Education Week* ($9,981,027 so far), which has received several grants specifically for reporting on Common Core;[38] the Education Writers

Association ($5,164,437);[39] *EdSource*, an education blog ($3,647,354);[40] *Chalkbeat*, an education news website ($797,444);[41] the *Hechinger Report*, a prominent education outlet;[42] and the *Atlantic*'s education reporting ($307,505 in 2015).[43]

Foundations often fund both research and activism, according to Scott Thomas, dean of Claremont Graduate University's education school. "It's the way [Gates is] doing it that we think is curious. It's an intrusion into the public sphere more directly that has not been seen before. They're jumping into the policy process itself. That's an interesting position, for a nonprofit to be involved in things that look a lot like lobbying."

It is flatly illegal for nonprofit, 501(c)3 organizations, including the Gates Foundation,[44] to lobby public officials or engage in other direct political activity, such as endorsing candidates. People and organizations that do lobby public officials are subject to heavy federal and state regulations and disclosure rules that nonprofits are not. Nonprofits found or suspected to have violated their tax status may face IRS investigation and prosecution. The Obama IRS has found time to harass smalltime, conservative-minded nonprofit groups – leading to several years of congressional and Justice Department investigation of IRS activity – but apparently it has not had time to check into the Gates Foundation, despite weighty evidence that this massive private organization essentially directed U.S. education policy. Doing so would mean acknowledging that the administration has participated in what could at best be called ethically dubious behavior.

Reckhow labels big education foundations a "shadow bureaucracy" whose activities in crafting and advocating for education policies cloak the process from ordinary citizens. This is what bothers Alisa Ellis, a Utah mother and grassroots leader known nationally for her criticism of Common Core. Because the standards and tests were incubated in nonprofit organizations, citizens can't find out who makes decisions, what organizations they're working with, what information they take into account, or how much anything costs, as they can when state boards of education or legislatures make policy, Ellis said, because open-records laws do not apply to ostensibly private organizations. In Arkansas, Common Core became law only because "private foundations are making decisions that would normally be left up to a public institution that would be accountable to the taxpayers," said Betty Peters, a member of the state school board.

"I don't think many people will quibble the good intentions of these foundations," said Thomas, "but that they subvert the basic democratic processes designed to help encourage liberty and equality is what we should be concerned about."

The Shadow Bureaucracy

After Gates agreed to pay for Common Core and its gravy train, the political stars aligned for the foundation to become part of a shadow bureaucracy within the federal government when the Obama administration came to office a few months later. One reason for the foundation's previous resistance to getting involved in federal policy was distaste for the George W. Bush administration. A Gates employee told Reckhow, "Particularly back in the day when people didn't like the Bush administration … all federal politics for people in Seattle looked like doing stuff with the Bush administration." Another employee described the shift that occurred with the election of Barack Obama: "It was much more legitimate to be involved with policy post-2008 with Obama."[45]

This post-2008 posture is directly contrary to Bill Gates's presentation of himself and his foundation's work as apolitical. In the *Washington Post* interview in 2014,

> Gates grew irritated … when the political backlash against the standards was mentioned. "These are not political things," he said. "These are where people are trying to apply expertise to say, 'Is this a way of making education better?' At the end of the day, I don't think wanting education to be better is a right-wing or left-wing thing."[46]

If Gates meant what he said – despite contradicting his own employees – he was wrong. It's impossible to be apolitical regarding public education, which is, after all, established by political institutions known as states and funded politically by taxpayers through state force. (If you don't pay the taxes that fund public schools, ultimately you get jailed.) The idea of nonpartisan or apolitical decisions in public policy is a progressive notion that goes back at least to Woodrow Wilson, whose ideal government would consist largely of unelected "experts" who managed everyone else's lives for them, untainted by political concerns – i.e., the will of the people.

Whether it's even possible for anyone to make unbiased "expert" decisions in anything is an old debate. But here's why Gates's "not political" claim about his education activism is an inherently political statement: Conservatives generally favor local control of education because they believe that people tend to abuse power and that good government therefore disperses power and sets limits on it. Progressives are more likely to believe that power doesn't necessarily corrupt, so they are more comfortable with government officials amassing and centralizing power, with advice from "experts" of their choosing. Thus, to insist that unfurling Common Core across the nation isn't a political matter is itself an expression of a *progressive* political viewpoint.

Moreover, Common Core's originators gleefully employed political muscle to spread their agenda nationwide. Because the Gates Foundation saw the Obama administration to be in sync with its own educational vision, four Gates employees went to work in the new administration in 2009. The two who headed to the Department of Education violated the administration's conflict-of-interest policy banning lobbyists from becoming high-ranking federal employees.[47] While interviewing Gates employees, Reckhow and Tompkins-Stange heard "several informants" mention that a number of the education secretary's staff appointments

> were either former Gates officials or former Gates grantees. One informant noted that, "Once Obama was elected, I mean, Gates literally had people sitting at the Department of Education, both formally and informally." These officials included Jim Shelton, assistant deputy secretary for innovation and improvement and former program director of the education program at Gates, and Joanne Weiss, director of the Race to the Top competition and a former partner at the NewSchools Venture Fund, a major Gates grantee that served as an intermediary funder for charter school management organizations.[48]

The new education secretary himself, Arne Duncan, also had Gates connections in his background (as alluded to earlier): while Duncan headed the Chicago Public Schools, the district received more than $47 million from the Gates Foundation.[49] Gates officials told Reckhow and Tompkins-Stange that Duncan was "a linchpin in the partnership between Gates and federal policymakers."[50] Duncan's chief of staff, Margot Rogers, was one of the former Gates employees who needed a conflict-of-interest waiver to join the administration.[51] The relationship between the two organizations was so close that Gates staff had regular phone conversations with Duncan and Shelton while the latter ostensibly worked for taxpayers.[52]

This cabal of former Gates employees and grant recipients basically walked into the White House with Obama, ready to implement the education plan that the foundation, along with employees of the Council of Chief State School Officers (CCSSO), had drafted beforehand. Between Coleman and Wilhoit's conversation with Gates in the summer of 2008 and the day that Obama assumed the presidency, the Gates Foundation cosponsored a paper titled "Benchmarking for Success: Ensuring U.S. Students Receive a World-Class Education." Written by employees of the three organizations that would go on to construct Common Core — CCSSO, the National Governors Association (NGA), and a nonprofit called Achieve, Inc. — the paper envisioned how the federal government could establish a national curriculum and tests (notwithstanding the legal prohibition). Federal policymakers "should offer funds to help underwrite the cost for states" to implement "a common core of internationally benchmarked standards in math and language arts," with new curriculum, assessments, teacher training, and other resources.[53] The paper refered to this effort as the "Common State Standards Initiative."[54]

The Obama administration ultimately didn't have to offer funding for Common Core to be written. Gates paid for that. Instead, the administration ponied up the one thing the federal government is uniquely qualified to provide: pressure, verging on coercion. Before we get to federal force-feeding, however, let's spend a little time talking about the chefs who made this meal of worms. They, too, are part of the shadow bureaucracy.

"Outsourcing a Core State Function"

Who called the shots during the obscure process that brought Common Core into the world? We don't know. As Alisa Ellis noted, the organizations that wrote and pushed Common Core, funded primarily with Gates money, are private and have no obligation to submit to open-records requests or hold public meetings, as state boards of education must do. No one inside NGA, CCSSO, or Achieve is elected by and accountable to voters and taxpayers. And these organizations have been remarkably unresponsive to requests for more information about the document that is up-ending U.S. education.

This is astonishing, not just because Americans are granted by law and tradition the right to govern our own affairs, but also because Common Core exercises so much power over a $620 billion industry that is mostly financed by taxes. The cost of implementing Common Core itself, according to one of the few estimates made, was between $5 and $12 billion.[55] That estimate was made by a Gates-financed organization and reflected its "middle-of-the-road" assessment. The only independent estimate of Common Core's costs nationwide concluded that its roll-out would stick taxpayers with a bill of $16 billion over and above existing tax support for education.[56] Gates assumed the right to direct between $5 billion and $16 billion in tax dollars with very little deliberation on the matter by elected officials in public forums created for that purpose. (Has he ever heard of "No taxation without representation"?)

Common Core was not "written by local school districts," as Ohio's governor and erstwhile presidential candidate, John Kasich, incorrectly told a Cleveland radio audience.[57] The National Governors Association seems to have been the primary initiator of Common Core, with CCSSO and Achieve doing more of the hands-on work. To use a metaphor, NGA was the Mafia don and the other two its henchmen. A 2013 paper by Dane Linn of NGA, titled "Governors and the Common Core," reinforces this educated guess.[58]

Taxpayers have some claim on the activities of NGA, CCSSO, and Achieve, not just because of these organizations' outsized influence on public policy, but also because taxpayers help fund the organizations directly. That's right: American taxpayers financially support meetings they cannot attend, where decisions they cannot influence are made about how their tax dollars are spent and how their children are educated.

NGA and CCSSO are basically clubby interest groups for governors and state superintendents, respectively, but states pay dues to belong, said Emmett McGroarty, director of the American Principles Project's education division. NGA would not release information on member dues to APP, he said. CCSSO did give a generic membership cost, but not what is paid by specific states, a sum that varies.

NGA's spokeswoman would only say, "we consider all governors members of the association," but at least five governors in office during the years of Common Core's emergence and implementation withdrew (or had already withdrawn) their membership publicly and refused to pay dues: those of Florida, Maine, North Dakota, South Carolina, and Texas, all Republicans. Spokesmen for those governors said NGA membership provided too little benefit for the money.

Former governor Rick Perry of Texas withdrew membership in 2003. In 2014 his spokesman Josh Havens said the state's NGA dues had been running $125,000 to $150,000 per year, and the governor "didn't feel that active membership was a smart use of taxpayer funds." Idaho suspended its membership in 2009 for financial reasons, but resumed paying about $40,000 for membership (plus $30,000 for travel to meetings) in 2013, said Jon Hanian, a spokesman for Governor Butch Otter. He explained that the governor "believes states are the laboratory of the republic" and "values sharing his experience as well as sharing the experience of other governors as he crafts public policy."

When Maine's governor, Paul LePage, pulled out of NGA in 2012, he told the *Bangor Daily News*, "I get no value out of those meetings. They are too politically correct and everybody is lovey-dovey and no decisions are ever made."[59] NGA's communications director told the paper that governors *cannot choose to leave*; they are all NGA members even if they don't pay dues. That raises the question why states pay dues at all.

In any case, 38 percent of NGA's revenue comes from taxpayers, according to its 2014 financial report.[60] In 2013-14, NGA's $25.8 million in total revenue included $5.3 million from the feds, $4.5 million from states, $7.9 million from private foundations, and another $2.3 million from corporate sponsors.[61] This has been its general pattern of income distribution for years. In the fiscal year during which Common Core was created, tax dollars provided 50 percent of NGA's revenue.[62] A spokeswoman for NGA referred questions about cash flow to NGA's communications director; neither of the two responded to several follow-up calls and emails.

NGA offers businesses and advocacy groups access to governors at its semiannual meetings. As governor of Virginia, George Allen attended the meetings largely to recruit IBM into his state, but he said the organization "didn't have much of an impact on my decisions as governor.... Not saying it's a bad organization, but we had our own agenda." At NGA meetings, governors play-act at making policy by voting on nonbinding resolutions to express shared priorities, said Allen, but "by the time they vote on a position," the resolutions "get watered down so much any objections are already accommodated." Moreover, NGA has no legal power to commit states to anything without the explicit consent of their legislatures. Yet it obviously has de facto power to influence states, as we'll see.

NGA's counterpart for state superintendents is CCSSO, which makes money partly by charging states to participate in a variety of committees. Membership in each committee costs $16,000 per year per state, and states can participate in several. Indiana, for example, participated in the math and social studies committees in 2012, said Adam Baker, spokesman for the Indiana Department of Education. CCSSO reported $2.5 million in revenue from membership dues in 2014.[63]

CCSSO also receives millions from the federal government. "Approximately 13% and 33% of the Council's revenue and 25% and 34% of accounts receivable were provided by U.S. Department of Education grants or contracts for fiscal years 2011 and 2010, respectively," according to the nonprofit's 2010-11 financial statement.[64] In 2011, CCSSO received $558,000 from the 2009 stimulus bill for working with one of the two federally funded networks that created national Common Core tests. In 2010, the U.S. Department of Education granted those two networks $330 million in stimulus funds. Since Common Core and its tests were released, federal funding as a percentage of CCSSO's revenue has declined to single digits, but the organization still received $1.8 million in federal dollars in 2014.[65]

Heather Crossin heard that CCSSO would be meeting in her hometown of Indianapolis in October 2012 to discuss national social studies mandates as a follow-up to Common Core. She called Michele Parks, a CCSSO meeting planner, and asked if she could attend. Crossin wanted to know what state officials were planning to do to her children with her money. Parks told her she could not attend the meeting. Crossin asked who was on the writing team for the social studies standards, and was told the information "was not available for public release."

According to the organization's meeting webpage, "the Council of Chief State School Officers holds over one hundred meetings per year. CCSSO meetings are closed to the public and attendance is by *invitation only* unless otherwise denoted" (emphasis in the original).[66]

Over a period of ten weeks, I sent dozens of emails and made numerous phone calls to at least six CCSSO spokesmen and personnel asking for access to the Indianapolis meeting or any others. At last, I got an email from Kate Dando in December 2012, long after the meeting had passed, saying: "our meetings/sessions at our meetings are open to press really on a case by case basis," and adding that a few reporters have attended CCSSO meetings, usually on background, which means they cannot directly quote what they hear.

Why not? "It's going to be reported that X state said this about their progress," said Carrie Heath Phillips, CCSSO's Common Core director. "When they have those conversations, we keep that protected, but it depends on the meeting and topic." In other words, public officials are scared to tell the public how well they are managing public resources, and CCSSO provides them private forums to relieve that anxiety. How comforting — for everyone except parents and taxpayers.

Somehow, those two unauthoritative networking forums of governors and state superintendents became serious drivers of education policy for the nation, along with Achieve, which describes itself as "an independent, nonpartisan, nonprofit education reform organization."[67] This third member of the triumvirate has benefited greatly from shepherding Common Core: it received a $186 million federal grant to run one of the two national Common Core test organizations, the Partnership for Assessment of Readiness for College and Careers (PARCC). There's some job security. Achieve continues to receive public money because states contract with it for Common Core tests. Its public tax filing for 2012 shows that these tests raked in $4,830,044 for Achieve that year.[68]

Although we don't know what the people who actually wrote Common Core earned for doing so, the leaders of all its parent organizations have been generously compensated. Michael Cohen had a salary of $311,602 as Achieve's president in 2012.[69] Wilhoit, the fellow who with Coleman had convinced Gates to put his money behind Common Core, made $349,615 in 2011, his last full year with CCSSO.[70] Dane Linn, who directly oversaw the creation of Common Core when he worked for NGA as its education director, got a salary of $222,122 from NGA in 2010.[71] These are comfortable incomes, easily outpacing the pay of most governors, and taxpayer money helped pad them.

In "Governors and the Common Core," Linn wrote, "In my 16 years as director of NGA's education division, I have spearheaded many national initiatives for the organization; few people have had the opportunity to influence state policy the way that I have over this time."[72] How jolly for him. But who elected Linn to "influence state policy"?

NGA has not released what resolution, if any, the governors voted on in 2009 to authorize its subsequent work to develop and promote Common Core. A researcher in Kentucky managed to get a copy of the "memorandum of agreement" that governors signed to kick off the project – not from NGA or CCSSO, but from the Kentucky Department of Education.[73] Signed copies of this memorandum are nestled among the thousands of pages (often deep within unsearchable PDFs) that states submitted to the Obama administration to win education grants from funds supplied in the 2009 stimulus bill, for reasons to be explained.

States have historically created education standards in public meetings, with related documents also a matter of public record, noted Bill Allison, editorial director at the Sunlight Foundation, a public transparency watchdog. But the Common Core process was quite different. "What was behind those policies, what was considered, the different elements that went into them, the ideas that went into them – it's a black box," he said. "The public do have the right to know the laws that are going to affect them and their families, especially when they're paying for them."

Do governors have legal authority to overhaul K-12 policy in their states merely by signing a series of contracts with each other, with private organizations, and with the federal government? Does any private organization have legal authority to formulate state policy? No, and no. The only legal way to authorize "state-led" initiatives is through state legislatures, by constitutionally established processes.

With Common Core, that happened only after the fact, if it happened at all. According to the National Conference of State Legislatures, in only four states did Common Core ever pass through the full state legislature. Almost everywhere else, it passed through the state board of education.[74] Only seven states have elected boards of education, while four have a mix of elected and appointed members.[75] So it was mostly unelected officials who locked states into an overhaul of education policy, with little to inform the public of what they were doing. But the real work of crafting the policy had been done by *private* organizations.

As Allison put it, "The state is outsourcing a core state function to an outside organization that is then outsourcing to other organizations, and you can't have the parental and legislator input you normally should." He added, "Education is the future, and I do think people have the right to know who is writing the curriculum."

How NGA Conjured Up Common Core

The National Governors Association first brought governors directly into the project of nationalizing education standards in June 2008 when it cohosted an education forum with the Gates-funded Hunt Institute,[76] a project of the former North Carolina governor James Hunt Jr. In September that year, NGA announced it was joining with CCSSO and Achieve to "promote international benchmarking of U.S. education performance."[77] The following December, the triumvirate released the "Benchmarking for Success" report calling for national curriculum mandates and tests, and recommending "a strong state-federal partnership" to accomplish that goal.

This chronology demonstrates that Common Core's originators requested federal backing before the project had a name, contrary to their later insistence that the initiative was independent of the federal government. Linn's paper reveals that "[Obama] administration officials were regularly updated about the effort to develop common standards," although he stresses that "they played no role in developing, reviewing, or approving the standards."[78] No role at all – if you don't count the deep professional relationships, the regular phone calls, and the funding streams between the U.S. Department of Education, Gates, NGA, Achieve, and CCSSO.

Over the next few months, the nonprofit triumvirate set about to commission new education standards. No more than a handful of sitting elected officials are named as endorsing the project in the press releases from NGA and Hunt during that time. (NGA spokesmen refused requests for comment.) Most of the governors Linn named as influencing the process were *former* elected officials.

On June 1, 2009, NGA and CCSSO announced that forty-six states (along with three territories) had committed to "joining a state-led process to develop a common core of state standards," but did not explain what "joining" entailed.[79] An education forum sponsored by NGA and the Hunt Institute two weeks later featured direct advocacy for national standards to twenty-one governors and their staff.[80] The organizations did not release the names of attendees at the invitation-only event.

At the forum, Secretary Duncan spoke of national education standards as a federal-state partnership. "[M]y job is to help you succeed" in adopting "common national standards," he told the assembly.[81] States had initiated Common Core, Duncan said, because a commission of fifteen people headed by two former governors and funded by the Gates Foundation had recommended national standards in 2007.[82] The federal government "empowers states to decide what kids need to learn and how to measure it," he noted, adding that one of the ways it would do so was by funding national tests. State-led, indeed!

By the beginning of July, NGA and CCSSO had formed more committees. There were two work groups, with a total of twenty-five members (four of whom sat in both committees), to write standards in math and in English. These twenty-five people included a few professors but no K-12 teachers. There were also two feedback committees to provide research and advice to the writers. The feedback groups together included thirty-three people (again, with four involved in both), mostly professors but with one middle school math teacher.[83] That's only *one* K-12 classroom teacher out of nearly sixty people selected to write or advise on K-12 standards. In September, NGA announced a "validation committee" whose job was to ensure that the standards were "research- and evidence-based," as had been promised.[84] In addition, says Linn, six states formed their own committees of teachers to send comments on drafts to the NGA/CCSSO committees.

According to Mark Bauerlein, an Emory University professor who sat on a feedback committee, the lead writers were David Coleman and Susan Pimentel in English, and Jason Zimba, Phil Daro, and William McCallum in math. Linn points to Coleman and Zimba as the top dogs for what went into the English and math sections, respectively,[85] and neither of them had previous experience writing education standards. None of these five lead writers had ever been a K-12 teacher before being appointed to tell K-12 teachers across the nation how to do their jobs. For some reason, that apparently mattered little to whoever hired them.

The writing process and surrounding discussions were sealed by confidentiality agreements. Feedback committee members weren't sure what effect their advice had, said Bauerlein. "I have no idea how much influence committee members had on the final product. Some of the things I advised made their way into the standards. Some of them didn't. I'm not sure why or how," he said.

Several people on the validation committee said the same: they had no idea what happened to the comments they submitted. James Milgram, a Stanford University professor who sat on the validation committee, described how the "facilitators" for the committee meeting "were virtually impossible to deal with." In an email, he explained, "The facilitators were emphatically trying to not let us act according to our charter, but simply sign or not sign a [final approval] letter when the charter said we had final say over the quality of the final [Common Core] and could revise or rewrite it if we deemed it necessary."

Milgram was one of only two subject-matter experts on the validation committee, meaning the only ones with doctorates and field experience in their specific subjects – Milgram in math, and Sandra Stotsky in English. Both had a large hand in writing the nation's best academic standards, those of California and Massachusetts, respectively.

Five of the twenty-nine people on the validation committee refused to sign off on Common Core. Stotsky told me that she and several others had sent objections in writing to their NGA and CCSSO handlers. But the validation committee's final report does not mention those objections.[86] Stotsky said the report's author told her after it was completed that he had never received any written objections and would have included them if he had.

When government agencies solicit public comments on proposed policies, standard procedure is for the agency to publish all comments submitted and a response to each general line of criticism. This didn't happen with Common Core.

Fed-Led Ed

Common Core supporters were able to piece together their creation behind the closed doors of private foundations, but no private organization could *make* anyone submit to it. A private foundation can *bribe* people, but not even Bill Gates could bribe every state to adopt his favored curriculum model. The federal government could bring muscle. Under the Obama administration, it did.

Proponents of Common Core know that Americans are generally wary of the federal government getting too close to education, so they use the "state-led" label almost obsessively when confronted with concerns about who brewed up the scheme and the extent of federal involvement in it. Prominent Core supporters have echoed the refrain everywhere their platforms have taken them in recent years. Bill Bennett, the Reagan-era education secretary, described Common Core in the *Wall Street Journal* as "a voluntary agreement among states."[87] Jeb Bush, former governor of Florida, opined in 2014 that the opposition to Common Core "has been mostly fueled by President Obama and his administration attempting to take credit for and co-opt a state-led initiative."[88]

So what do the advocates mean by "state-led"? Did an assembly of state officials sit down and write the national standards? Did state legislatures or boards of education initiate and carry out this project? No. Its creators and promoters included practically no elected officials. None of the governors who worked directly on the project were serving in office at the time of their involvement. Elected or even appointed state officials became formally involved only after Common Core appeared as a finished product.

Rather than "state-led," it is far more accurate to call the initiative "special interest-led" or "Gates-led." Common Core was developed within private organizations, in coordination with the Obama administration. It is true that governors and state superintendents signed a "memorandum of agreement" with NGA and CCSSO to kick off the development of Common Core, but that document itself contradicts the "state-led" talking point in two ways.

First, like the "Benchmarking for Success" report that NGA, CCSSO, and Achieve published in 2008, this memorandum *explicitly requests federal involvement* in Common Core, saying there is "an appropriate federal role in supporting this state-led effort."[89] This role was expected to include funding the development of the Common Core standards and the corresponding national tests; giving states "incentives" to adopt the standards and restructure their education systems around them; giving states money to train teachers in Common Core and otherwise move it into place; and changing federal education laws to fit the experiment. The Obama administration subsequently did all these things.

Second, the agreement defines Common Core itself as a set of blueprints not just for curriculum, but also for national tests. Those tests are to enforce the curriculum mandates by measuring how well schools have instructed children in what the document demands. "High quality assessments go hand-in-hand with high quality instruction based on high quality standards. You cannot have one without the other," said Laura Slover, CEO of PARCC, one of the Common Core testing organizations funded by the federal government. "The PARCC states see quality assessments as a part of instruction, not a break from instruction."[90] The Obama administration not only provided the money to develop these tests, as NGA and CCSSO requested, but also directly supervised the process, as we will see.

In short, the federal government was closely involved in building Common Core, according to the initiative's founding documents and leaders. To say otherwise is either the result of ignorance or an exercise in deception.

In 2009, the new Obama administration obliged NGA and CCSSO's request for a "federal-state partnership" to "leverage" states into Common Core. Congress, in its wisdom, had granted the incoming education secretary a $4.35 billion slush fund in the stimulus bill. Duncan decided to turn that money into the grant competition he called Race to the Top (RTT). To get a slice of that pie, states had to explain how they would spend it. The Education Department judged state proposals according to four main criteria. One of these was that a state had adopted or committed itself to adopt "education standards common to a significant number of states."

That definition, then as now, fits only Common Core. Indeed, the final regulations for RTT applications said "a State will earn 'high' points if its consortium [curriculum standards group] includes a majority of the States in the country; it will earn 'medium' or 'low' points if its consortium includes one-half or fewer of the States in the country."[91] Translation: Want to improve your chances of getting some of this money? Adopt Common Core, sight unseen.

Or as Joanne Weiss, who ran RTT as Duncan's chief of staff, put it bluntly in a 2015 paper, "[W]e forced alignment among the top three education leaders in each participating state – the governor, the chief state school officer, and the president of the state board of education – by requiring each of them to sign their state's Race to the Top application."[92] There's that federal muscle.

In its 2014 retrospective on how all this happened – published four years after states had locked themselves into the scheme – the *Washington Post* reported that the Obama administration had actually written the words "Common Core" into its initial RTT grant requirements. But the straightforwardness of this language alarmed Wilhoit. "Those kinds of things cause people to be real suspicious," he told the *Post*. So he got Weiss to delete the words "Common Core" in favor of the euphemism "college-and career-ready" standards.[93]

States had one other option for fulfilling the "college- and career-ready" criterion. They could have all their higher education institutions certify that the state's existing standards would graduate students ready for college with no need for remediation, something no high school diploma has ever certified. Doing so would either pull college down to the level of the average high school graduate or raise high school diploma requirements to a level most students would fail to reach. No state chose that option.

There was little time to do so, anyway. The U.S. Department of Education issued its Race to the Top guidelines on November 19, 2009.[94] The first deadline for states to return applications – which averaged three hundred pages in length, with an additional two hundred pages of appendices[95] – was January 19, 2010. The first *draft* of Common Core would not be released until March. Yet forty states and the District of Columbia submitted applications including pledges to adopt Common Core, whatever it was.[96] Merely applying for a federal grant functioned, in effect, as a contractual promise.

The Gates Foundation sent twenty-four states a total of $2.7 million to pay for consultants who helped write these applications,[97] which may explain why they all looked similar. So much for "competition." Really, there was one competitor: the Gates Foundation. And it was competing on criteria it helped create. So it isn't surprising that fourteen of the sixteen RTT-winning states had crafted their applications with the assistance of Gates-funded consultants.

"The Gates Foundation's agenda has become the country's agenda in education," said Michael Petrilli, vice president of the Thomas B. Fordham Institute, to the *Puget Sound Business Journal* in 2009.[98] Indeed, it has. But again, who elected Gates?

The second deadline for a shot at RTT money was June 1, 2010.[99] At least there was a draft of Common Core available by then, but the final edition would not be published until the following day. During this round of applications, thirty-five states and the District of Columbia renewed their promises to adopt Common Core.[100]

These pledges were yet another reason Common Core went into effect years before voters or parents had any idea what was happening. States' subsequent adoption of Common Core was just a formality. After the mandates were officially published on June 2, it took only thirty-five business days for a majority of states to issue the regulations locking themselves in.[101]

Tennessee was one of the first two RTT winners. Its state board of education unanimously rubberstamped Common Core on July 30, 2010, noting in its meeting minutes, "The verbatim adoption of these standards is required for Race to the Top approval."[102] Connecticut, the other initial winner, followed the same course of action, for the same reasons. The minutes for its state board meeting on July 7 likewise show unanimous approval of Common Core standards "in their entirety" as a mandatory follow-through on the state's RTT promises.[103]

The language of "verbatim adoption" and "in their entirety" is noteworthy because state officials who support Common Core now insist that states "can do as they please with the standards and make changes as they wish," since they own the copyright, as the CCSSO director Chris Minnich told a reporter.[104] The copyright assertion has appeared in a number of state debates over a Common Core repeal. But it's clear from original documents that states had to replace their curriculum mandates with Common Core in order to have a shot at RTT grants, a requirement that state officials clearly understood.

The Obama administration followed the RTT grant inducements with another Common Core ratchet. On September 23, 2011, Duncan unilaterally suspended the No Child Left Behind law (passed in 2001) in favor of direct contracts with states that met his personal education policy preferences, rather than complying with the law. It's not clear this was legal. In fact, two of the top Department of Education lawyers from the George W. Bush administration argued that Bush's signature law gave the secretary no such license.[105] But Duncan went ahead anyway, and congressional leaders did nothing about it except complain flaccidly.

The NCLB waivers lifted legally prescribed sanctions on low-performing schools – such as a possible takeover by a private management company – in exchange for an extralegal requirement that states essentially adopt Common Core. As with the RTT grants, the states could use "college- and career-ready standards" that were "common to a significant number of States," or have state institutions of higher education certify a state's standards on Common Core criteria.[106] Only one state, Minnesota, chose the second option in its initial waiver application. Forty-five states have applied, and all but two of them have received the waivers so far.[107] When Oklahoma repealed Common Core in 2014 and formed a committee to write a replacement, Duncan yanked its NCLB waiver until the state's institutions of higher education quickly certified that Oklahoma's previous curriculum mandates (which were being used in the interim) met federal requirements.

Nationalizing Tests

Still think Common Core was state-led? The federal government, as noted earlier, also funded and oversaw the development of the national tests that constitute the second half of the initiative. In 2010, the Obama administration provided four-year grants totaling $330 million to the Partnership for Assessment of Readiness for College and Careers (PARCC) and the Smarter Balanced Assessment Consortium (SBAC), for the purpose of writing tests aligned with the Common Core curriculum.[108] In return for this largesse, the two organizations submitted to monthly and quarterly meetings and regular conference calls with U.S. Department of Education employees,[109] and to oversight by a specially appointed federal board that had access to and power over every aspect of the tests, down to the specific questions.[110]

PARCC and Smarter Balanced are not just testing organizations. Their grant agreements with the federal government reveal that they have directly written curriculum materials and models for classroom activities.

SBAC's contract with the federal government said the consortium would provide "curriculum analysis tools, [and] professional development related to the new standards and assessments including support for educators to better understand the content of the new standards."[111] Its grant application promised it would provide teachers with "exemplary instructional materials linked to CCSS [Common Core State Standards]"[112] and with "model curriculum and instructional modules that are aligned with the CCSS," as well as training.[113] It would send teachers "recommended readings, focused group discussions, use of online tools, and sharing of annotated examples of best practices and exercises."[114] The organization budgeted $5.125 million in federal funds to contract with yet another organization to develop such "instructional and curriculum resources for educators."[115]

PARCC's federal contract said it would distribute sample test items that "model the kinds of activities and assignments that teachers should incorporate into their classrooms throughout the year."[116] The contract included plans for PARCC to create an online resource with curriculum frameworks for teachers to use in lesson planning.[117] PARCC would also write "model curriculum frameworks" and "exemplar lesson plans."[118] In 2015, Joanne Weiss wrote that "new curriculum materials funded through Race to the Top and released in 2014 are already in use in 20 percent of classrooms nationwide."[119]

Recall that Achieve, the nonprofit that coordinated the writing of Common Core, runs PARCC and should thus be well aware of this federal oversight and involvement. Yet the organization routinely proclaims independence from the feds. For example, when Michigan's legislature was rethinking its commitment to Common Core in 2013, Achieve's president, Michael Cohen, testified to the state house of representatives that the vision of Common Core was for "no federal participation in the process at all – no federal funding, no federal review or involvement."[120] At that very time, Cohen was leading a Common Core testing organization that submitted to monthly oversight calls with federal officials and was using federal funds to write national curriculum materials and tests. That same organization had helped coordinate memorandums of agreement in which signatories asked for federal assistance to launch the Common Core project.

Remember, too, that it's flat-out illegal for the federal government to have anything to do with curriculum. Federal agencies have historically avoided the explicit legal prohibition by paying other people to write curriculum. So the feds aren't doing it themselves, but these projects are definitely carried out under federal auspices and authority; they rely on federal funds; and their shape is influenced by federal officials. They are federal products in all but name, though Common Core supporters have clutched at technicalities to cover their rears.

The U.S. Constitution grants the federal government no power whatsoever in education policy. It's legally a state and local responsibility. Full stop. But that changed in practice after a Supreme Court decision of 1937. In *Helvering v. Davis*, the Court reinterpreted the Constitution's "general welfare" clause in a way that "allows Congress to use money to induce states to adopt policies the federal government could itself not impose," explained James L. Buckley, a retired U.S. senator and federal judge. "The federal government cannot force states to do things, but it can bribe them to do things." His book *Saving Congress from Itself* jumps off from research showing that one-sixth of the federal budget is consumed by grants to states, private organizations, and local governments to fund activities that technically fall outside the federal government's constitutional limits.[121]

Running that money through the federal bureaucracy before it filters down again through local organizations to the American people is a way to increase the cost of any enterprise. It also diminishes the accountability of public officials and programs, Buckley pointed out, because it's hard to hold local officials accountable for the failure of a federal program. They didn't think it up, they just went along to keep their jobs or to get back some of the money their constituents were obliged to send to the federal government. "The public at large has got to become aware of how much this affects them" not just in their pocketbooks, said Buckley, but also in terms of "the democratic ability to determine what's going to happen in their back yard and how their money is going to be used."

Passing Common Core to Find Out What's In It

Remember that forty states and the District of Columbia signed RTT contracts with the Obama administration in 2010 promising to use Common Core before even a *draft* of it was available.[122] This helps explain why almost nobody had heard of Common Core until well after it was etched in stone. Even education reporters said little about Common Core until parents began complaining about what was happening in their children's classrooms.

A search of "Common Core standards" in all English-language newspapers in the LexisNexis search engine brings up 371 stories in 2010.[123] That's an average of seven news stories per state for the whole year, in all publications. For the year 2009, when the project was germinating, a search finds barely more than thirty stories in all.

In the nation's dominant newspapers, the *Washington Post* and the *New York Times*, a total of twenty-one print articles on Common Core appeared in 2009-10. Only one article in each publication during that time referenced a critic of the initiative. In the *Times*, it was a Chicago parent worried that national tests would lead to overtesting. In the *Post*, it was Neal McCluskey from the libertarian Cato Institute making one critical point alongside positive statements by three other people plus reference to a supportive study.

The *Wall Street Journal*'s archives do not appear on Lexis, and their own online archives don't show results earlier than 2011, but in that year the *Journal* published only six stories containing those search terms. One was a supportive op-ed by Jeb Bush and Joel Klein, former New York City schools chancellor. The others were routine reports on the standards rolling out into schools, a done deal.

Once parents noticed the changes coming into their children's schools, their outcries prompted more extensive news coverage. In 2011, a Lexis-Nexis search for the terms "Common Core standards" turned up 448 articles. The number doubled the next year, to 889. Then came a surge in 2013, with 2,273 stories – more than six times as many as in 2010, the year that Common Core effectively became national policy. In 2014, the number more than doubled over the previous year, to 4,847.

Print mentions of "Common Core" and "standards," 2009-2014

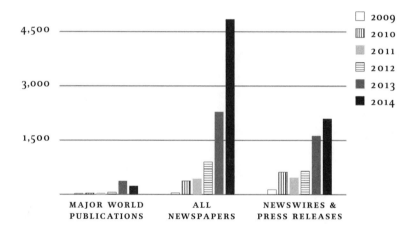

These statistics indicate that reporters failed to keep the public informed of the extensive changes afoot in education before the signatures were inked. By the time parents had enough information to voice their opposition, their school districts were legally obligated to keep the train moving.

Frederick Hess and Michael McShane of the American Enterprise Institute published a study of news reporting on Common Core in which they found that the initiative "received hardly any attention at all" in the popular press while it was being created and adopted by most of the states.[124] The media attention spiked only when the curriculum mandates were actually in the classrooms. Here's their graph of the news coverage by month from 2009 through 2013:

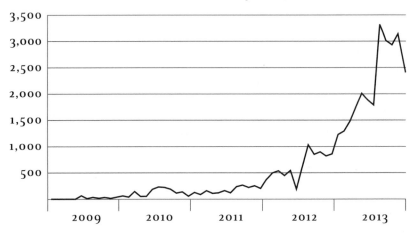

Common Core referenced in articles by month, 2009–2013

Hess and McShane also compared the media coverage of Common Core with that of another controversial education policy, school vouchers, by number of stories per year in relation to the number of children affected. In 2013, the year of highest Common Core coverage they reviewed, reporters wrote one article for every four children who received a school voucher, but one for every 1,100 children whose schools had to use Common Core. That's a difference of 27,500 percent.

They further searched for "Common Core" together with descriptive terms relating to political conflict, such as "supporter" and "opponent." This led to "a straightforward conclusion: the coverage of the standards at the outset was generally glowing, rarely referencing any kind of conflict until it had already bubbled over."

Despite the surge of media attention in 2013, a national PDK/Gallup survey in May of that year found that 62 percent of Americans had never heard of Common Core. Among parents with children in public school, 55 percent had never heard of it.[125] That might be expected in a closed society where citizens are not involved in governance by design, but our laws and traditions grant the American people the power of self-government through elected representation. To govern their own affairs, however, people have to know what's being planned for them before it's done.

The way Common Core was quietly implemented left many Americans feeling tricked. As Hess and McShane concluded, "the mainstream media dropped the ball on covering the Common Core," and ultimately this negligence "only fomented opposition to the standards. When parents and taxpayers found out that the standards had already been adopted, they thought the wool had been pulled over their eyes."[126] Those parents and taxpayers thought correctly.

The convoluted and opaque way that Common Core was developed and imposed has deprived parents and taxpayers of the right to know and influence the rules that affect our lives, and to know what is being done with the money we send to the government. The general public had no opportunity to give genuine consent to Common Core and all its baggage. So the average folks paying the bills and supplying the human guinea pigs for this experiment had to wait until it was passed to find out what was in it – to borrow Representative Nancy Pelosi's immortal words about Obamacare, which at least was put to a vote by duly elected legislators. In that respect, Common Core is a greater affront to democratic governance.

CHAPTER 2

Experience —
The Common Core
Classroom

I N FALL 2013 it took inquiries at nine schools in various districts across three states to find someone willing to show an outsider what Common Core looks like.

An English teacher at a classical charter school in Indianapolis initially welcomed a school visit; she had testified before Indiana's legislature in support of the national curriculum and testing standards. Then she emailed to say she could not invite people into her classroom to see the standards in action. "My principal told me that I am not allowed to engage with you on this," she wrote. "It is frustrating that something that should not be political is. I apologize that I could not be more helpful."

No one that she recommended I talk to would even reply to my repeated inquiries. I got the same brushoff from several districts in nearby states. But staff from the Metropolitan School District of Warren Township, in southeast Indianapolis, were quite willing to have me visit.

Warren was one of sixteen school districts nationwide to win a federal Race to the Top grant directly, rather than through the state, in 2012. Its application stressed the district's embrace of Common Core, and in less than a year the resulting $28.5 million had already produced detailed curriculum maps and teacher training programs. The Warren schools' eagerness to welcome my visit in autumn 2013 suggested I would see a well-organized local rollout of the national initiative, assisted by federal funds.

Of the roughly twelve thousand students in Warren schools, 58 percent qualify for federal free or reduced-price lunch, a proxy for low-income status, and 59 percent are ethnic minorities. On the National Assessment of Educational Progress, Warren students rank in about the 50th percentile in math and reading.[1] The district's spending per pupil, $11,600 a year, is close to the state average.[2] The RTT grant has amounted to about 5.6 percent of Warren's annual $128 million budget in each of its four years. (When RTT grants go to states as opposed to districts, the funds typically make up 1 to 3 percent of the state's education spending.) To have a better chance of receiving those funds, again, districts and states committed themselves to Common Core.[3]

President Obama did indeed leverage a relatively minuscule amount of money into huge political and educational changes, just as he boasted in his 2012 State of the Union address, saying: "For less than 1 percent of what our nation spends on education each year, we've convinced nearly every state in the country to raise their standards for teaching and learning – the first time that's happened in a generation."[4] This line was a rerun from his 2011 State of the Union,[5] and the 1 percent bargain appeared again in 2013.[6] By 2014, however, opposition from Americans on all sides of the political spectrum had made Common Core no longer an applause line, so Obama's speechwriters dropped it.

When I visited Warren schools, Indiana was one of some sixteen states that were formally reconsidering Common Core. Under public pressure, Governor Mike Pence and legislative leaders had come out in favor of submitting the standards to review, and that spring the legislature had passed a law suspending Common Core implementation during the 2013-14 academic year while the review proceeded. The grassroots furor that was building against Common Core in Indiana and nationwide explained why many teachers and administrators feared to discuss the standards. But not those in Warren Township. They were proud of what they had already done to align their teaching with the new curriculum mandates. Expecting that Common Core would survive the political challenge, they saw no reason to backtrack.

It was a rainy October afternoon when I spoke with Ryan Russell, the director of teacher effectiveness for the Warren district. He flicked through a series of documents and apps on his iPad in a few smooth motions, displaying some results of the twenty thousand man-hours that forty or so teachers and administrators had put into redesigning staff evaluations. Approximately three-quarters of Indiana districts were using the state template for teacher evaluations, but Warren chose to design its own. Russell then pulled up the curriculum maps that district teachers had written over the summer, a project the federal grant supported.

The maps would have made many a teacher drool. Teachers every-where were scrambling to align their classrooms with Common Core. A Scholastic poll of twenty thousand teachers conducted in autumn 2013, around the same time as my Warren visit, found 48 percent saying that integrating Common Core into their classrooms had just begun, three years after their states had signed on to the standards. About three-quarters of teachers polled said they needed more planning time and training.[7] A follow-up poll a year later found that a full 78 percent of teachers said they still needed more planning time, and over 80 percent said they needed more training and materials.[8]

The Warren district seemed to be ahead of the game. Its curriculum maps arranged Common Core's learning goals into an instructional cal-endar, giving date ranges for teaching specific math and English concepts. For example, second-grade teachers might spend October 16–27 on counting to a hundred by twos, working with triangles, and so on. Each date range in the map contained links to the corresponding sections of the district's online textbooks from Pearson, the world's largest education publisher (and a Common Core testing contractor), and to related resources such as explanatory videos and suggested class activities. Teachers could access those resources instantly, as Russell did, by touching the link on their iPad or Chromebook. (The RTT grant also funded a raft of iPads for kindergarteners and Chromebooks for the other students.)

Asked if other districts were this organized, Russell emitted a little puff of air: "No," he said emphatically. Warren planned to make its curric-ulum maps public since they were created with federal funds, he said, though he added an important caveat: "I could give them to a district and they wouldn't have the same success because it was the work on this and our teachers doing it that made us so prepared."

Fuzzy Math Makes a Comeback

Liberty Park Elementary School is a spacious building erected in 2002 beside a leafy middle school and an aquatics center. With Russell, I visit a classroom where Sarah Latdrik is working with six first graders who scored low on the district tests she gives every three weeks. The children are sitting in front of a smartboard, taking turns jumping up to touch two-digit numbers displayed on melons and strawberries bouncing about the screen. They win points if they match the fruit number to the sum of "ten-sticks" and "one-cubes" displayed in a corner.

Ten-sticks and one-cubes reappear in the math lesson Latdrik begins when her other sixteen students bound into the room, accompanied by an aide. The sticks and cubes resemble a sort of Tetris set. Ten small cubes, each representing the number one, can stack up in a column (or stick) to represent ten. The sticks lined up in a row of ten would form a large square, which represents one hundred.

Russell's first-grade daughter gasps when she notices him in her class-room and trots over to hug him. Then, slightly embarrassed, she quickly returns to one of several irregular trapezoidal tables that take the place of desks. The children wear collared shirts, mostly polos, and no jeans – a loosely defined uniform the Warren district requires.

Latdrik gathers all the children in front of the smartboard. "I'm ready to teach," she announces. "I'm ready to learn," the kids chorus.

She walks them through several ways to write the day's date on a smartboard-projected calendar, writing directly on the screen. Then they clap and slap their legs, chanting in unison as they move through a series of simple addition problems: "Three plus three is six – kicks! Four plus four is eight – great!"

Latdrik switches over to a large paper pad on an easel, with more ten-stick and one-cube groupings, and calls on kids to tell her what number each represents. A girl gives a correct answer, and Latdrik asks her, "Raven, what strategy did you use to find out what number that is?" Raven responds, "First I counted by tens, then by ones."

The teacher then discusses two good answers to the previous day's homework problem. Finally she says: "If you want to help me solve my math problem, give me a wink."

Liberty Elementary has four first-grade classes. The smartboard dis-plays the names of each class's teachers, and below each the number of students in that class: 22, 22, 21, and 23. Latdrik wants to bring a treat to school for all the first graders next week, she says. So how many should she make? This is a "real-world problem" of the kind that many teachers are emphasizing thanks to Common Core, whose math benchmarks use the term "real-world" fifty-one times.[9] She tells the children to return to their desks and take out their math manipulatives – foam versions of the ten-sticks and one-cubes on the screen. The children cluster in twos and threes, pulling out their "math journals" to help solve the problem. Latdrik moves among the tables, giving suggestions and answering questions.

Two little girls sitting at a table nearby are working independently. One with pigtails gathered all over her head by colorful plastic bobbles draws on her paper a stick-and-cube diagram that matches her manipulatives, which in turn correspond to the numbers on the board:

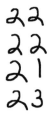

She counts up the sticks and writes down the results: $10 + 10 + 10 + 10 + 10 + 10 + 10 = 70$. She missed one. Finally, she counts the cubes, and writes her answer to the problem: 78.

Her partner, a girl in a yellow polo shirt, with hair in thin braids, writes in her math journal:

$$22$$
$$22$$
$$21$$
$$23$$

Instead of proceeding to add these numbers in the traditional way, beginning with the right-hand column, the girl counts up the tens from the left column and takes out eight ten-sticks. She does the same for the ones column using the little cubes, and then counts up all the manipulatives. On her paper she writes "86." She has counted the one-cubes incorrectly.

But she doesn't know it yet, so she plays with the remaining foam blocks until Latdrik tells the children to put away the manipulatives and discuss their answers. It has taken the group approximately eight minutes to work this problem. To answer it the traditional way would take an average first grader about fifteen seconds.

On the wall are two posters suggesting different ways to add and subtract. They include tally marks, drawing a picture, a number line, and a number sentence: $7 + 4 = 11$. What's missing is the standard algorithms for addition and subtraction: stacking the numbers and computing them by columns, starting with the ones column. Common Core doesn't call for this procedure until the fourth grade. For first graders, it prescribes exactly what Latdrik has done: using "a variety of models, including discrete objects and length-based models (e.g., cubes connected to form lengths,) to model add-to, take-from, put-together, take-apart"; teaching children to compare "a variety of solution strategies"; and the like.[10]

Activities like those practiced in Sarah Latdrik's class have appeared in stories about Common Core's "new way of school" in newspapers across the country. These methods have actually been around for decades, variously dubbed "new math," "reform math," and even "fuzzy math." As critics point out, multiplying the things that children must keep track of leads to simple errors like those made by the two girls trying to add up two-digit numbers with a detour through sticks and cubes. Moreover, the amount of time eaten up by such convoluted methods means less time for calculating practice. Children are then hampered when they reach algebra, where success requires having routine math procedures down cold.

Most high-achieving countries call for fluency in three-digit addition and subtraction in third grade, says Ze'ev Wurman, a former U.S. Department of Education official who helped write California's well-regarded math standards. Those countries also typically introduce standard algorithms immediately, the way many of today's parents learned math. In Wurman's view, "The rubbish that fills [Common Core] in earlier grades about 'strategies' 'relationships' and 'properties' ... is not truly 'rubbish' – and one can find some good explanation for a little bit of need of them – but it is repeated ad nauseam." Thus the curriculum "opens itself up for easy interpretation of fuzz and invented algorithms, which most implementations and textbooks gleefully (or ignorantly) proceed to make."

Parents have raised many complaints about the time-devouring Common Core math processes and the incomprehensible problems their young children are assigned. Many examples of confusing math homework have gone viral.

Jeff Sevart, an electrical engineer who lives in Indiana, posted his second-grade son's Common Core math homework on Facebook. The instruction for the assignment read: "Jack used the number line below to solve 427-326. Find his error. Then write a letter to Jack telling him what he did right, and what he should do to fix his mistake." After spending two hours trying to help his son figure out the answer, Sevart himself wrote the letter:

> Dear Jack,
>
> Don't feel bad. I have a Bachelor of Science Degree in Electronics Engineering which included extensive study in differential equations and other higher math applications. Even I cannot explain the Common Core Mathematics approach, nor get the answer correct. In the real world, simplification is valued over complication.

Sevart then demonstrated the traditional, straightforward method of subtraction. "The answer is solved in under 5 seconds," he wrote, whereas the process that "Jack" used was "ridiculous and would result in termination" in the workplace. He signed his letter "Frustrated Parent" and put it online. Sevart's outraged post soon appeared on Yahoo! News, Glenn Beck's radio program, the *Huffington Post*, and *Time* online, among other media outlets.

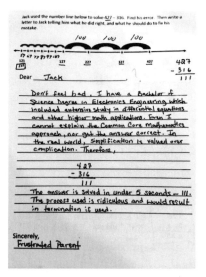

Another angry dad was the comedian Louis C.K., who took to Twitter to express his vexation over his daughter's third-grade math homework.

My kids used to love math. Now it makes them cry. Thanks standardized testing and common core!
— Louis C.K. (@louisck) April 28, 2014[11]

He then repeated his complaints on the *Late Show with David Letterman.*

The usual response from Common Core supporters to such complaints is: Common Core is not a curriculum; it's only a set of standards for curriculum and testing, which publishers and teachers then use as the basis for writing math problems and other assignments. Imagine a recipe book that lists ingredients but doesn't specify quantities or processes; the cook can figure that out. So if the dish isn't tasty, blame the cook, not the recipe book.

But if all the cooks are turning out similarly unpalatable dishes, that means the recipes deserve some criticism. Tom Loveless of the Brookings Institution observed that Common Core tells curriculum publishers and teachers to write math problems like the one Sevart posted on Facebook — but not directly. In a Brookings podcast where Loveless discussed Sevart's post, he noted that it came from a textbook published *before* Common Core came out. Bad math instruction has been around forever. On the other hand, parents aren't crazy to see a connection between bad math and Common Core, because "in school districts, and in schools, and in classrooms, people hear a certain message from Common Core. And one of the messages is: kids need to be doing this kind of 'deeper learning, deeper thinking, higher-order thinking' in mathematics.... It gives local educators license to adopt a lot of this garbage, this really bad curriculum. And they do it under the shield of the Common Core." When teachers have no choice but to use Common Core, it's harder to hold them accountable for bad instruction.

Terms like "deeper learning" and "real-world problems" mean special things in the education world. Loveless calls this terminology "a dog whistle to a certain way of approaching mathematics that has never worked in the past." It was tried nationally in the 1960s and again in the 1990s. "It failed both times. And we are seeing a resurrection of some of these bad materials and these bad practices again. And it's partially the Common Core's fault."[12]

Common Core English

Not far from Liberty Elementary School, with the one-cubes and ten-sticks, Tessa Bohonos is giving an English lesson to her class of advanced freshmen at Warren Central High School. It's the last lesson of the day, and the kids are quiet. That's partly because they spend about half of the class time using their Chromebooks. Bohonos has just earned her master's degree in education technology from Ball State University, and she's eager to apply her new skills.

Her long ponytail swings as she walks about the room. The desks are arranged traditionally, facing the front in rows. The walls are not aflutter with a kaleidoscope of color like the first-grade room. In the back, dramatic black and white posters of Greek gods from classical mythology brush the ceiling in a neat row, but otherwise the room is subdued and focused.

The students hunch over their Chromebooks, squinting at the screens. They spend a few minutes entering new "academic vocabulary" into Google spreadsheets, then several minutes on a short lesson. Common Core says high schoolers should "use technology, including the Internet, to produce, publish, and update individual or shared writing products."[13]

Bohonos tells students to cluster around the whiteboard and write any story elements they can think of, because "I don't like to spend time on things you already know. That's boring." They write words like *conflict*, *protagonist*, *thesis* in deliberately random, multicolored verbal fragments across the board. One young man writes sideways. Then Bohonos hands the students a page filled with vocabulary terms, many of which have just been written on the whiteboard. They run through the list together. Anything a student doesn't know well, she says, should go into his academic vocabulary spreadsheet.

"I'm not saying this will for sure happen," she says, tilting her head and sounding secretive, "but these words *just might* show up on a future quiz."

Students spend the rest of class working on an essay due in four days, before they read *To Kill a Mockingbird*. Their "pre-reading" essay must be on one of three topics: race relations, banning books, or "the N-word in literature."

Bohonos reminds students to turn in a bibliography with their essay. She has put several articles related to each topic on an online pinboard for students to use as sources, including articles on the Scottsboro Boys and *Plessy v. Ferguson*. Bohonos tells me she's adding historical documents to her instruction because of Common Core's requirement that students read progressively more nonfiction. Warren's RTT application says that eighth-grade teachers in the district will assign readings that are 45 percent "literacy" and 55 percent "informational" passages, as Common Core directs, with the ratio shifting to 30/70 by twelfth grade.[14]

Common Core also mandates assigning books at the students' grade level rather than their reading level, so now Bohonos's nonadvanced students will read the actual book *To Kill a Mockingbird* instead of the simpler screenplay, as they did before. A Fordham Institute survey of 1,154 English teachers nationwide in October 2013 found that more than one-third of the high school teachers assigned *To Kill a Mockingbird*, the most commonly used book.[15] While this book's themes are appropriate for middle school or later, the reading level of the language is rated for elementary schoolers; one Common Core–approved scale says it's a good fit for a midyear fifth grader.[16] In other words, it's thematically but not linguistically complex, although Common Core claims to emphasize the latter.

Bohonos walks around, conferring with students individually as they write. Once the essay is finished, students must post it online and respond to at least three of their classmates' essays "with at least 75 words in your response," Bohonos says. There's a hitch: the Chromebooks won't allow cutting and pasting into the discussion board, so students have to upload their essays as attachments. But overall, Bohonos likes the online board: "It's what college students are using," she tells her students.

Bohonos is excited about helping students practice "collaboration" and "twenty-first-century skills" with another assignment based on *To Kill a Mockingbird*: they will choose approximately two pages of "descriptive text" from the book and add images to create a short YouTube video. The Common Core standards ask high school kids to "make strategic use of digital media" and "integrate and evaluate information presented in diverse media and formats." Since it's a new lesson for Bohonos this year, she'll try it out on the advanced students first, and then use their videos as examples in her other classes.

"Authentic, Collaborative" Teaching

Bohonos and Latdrik were among the teachers paid with RTT grant money to attend several Common Core seminars put on by the district in summer 2013. Teachers who participated in the Common Core planning committee, also compensated with grant funds, spent a week and a half thinking through the standards and writing them "in kid-friendly language," Bohonos said.

The standards document itself is heavy reading, laden with jargon. Here's a general standard for language arts: "Acquire and use accurately a range of general academic and domain-specific words and phrases sufficient for reading, writing, speaking, and listening at the college and career readiness level; demonstrate independence in gathering vocabulary knowledge when encountering an unknown term important to comprehension or expression."[17] Translation: Learn a lot of words, and look up words you don't know.

"The Common Core can be vague if there isn't an administrator saying 'This is how we take this,'" Latdrik acknowledged. The Warren district was methodical in helping teachers apply the mandates in their classrooms. Teachers met regularly with a Common Core coach. Every Wednesday morning, they met in groups both within and across grade levels to discuss a specified topic, such as the collaborative aspects of Common Core, or workshop approaches to math and writing. Warren's high school English teachers held a close-reading workshop for faculty in other departments; Bohonos worked with art teachers, explaining how close reading is "like analyzing art."

Latdrik said the first two years of Common Core were "rough," but she came to like it. "Rather than me standing up and teaching [students] a skill, it's me coordinating experiences where they can authentically engage in that on their own," she explained. "I've never felt more like what I'm teaching them in kindergarten and first grade is truly important."

Warren's professional development program highlights materials from self-described "constructivist" educators, who promote you're-on-your-own techniques rather than traditional teaching styles based on giving explicit instruction and imparting knowledge. In one Teaching Channel video, for example, a middle school math teacher has his students find the formula for the surface area of a cylinder without assistance.[18] The progressive educators who control teacher training tend to favor constructivist methods. Research has shown that this approach may be effective with well-off students, but is likely to be detrimental to poorer children whose families are less equipped to fill in the gaps left by self-led instruction.[19]

Ryan Russell said that the Warren district, from administrators to teachers and parents, greatly preferred Common Core, although there were scattered complaints from parents. Critics often mention teachers who are scared to object to the new curriculum and tests, but Russell had not heard any Warren teacher say that Common Core was less challenging than the old curriculum. As the state of Indiana considered reverting to its previous standards, his district's biggest worry was that students would then perform poorly on the SAT and ACT college entrance exams, which had been changed to fit Common Core. "I don't want kids to lose opportunities because of a political battle," Russell said. An often overlooked part of the standards debate is that school leaders and teachers cannot choose which standards they will use, no matter how strongly they prefer a particular set.

While national reviewers such as those at the Fordham Institute have rated Indiana's previous standards higher than Common Core – among the best in the nation, in fact[20] – Russell thought the state tests had set expectations too low. Indiana's tenth-grade English test measured an eighth-grade reading level, for example. As for complaints about diluted math instruction (remember the Furtado twins in Massachusetts?), he noted that Warren still offered advanced classes to students who wanted to go beyond the Algebra II that Common Core prescribes as a final math course, so they could enter college with calculus under their belts, ready for a science or math major.

As it turned out, Indiana largely retained Common Core with some minor changes, including a new name: Indiana Academic Standards.[21] The Warren district has continued to use its Common Core materials and practices, referring to Indiana's standards and Common Core as essentially a unit.[22] Recall that the district was lucky enough to get extra funding from the nation's taxpayers to support the revamping of its curriculum and the retraining of teachers – an advantage most districts cannot expect. So how have Warren students performed with their new and improved education?

Data on the Indiana state test results released in August 2014 showed that Warren was one of only two districts in Marion County (the state's most populous county) to see a *decline* in passing rates over the previous year. It just barely beat out the state's worst-performing district, Indianapolis Public Schools. The superintendent, Dena Cushenberry, blamed the Warren district's comparatively poor performance in part on the burdens of meeting the requirements for curricular changes and other mandates that the U.S. Department of Education attached to the RTT grant.[23] So much for that.

Hoping for the Best

In late June 2014, when teachers ought to be out sunning themselves, a trio of them perched on bright purple block chairs inside a Frank Lloyd Wright–looking new elementary school in Bensenville, a suburb of Chicago. They're enjoying a snack break at a teacher training conference, and discussing whether they can emulate a model Common Core lesson they've just seen.

"Most of my kids are not on grade level," says a youthful teacher in gray slacks, with black hair piled into a high bun. "Lots have no dads or moms, and are being raised by whoever. They've got their own problems."

A teacher sitting across from her, in a purple boyfriend cardigan and jeans, notes that her school isn't bright and airy like the one they're sitting in: "It's dark, and old. I think the kids pick up that feeling when they're inside." Teachers get two reams of paper per month for copies, she says with a sigh, so they buy more themselves. The other two teachers nod in empathy.

"I like how they told the kids first what they would learn, then they learned it" in the model lesson, says a wavy-haired blond teacher whose nametag reads "Angelique."

"How did they get the kids to be so quiet?" the gray-slacked teacher wonders. Probably because the model classroom had two teachers for fifteen students, she guesses. She doesn't have a teaching assistant or co-teacher, so "I got to keep my students from jumping out the window." And besides, "some parents you can't call [for help] because you know the kid is going to get a beating."

Teachers and staff in Bensenville School District spent two months putting together a three-day conference for nearby school districts on how to teach Common Core. Illinois agreed in 2010 to replace its state curriculum mandates and tests with Common Core, but in the summer of 2014, Bensenville was still one of only a few Illinois school districts already all-in.

It certainly helped that Bensenville, a bitty district of only three schools next to O'Hare Airport, received federal money to support its Common Core implementation, like Warren in Indiana. Bensenville got $20,644 out of a $43 million Race to the Top grant to Illinois in 2011.[24] In exchange for this RTT money, 35 of the 866 school districts in Illinois, including Bensenville, agreed to comply with new federal mandates in advance of the other districts. The money-getting policies included rating teachers at least partly on their students' scores on standardized tests, increasing science and math initiatives, and reorienting instruction around Common Core – all Obama administration priorities. Bensenville also volunteered to run trial versions of Common Core's federally funded national tests before all schools had to use them in place of their existing state tests in 2015. That gave them more time to align their teaching with the test format.

The $20,644 didn't cover the cost of making all these changes, but Bensenville wanted to be one of Illinois's few "reform exemplars,"[25] willing to strike out into a thicket of education policies that the Obama administration planted. The RTT provision to use standardized test results as the main basis for rating teachers and schools was expected to change teacher training nationwide in line with the new curriculum and its associated tests, but that process was going slowly. Bensenville's instructional leader, Kay Dugan, had just interviewed "a bright teacher candidate from a good school" and asked her what she knew about Common Core. The candidate replied, "I never heard of that."

Dugan, a petite lady with bright gray eyes, also co-chaired Illinois's Educator Leader Cadre,[26] a group of teachers and administrators who led workshops on Common Core for PARCC, one of its national testing organizations. She spoke of "pushback" against Common Core from teachers and administrators in other school districts on the ground that it's "too hard" for the students. That training conference with its model lessons in the summer of 2014 was designed to help other districts feel as confident in their new set of curricular clothes as Bensenville.

A Look at "Close Reading"

The Bensenville teachers leading the workshops are enthusiastic, if perhaps a bit nervous at having groups of outside teachers observe their summer-school lessons. The buzzword of the day is "close reading," a technique of literary interpretation that was popular in universities some time ago and entered K–12 classrooms along with Common Core. Adapted for younger children, it seems to mean anchoring their observations about a text (the teachers never speak of a "book" or an "article," but always of a "text") in direct quotations from the material.

In her second-grade classroom, Kristi Mullen pivots from child to child, handing out highlighters. The tykes have just read *Pop's Bridge* by Eve Bunting, a fiction picture book about two young San Franciscans whose fathers – one Asian and one Caucasian – are helping build the Golden Gate Bridge. Young Robert, the white boy, thinks his father has a more important bridge-building job than his friend Charlie's dad, who is a painter. But one day the two boys see several workers die in a fall, and Robert realizes that constructing the bridge endangers all the workers equally. Scholastic, the book's publisher, says the book is appropriate for readers in kindergarten through second grade.[27] Summer-school students, of course, are behind their peers. That's why they're in summer school.

"I'm going to ask some text-dependent questions," Mullen says to the children, emphasizing the last three words and flipping to a "warm-up" on a giant pad of paper stuck to an easel. It tells the children to underline, on copies of the book's first few pages: "Who are the important characters in the story? Why are they important?" The children's desks are arranged in three clusters of five, and Mullen walks among them repeating those two questions. "Charlie's father is important because he builds the bridge," one student offers. Mullen repeats the answer, then adds, "I like your text evidence."

After a few minutes of this, there's a "challenge question": "What are Robert's feelings about his pop and Charlie's father?" A girl raises her hand.

"Yes, ma'am," Mullen responds.

"He's proud."

"How do we know he's proud?"

"The book said that."

"Let's go to our book and highlight evidence that he's proud: 'He has an important job.' What does he keep calling the bridge?"

Another child: "The Golden Gate Bridge."

That isn't what the teacher is looking for. "At the beginning, what does it say? 'The impossible bridge.' If it's impossible and you do it, are you proud?" A few kids say, "No." Mullen looks at them and says firmly, "Yes."

Close-reading theory has told Mullen to stick to the text. Following that dictate costs her and the kids an opportunity to talk about the reasons for their "incorrect" answers, which would have made their discussion far more interesting and fruitful. Perhaps the teacher was just off her game, with fifteen grownups watching from the back of the room.

Mullen then tells the children to pair up and look for more evidence to help answer the challenge question. As they rearrange themselves, she sends about five who need extra attention off to a semicircle in the corner with the assistant (the object of envy among visiting teachers).

In another part of the school building in Bensenville, a pair of teachers are leading an eighth-grade class in close reading. For most of these students, English is a new language, so they are also using a picture book. *Grandfather's Journey*, by Allen Say, tells the story of a Japanese man who emigrates to the United States but keeps traveling between the two countries, in each place longing for the other. The prose is simple and spare, with just one sentence per page, but the watercolor illustrations are exquisite. *Grandfather's Journey* won the 1994 Caldecott Medal for American picture books, which emphasizes illustrations over language. Its publisher says the book is suitable for children ages four through eight, but Scholastic rates it at a third- through fifth-grade reading level.[28]

This classroom too has desks arranged in clusters of five. A bulletin board in the back displays "Grandfather's Journey Vocabulary": *evoked, homesick, towering, exchange*. In the front, a projector beams questions about the book onto a screen. After each question is a reference to a corresponding Common Core standard: "Why do you think grandfather surrounds himself with songbirds? RL.8.4." (The code means Reading: Literature, Grade 8, standard 4.)[29]

The eighth graders are much quieter than the second graders. They keep their answers short and low. The two teachers – Nick Georgopoulos, a young man with tousled hair, and Argiro Vranas, a petite woman in tall heels – energetically work the room, circling the students, pointing to their open books, querying. As students sequentially answer the questions on the screen, the teachers say to the class: "Do you guys agree...? Write down your text evidence." The teachers are clearly working hard, but it's difficult to tell whether the students are. Maybe visitors make them bashful, too.

The twenty-four visiting teachers watch several different lessons of this kind, and then gather in the school's music room, around seven folding tables topped with brightly colored plastic tablecloths and strewn with highlighters. The walls are covered in sound-absorbing pads and lined with a string of small American flags. The teachers who gave the model lessons, plus several of the district's instruction and curriculum coaches, sit around the room in canvas director's chairs. First, they answer questions.

An early one: "Where did you learn to do this?"

Caitlin Hare, a first-year Bensenville teacher with a kind, open face, takes that one on. "All through college we learned about Common Core, so I do feel comfortable with it," she says. Her third- through fifth-grade class will finish out summer school with another five-day close reading of one main fiction book about the Oregon Trail, accompanied by a number of nonfiction "texts" such as travelers' journal entries and historical accounts, to meet Common Core's nonfiction requirements.

Leah Gauthier, the district's instructional services director, then speaks up: "When we started, there was no textbook for Common Core. This did not happen overnight. We've taken baby steps the whole way."

Those baby steps included ditching textbooks, except for continuing to use Everyday Math curriculum as Bensenville's main resource for math. (Everyday Math is regularly pilloried as one of the "fuzzy math" textbook series.) A curriculum committee now pulls together all the materials each Bensenville grade uses, and integrates all the subjects. So an "English" class might use historical or science-based materials, and a science class might include math concepts.

"Because we jumped in, we're not flailing now and can add more," Gauthier says. "We were a textbook district, doing the same thing in every room on the same day. Now standards are ingredients."

Argiro Vranas chimes in: "Before, I didn't know how I could spend five days on one text. Now, this is how we do it in Bensenville."

Common Core supporters insist that the program doesn't restrict or control teachers. That claim conflicts with common sense and with what teachers hear in their districts. Quite plainly, Common Core is an instructional overhaul. It is intended to change what and how kids learn, which requires changing what and how teachers teach. There's no reason to go through all this trouble if it doesn't change much of anything. That's why teachers have to get in line and implement the required "instructional shifts."

In Bensenville's Q&A, the visiting teachers sound much like the summer-school students: willing but unsure; struggling to grasp the new paradigm. "What is a good resource for informational text?" asks a gum-chewing teacher with flipped blond hair. "How do you have *time* for this?" wonders another, with a pale pink manicure.

A Bensenville principal says he did practice lessons in close reading in order to understand how to give teachers feedback, and the first one was like "one of the rings of hell. If I were evaluating my [own] lesson, there would have been some hard conversations afterward."

After the Q&A, the conference participants dive into a practice set. The workshop facilitators hand everyone a one-page set of four excerpts from *Bud, Not Buddy*, a Newbery Award–winning book by Christopher Paul Curtis about a ten-year-old African American orphan boy who runs away from an unkind foster family during the Great Depression to search for his musician father. Scholastic rates it at a fifth-grade reading level.[30]

"We read full novels all the time," Kay Dugan says. "That we don't is a Common Core myth."

The teachers review some specific Common Core requirements, including the instruction to "annotate along the way" as the students did in the model lesson, and then work in groups to develop their own "text-dependent questions" about the book. Finally, they share their results with everyone.

The teachers at one table have it down. One sample question they came up with: "When it says, 'Jerry looked like he'd just found out they were going to dip him in a pot of boiling milk,' what does that mean?"

Teachers at another table are still confused. They twirl their pens and talk to each other in fragmentary fashion. "I don't get this," says one, pursing her lipsticked mouth and leaning her head on her hand. "What kind of questions are we supposed to ask? 'Where are Bud and Jerry going?'"

The idea, Gauthier explains, is to have children cite a source for their answers and steer them away from emotional responses, because their feelings are not the point of reading literature. After all, "You don't have to read *Jack and the Beanstalk* to answer, 'How would you feel if you were chased by a giant?'"

Is Close Reading Effective Teaching?

If one looks at supporting materials for Common Core, the time that Bensenville teachers spent instructing others in the close-reading method may seem warranted. An instructional guide from the PARCC testing organization, for example, says that close reading is "a key component of college and career readiness" and will be included in its exams.[31] David Coleman, a main architect of Common Core who now heads the College Board, gave a model lesson employing the technique to analyze Martin Luther King Jr.'s "Letter from a Birmingham Jail." He did the lesson in spring 2011 on behalf of the New York State Education Department, and the fifteen-minute video is featured in an extensive online collection of Common Core materials.[32] At a conference in summer 2013, Coleman argued strenuously that curriculum and tests should focus on specific reading assignments and that children should not rely on background information: "Let's just be very careful that we don't … rob the text as the source of information, and pleasure, and excitement."[33]

A key reason given for stressing this approach to reading is that children in poorer homes typically read far fewer books, hear far less complex spoken language, and have far less exposure to varied experiences such as travel, or visiting a farm or a museum, a local music festival or a zoo. These deficiencies limit their knowledge of the world, which in turn limits their reading ability, because the ability to read fluently on any particular subject depends heavily on prior knowledge of that subject. A baseball fanatic will read various team statistics with ease, but people with little knowledge of baseball will have a hard time getting through articles littered with unfamiliar terms such as "RBI" and "closer," as I learned after taking on the baseball beat for my college newspaper. This is true of any subject, as the linguist E. D. Hirsch has demonstrated.[34]

Hirsch advocates that all children therefore be taught an explicitly defined core of knowledge in school, and he established his Core Knowledge Foundation for that purpose. Schools affiliated with this organization boast significantly higher student achievement than others.[35] Common Core seemingly nods to Hirsch's findings by saying in the introduction that the mandates need to be accompanied by a curriculum that is "intentionally and coherently structured to develop rich content knowledge within and across grades." Hirsch officially endorsed Common Core for that reason in 2013, writing that the authors "break the fearful silence about the critical importance of specific content." In the very same endorsement, however, he noted that the mandates contain no "specific historical, scientific, and other knowledge that is required for mature literacy."[36] After giving a little nod to Hirsch, Common Core runs contrary to the substance of his work.

Common Core requires little content whatsoever for English language arts. The mandates are mostly a set of procedures that can be applied to just about anything. That's why organizations completely unrelated to teaching English, such as the Girl Scouts or the Future of Sex Education Project, can claim their materials are "aligned to Common Core." Instead of giving specifics on what children must know about the English language and literature in order to be educated adults, Common Core mostly tells teachers what to do with content-bearing material, whether it's "text" or conversation. It does recommend some books in an appendix (including *Bud, Not Buddy*, though not *Pop's Bridge* or *Grandfather's Journey*).[37] One likely reason for not specifying content is to avoid curriculum wars. So while Common Core's introduction says a few positive things about "content knowledge," the mandates remain mostly silent on what such knowledge ought to be. It's a little like requiring schools to provide vitamins every day, but not specifying which ones or at what dosage.

But Common Core doesn't merely remain open-ended on content. It actually undermines the teaching of specific core knowledge by promoting classroom methods that emphasize academic skills or practices instead, supposedly to help eliminate the environmental advantage that better-off children bring with them. That's why "close reading" calls for answers drawn strictly from the text at hand, not from the wider store of knowledge that children may have amassed. It's an attempt to level the playing field.

Trying to separate skills from knowledge in this way is a fool's errand, according to Robert Pondiscio, a former teacher turned pundit.[38] To illustrate the point: you can't learn how to build a house without knowing about materials or the use of tools; and conversely, using the tools and materials deepens your knowledge of them. Reading about baseball or the phases of the moon or the Oregon Trail increases your knowledge of those subjects, and the acquired knowledge then improves your ability to read about related topics, in a kind of feedback. When you read the daily news, you will comprehend it more thoroughly if you start from a solid base of civic and cultural literacy — something that too many citizens do not have.

A survey in 2011 found that only half of Americans could name the three branches of government, and just one in five could identify the origin of the phrase "a wall of separation" between church and state from among four options.[39] The remedy for this problem does not lie in the content-light standards of Common Core, with all its emphasis on "informational text" but no coherent principles for selecting and organizing it. If children read only a haphazard list of materials their teachers happen to like, compiled with no thought to building a focused and delineated core of cultural literacy, their knowledge level will be laughable and their reading fluency will be underdeveloped, too.

As for the merits of "close reading," there is very little research on its use in K-12 classrooms. The theory arose in Yale University in the 1930s and has largely stayed in universities ever since, as one of many methods for studying and critiquing literature, primarily poetry, and hardly the most prevalent one. A search of ERIC.gov, a federal repository of education research, finds no statistical studies prior to the Common Core era on using the technique in K-12 classrooms, although it turns up a small handful of theoretical papers about how it might be done. Since Common Core arrived, there are still no serious studies in the database, although it shows a slight uptick in theory papers, which all cite Common Core as their reason for existing. A serious study would do something like compare students in close-reading classes with students taught by other methods. The best kind of study would randomly assign the instructional style to classes of students and then compare the results with other classes, as has been done for math curriculum.

At any rate, close reading is now all the rage not just in Bensenville and Warren, but across the nation, thanks to Common Core. Pondiscio is a Common Core supporter and a former employee of Hirsch's foundation, but he was aghast when he saw a model Common Core lesson in New York using the close-reading method in the summer of 2013. So he posted a critique online:

> Excerpts. No complete works. Bleeding chunks of literature chosen because they presumably offer opportunities to learn and practice a reading "skill." The Common Core standards are supposed to give students the opportunity to grapple with texts worth reading. If nothing else, it should mean a transition from skills-driven literacy to curriculum-driven literacy. Skills are tools for analyzing text; literature is not a delivery mechanism for teaching skills. And fifty-three lessons on character development?

He quoted a model teacher saying "It takes two to three days to complete a lesson" in Common Core, and he asked, "Is this one unit on character development going to last *all year?*" Instead of observing "a great reading lesson," Pondiscio saw something "dull" and "uninspiring."[40]

The teachers at Bensenville's three-day training seminar all clearly wanted to provide a good, inspiring education for the children in their classes, or they wouldn't have spent precious summer days on the other side of the desk. Surveys were finding that most teachers felt two things about adopting Common Core in their classrooms: optimism and worry. A survey in summer 2014 by Scholastic and the Bill and Melinda Gates Foundation found that 68 percent of teachers strongly or somewhat agreed they were "enthusiastic" about Common Core, but that was a five-point drop from 2013.[41] At the same time, 81 percent agreed strongly or somewhat that getting it into place would be "challenging," an eight-point *increase* from the previous year. While Scholastic seems to have discontinued its poll on the subject, another one by the journal *Education Next* found a sharp drop-off in teacher support for Common Core between 2013 and 2015, from 76 percent to 40 percent, while opposition jumped from 12 to 50 percent.[42] This stunning reversal has been met with renewed PR efforts by Common Core proponents, despite the failures of that tactic to date.

Standards-Based Grading

It would take an encyclopedia to cover everything that Common Core changes in U.S. education. As an illustration of how far-reaching the mandates are, consider the effect on how teachers grade their students' work.

Even before Common Core, many teachers were shifting toward what is known as "standards-based grading" as a consequence of federal requirements that schools conform to centrally determined standards. In this form of grading, students are rated on a number scale like 1-4, or with letters like P for proficiency and M for mastery, instead of the familiar 0-100 percentiles or A–F letter grades. The mandate of No Child Left Behind (2001) that states test all students in math and reading increased the interest in standards-based grading nationwide, said Tammy Heflebower, vice president of the Marzano Research Laboratory, an organization that promotes standards-based instruction. She described "a natural trajectory over the last seven, eight, maybe ten years" toward the new grading style. "But now Common Core is going to help focus us because we have a common metric by which to measure kids.... I would anticipate a resurgence of interest because we're going to look at competency over point-grabbing, so to speak."

Ken O'Connor, a Canadian consultant who has worked with hundreds of schools across North America, saw an uptick in standards-based grading after forty-six states adopted Common Core. More middle schools and high schools have been showing an interest, and some states have mandated similar approaches, often called "proficiency-based grading." An Oregon law in 2013 and a more recent law in Maine require teachers to assess students by state standards, accelerating the trend toward standards-based grading. In 2016, the nation's tenth-largest school district, Fairfax County Public Schools in Virginia, adopted standards-based grading.[43] "There definitely is, as far as I can see, momentum gathering," O'Connor said.

In standards-based grading, teachers rate students on specific skills, often giving several different ratings per assignment if it involves several measurable skills. Report cards are typically longer and more detailed than they used to be. For each skill, teachers might give an assessment of "mastery," "progressing," or "insufficient progress," to cite one variation on the concept.

"In a pure standards-based system you would have only two levels: proficient and not proficient," O'Connor said. "The symbolic representations – A to F, percentages – they're artificial constructs that very often are only identified in symbolic terms. A is 90 to 100, B is 80 to 89. That doesn't mean anything because ... if it's an easy test on an easy skill, a high score may mean a low level of performance." A central goal of standards-based grading, he explained, is to relate grades and teacher comments directly to the learning outcomes that states demand, and thus make grades more objective because they are based on outside criteria rather than a particular teacher's judgment.

Heflebower observed that this kind of grading system is part of a larger trend toward standardization in schools: "When I went to school twenty-five years ago, teachers decided what they taught, how they taught it, and how to grade it. The standards movement has helped make more consistent what we teach [from] teacher to teacher, school to school, across a state." A standardized grading system goes along with standardized instruction.

As schools adopt standards-based grading, whether to tie instruction more closely to Common Core or for the other benefits that its proponents claim, some parents say the grading scale is confusing. Some teachers say the system grants too much authority to people outside classrooms. And that may be the point. Shifting authority away from teachers appears to be a central objective of advocates for nationalizing education. Many of them blame teachers for subpar academic performance in the United States, so they believe that teachers need to be micromanaged.

Some teachers like the new grading practice, and some don't. When Tracie Happel's school district in southwestern Wisconsin began phasing in Common Core, it also decided teachers would use standards-based grading. Happel, a second-grade teacher, joined the committee that designed the new system. Their new quarterly report card was initially eight pages long, but the committee pared it down to one double-sided page. Now, K–8 students are graded M for mastery, P for progression, and L for learning.

Most of those on the committee were enthusiastic about the change, said Happel, recalling their attitude mockingly: "We're so in the twenty-first century!" But she was uncertain about the results. "Kids were more excited when I told them they got an A-plus, or a B. They know that's pretty good. But when you give them a P or M they don't know what that means." The rest of the teachers in her grade level were also unpersuaded. "They said, 'Why are we doing this? How am I going to grade that? How do I know what an M is?' Some just said, 'I'm converting them to percentages.' … I think people grade based on feeling and keeping score."

It was a different story for Patricia Scriffiny, a twenty-year high school math teacher in Colorado. Before switching to standards-based grading nine years ago, she said, "I had some students, they tended to be mostly girls, who would work very hard, do every scrap of extra credit, and fail miserably on tests. They really weren't learning, but they were being compliant. Students who were more likely to be boys would fall apart on student management issues like staying organized and turning in homework. They would just sort of disappear, get Ds or Fs, and quit engaging because they were learning the math but their grade never reflected their learning."

Changing her methods was the only thing that kept her teaching, Scriffiny told me. Now she crafts and grades assignments according to specific learning objectives from Common Core standards and Advanced

Placement (AP) curriculum. As a result, she and her students are "having the right conversations now where we're talking about the right things." The new grading method incentivizes students to edit their own work and to meet with her for help. "It is so much more respectful to kids and so much more useful for learning rather than a tool for punishment," Scriffiny said. She also finds that parent-teacher conferences are more fruitful when she can tell parents the specific areas their child needs to work on. "If I can prove I know their child and know what they're struggling with, they're on board."

One of her colleagues felt exactly the opposite way about standards-based grading. Scriffiny recalled her saying, "If I was mandated to do that, I would retire." Scriffiny sympathized, and she questioned the wisdom of making the new system mandatory: "If teachers are told, 'You're going to do this' and they don't understand why, that tends not to work very well."

Jenny Larson, a high school English teacher in Minnesota, changed her view on such a grading system over time, but only after her school district made some adjustments in response to complaints about it. The district moved into standards-based grading along with Common Core, but the attempt to micromanage teachers from afar ran into resistance. At school board meetings, Larson criticized four aspects of the grading system.

First, the district had told teachers they could not assign a zero for work that students didn't turn in; they could only grade the work that *was* turned in. Many students therefore stopped turning in work. Second, teachers couldn't penalize students for late work, so one-third of Larson's AP class turned in everything right at the end of the semester, leaving her with hundreds of pages to grade in just a few days.

Third, the district had told teachers to stop including behavioral issues in grades. That was "a big problem" for physical education teachers, said Larson. They believed that behavior "should be part of the standard because sportsmanship is one of the rules for professional sports."

Fourth, work done in class throughout the year could be worth only 20 percent of the final grade. Many of Larson's students decided that in-class work didn't matter much, "not realizing there's a payoff" from it because regular practice improves performance on big items like tests and papers.

After one year and many complaints, the district changed its grading policies on the first two items, allowing teachers to give students a "drop-dead date" for assignments and a failing grade for assignments they didn't turn in.

In practical terms, the new system is more complex and time-consuming. "When I'm scoring a sixty-question literary terms test, I have to translate that into a number: 4, 3, 2, 1, 0," Larson explained. "I write down the number they get – 57, 44 – and then translate that into 4, 3, 2, 1. And I also want them to know how close they came, so I have to enter both of those in my gradebook." It gets more complicated: "If we have six different things we're measuring in a paper, I have to enter each separately or figure out how to average them, so it's taking twice as long. And I'm more prone to error, too, especially with a ten-point quiz. Ten would be [graded] a 4, but sometimes I don't enter 4 so I have to double-check."

Two years into the practice, after lots of rethinking and explaining to students and parents, Larson came to like standards-based grading. For one thing, there are no extra-credit options to bump up a C or D grade to a B, so students "actually have to work" on the assignments. "I also like to give them assignments related to a standard," she said. "It removes the idea from students that they are getting busywork; it makes it very purposeful."

A big reason that Tracie Happel dislikes standards-based grading is that it distances parents from their kids' education (as does Common Core math, when parents cannot help even their elementary school children). "It's too detailed and parents don't know what it means," she said. Unlike Scriffiny, she finds that the new system makes it harder to give parents a clear sense of how well their children are doing, partly because it discourages making distinctions between a pass-with-flying-colors and a just-adequate performance. "Parents say 'How come my child doesn't get an M [for mastery]?' So then you have to bring out evidence of how the child is doing. And in the state of Wisconsin everyone passes, but we've been told you can't give an M unless you can absolutely prove it, so no one ever gets an M."

Parents often require lots of explanation if teachers and schools switch to the system, Scriffiny said. "I've had every reaction on the spectrum you can imagine, but I've had parents come in and say, 'This makes more sense to me because this is how I'm evaluated at work.' The ones who fight it the most are the parents of honors kids. They're the ones who are good at playing school, aren't they? They're very good at jumping through hoops."

James Wilson is a parent and teacher in the Puget Sound region of Washington State. He has also overseen curriculum for Georgia's department of education and has been a principal of several schools. His daughter's school district uses standards-based grading, and he has been required to use it as a teacher. "As parents, we hate it," he said. "It tells us nothing other than our schools have implemented another screwball idea."

Depending on the district, a child's grade under standards-based grading will often rest mostly on large assignments like tests, with the remaining 10 to 20 percent coming from daily work, Wilson said. One consequence is the same problem Jenny Larson found in her Minnesota school: "The kids understand and they work it, and they say, 'Hey, why should I do this? It doesn't count for anything.' So as a result they don't do the practice that they really need to do to perform well on the assessments when it does count."

Districts typically convert standards-based grades into A–F grades or a 4.0-based system for a transcript, since colleges are accustomed to those grading scales. To Wilson, that makes the entire enterprise seem a waste of time. He said he's seen no evidence that the new approach to grading improves learning, and so it looks like just another of the fads that administrators pass around at conferences.

Wilson's larger problem with standards-based grading is philosophical: "We've moved away from content knowledge to wanting process," just the way Common Core emphasizes skills rather than knowledge. When learning is centered on process, students and teachers zoom in on tiny fragments of information and miss the big picture of how it all fits together. "You're taking standard C, whatever standard C is, and you're focusing on that to give a kid a rating," without providing a deeper education in the liberal arts. "You focus on such a minute part of something that is so much larger … and you realize the kid can do this and it looks like the kid is doing well, but they really can't do anything with the larger subject area."

Because she decided to use this kind of grading on her own, Scriffiny has had many conversations with colleagues about what it means to evaluate student work. Teachers' beliefs about human nature and how to mold young people's character influence their grading, she said. Some of her colleagues believe that kids should be penalized for late or poor work because the real world often won't give them second chances. Scriffiny, on the other hand, believes that kids need to learn the power of forgiveness and their own ability to change labels that others have pinned on them.

"I feel like a priest," she said. "People I've just met tell me these horrible experiences they've had with math teachers. How you value people, it's an infinite part of what we do. It's visceral.… Sometimes the powers that be forget that. They think it's just an instructional strategy, no big deal, we can just change it."

That sometimes seems to be the attitude of the social planners who cooked up Common Core. They seem to have given little thought to the many consequences of taking local control away from schools, or to the possibility that some things, such as a grading scale, might work well for some schools and teachers but not for others. The people most affected – school staff, parents, local leaders – are not being allowed to decide what works best for their students and their children, and that lack of choice inflames the political and academic disagreements over Common Core. The central planners making those decisions are so far away from class- rooms they may forget they're playing with human beings. It's a little like kids bulldozing and rebuilding houses in a video game, except it isn't a game. It's real.

CHAPTER 3

Control — One Test to Rule Them All

A MOTHER EMAILED ME in March 2014, worried her children were being targeted in school in retaliation for her disagreement with their superintendent over Common Core. Sarah Lewis had sent a letter to Jesse Steiner, superintendent of Celina City Schools in western Ohio, asking to opt her three children out of state tests. A few days later, Steiner sent Lewis an email saying her children would not be excused from anything: "[O]n the recommendation of legal counsel, I am rejecting your request for your child to 'Opt Out' of any and all testing. Your child will be expected to follow the same educational procedures as the rest of the student body."

That same day, the superintendent drove to her kids' school and demanded to have the three Lewis children weighed and measured, even though their principal, Dan Pohlman, had allowed them to opt out of an earlier body-mass-index screening. Lewis had wanted her kids released from the BMI screening for two reasons. First, her family considers health information to be private. "We would rather have that information kept between our family and our physician," she told me. Second, her daughter was distressed when she came home from school one day the previous year with a report saying her BMI meant she was overweight. "This is a nine-year-old girl that is already uncomfortable with her body as it starts to change," Lewis said.

Nevertheless, on Steiner's order, the Lewis children were pulled out in front of their class to have their weight and height measured separately from all the other kids. No one notified Lewis that this was being done until the kids came home from school upset. "They were singled out and weighed and measured. They were humiliated," Lewis said over the phone, almost in tears. She believed that the superintendent was angry at her temerity in asking for the testing opt-out, she said, so "he decided to take it out on my kids."

Lewis was just one among hundreds of thousands of parents who requested to have their children excused from Common Core tests, which were administered in pilot versions to randomly selected students across the country in 2013 and 2014. Those trial runs were intended to prepare the tests for full implementation in 2015, when they would replace the existing state tests in reading and math that the No Child Left Behind law mandated annually for third through eighth grade and once in high school. As they rumbled into schools, however, the tests self-destructed spectacularly, nullifying hundreds of thousands of hours spent on them by millions of children, teachers, parents, and bureaucrats, not to mention wasting hundreds of millions of tax dollars. Consequently, citizens have grown more distrustful of those who run America's public schools.

When Lewis emailed me about her concerns, the Common Core debate had been heating up in Celina City. Lewis and her husband began discussing the national standards and tests when their third grader started getting new kinds of math problems. He was also "constantly coming home talking about how they were taking practice tests. It seemed like that was all he was doing," Lewis said. One night, he cried because he was so stressed about the tests.

She asked her kids' teachers about the new math, and they told her, "We have to do it this way because it's going to be on the test." Lewis said to me in exasperation: "Test, test, test – that's all we heard!"

Lewis and some other mothers started talking to each other about Common Core and researching it online. They began giving public presentations, writing to local newspapers, and inviting experts to speak. In February 2014, they invited Heidi Huber, a grassroots leader who founded Ohioans Against Common Core. In March, they hosted Terrence O. Moore, a riveting public speaker who was then a professor at Hillsdale College and still advises its Charter School Initiative. It was standing-room-only in the Celina High School lecture hall that evening, according to Celina's *Daily Standard*. The next day, Steiner sent his email to Lewis and visited her kids at school.

"Some people don't think it's a big deal. Who cares if they weigh and mess with your kids?" Lewis said. "It doesn't matter why. What matters is that we asked them not to do it." (Steiner and Pohlman did not return phone messages requesting comment.)

Lewis is concerned that disagreements among adults on education policy may hurt her kids again. "I support our teachers," she said, "but I am very fearful that they are going to start treating [my children] differently because of all of this."

In fact, the BMI incident wasn't the end of insults the Lewis family endured at the hands of "public servants." The week before her children went back to school that fall, Sarah asked her school board if her sixth grader could be excused from a world religions segment in social studies. The previous year, students had spent a month studying Islam, and Lewis believes that school is not the place for children to learn a religion. Steiner asked her to meet with him to discuss the matter.

In that meeting, Lewis said, Steiner told her she could not excuse her daughter from those classes and she must route all communications with her children's teachers through the school office. He gave her the state forms for homeschooling and encouraged her to withdraw her children from public school. He handed her a piece of paper with the word "bigot" and its definition, telling her the description fit her, she said. Steiner also told her that the school district considered her requests to be "harassment," Lewis said.

"I must be living in a nightmare because none of this seems real," she told me. "I am a homeowner and a taxpayer. I support public education and am appalled that I would be treated this way as a parent. What, if any, recourse do I as a parent have?"

Lewis's experience illustrates several harmful trends in public education that Common Core exacerbates. One is a heavy emphasis on standardized testing, to meet state and federal mandates. The second is that schools are functioning as data-collection agencies to funnel personal information about their charges to myriad private and government entities, with very little security or oversight. Third is a wresting of authority away from the parents who pay for public schools through taxes and send their children there to be educated, yet have little power to decide what kind of education they will receive. In all three of these trends, the issue comes down to who controls the public schools: parents and local taxpayers, or a coalition of largely unelected government officials and advocacy groups? Most people may believe it's the former, but Common Core and its testing mandates reveal that it's really the latter.

An Absolute Game-Changer

When Arne Duncan announced in 2010 that the U.S. Department of Education was awarding $330 million to PARCC and SBAC to create national tests linked to Common Core, he declared, "Today is the day that marks the beginning of the development of a new and much-improved generation of assessments for America's schoolchildren. Today marks the start of Assessments 2.0." The new tests would be "an absolute game-changer in public education."[1]

The money was to cover operating costs for PARCC and SBAC during the four years they were developing the tests. The two nonprofits might be thought of almost as a unit because they have shared test questions and coordinated their test results, with the aim of fulfilling the promise of "national" tests. Recall also that PARCC is run by Achieve, Inc., part of the triumvirate that developed Common Core in the first place. There's a handy little built-in kickback designed to provide ongoing revenue, since states now pay annual fees for the tests. PARCC and SBAC worked with bureaucrats from almost every state to create their "game-changer" tests from scratch.

The consortia appeared to be involving teachers in the process, but in Brad McQueen's experience it seemed to have little effect. McQueen, a fifth-grade teacher in Tucson, had helped write Arizona's state tests for five years before he was invited to participate in writing the PARCC assessments in 2013. He thought this would be an advantage in his classroom. "There are standards every which way," he said, "but until you really see what they're looking for [in the tests], you don't know how to adjust your teaching. A lot of teachers were saying, 'We'll wait until the test comes out, we'll see what this looks like.'" McQueen saw the invitation from PARCC as an opportunity to get a head start on teaching his kids what the Common Core tests would require them to know, so he traveled to Chicago with four other teachers from Arizona during spring break.

When teachers write questions for standardized tests, they work from "rubrics," or criteria for the test questions, to make sure they measure what the test's creators want. It might be a certain vocabulary level, or specific abilities such as finding the main idea of a paragraph. The rubrics were already written for McQueen and the other teachers working that week in Chicago writing and reviewing test questions, which were then tried out on kids.

"The rubrics didn't seem to be working to me," McQueen said. "All the kids were failing. The essay questions made no sense. As a teacher, when I write a question I know what is confusing for a student. But these were confusing as to what they wanted. A teacher doesn't ever write it that way." He and several other teachers started asking who wrote the rubrics, and whether they could improve them.

The short answer was no. Certain styles of teaching were built into Common Core, such as the requirement that students only use information from a given text, as we saw in Chapter 2 with the teachers' requests for "textual evidence." McQueen said a PARCC official told him, "We don't ever want [students'] opinion, we want them to look at the experts' opinions and they repeat back the experts' opinions." McQueen replied, "We don't teach that way ... to just believe whatever you read." The official said, "We expect when the test comes out, teachers will reflect the Common Core way of thinking in their classroom."

"That was kind of a kick in the stomach, and I thought *there's something wrong here*," McQueen told me. "There were a couple more days [to the meeting], so I just kept my head down. There weren't a lot of teachers there. It was heavy with the bureaucrat type."

That interaction and others like it felt "odd" to McQueen. When he wrote tests for Arizona, teachers "had so much control and input over the test. We could change or alter it if it didn't work. Here decisions were made by different committees, so I really got the idea that there's a lot more bureaucracy. Decision making has been removed from Arizona to this other group."

The resistance to feedback extended down to very small things, such as bolding text or giving students an excerpt when asking them a vocabulary question instead of requiring them to work from a larger reading assignment. "They would say instantly, 'That's already been decided.' But that's not how we would do it in the classroom," said McQueen.

The PARCC folks also used words from Common Core that teachers didn't use, and it resulted in communication problems. Rather than consider altering Common Core or its tests to fit classroom practices, PARCC employees would repeat the line: "Teachers will have to start using this language in the classroom." McQueen wondered, "Shouldn't you make your standards from the ground up, not the top down?" Then he laughed. "They're not a ground-up type organization."

That experience prompted McQueen to look into Common Core more deeply when he returned home. He attended another PARCC question-writing session in November, where he asked more questions and got even colder responses. He was invited back to several more sessions, but they were all held while school was in session, and he didn't like to leave his students with substitute teachers so long.

Most of the test developers he met "had the flexibility to leave for a week. Teachers can't do that," he pointed out. Participants had at least a week of preparation to do before these events, and they were expected to take part in Skype conference calls afterward. "You're not going to get a teacher to do that unless it's a teacher that is okay leaving a class for a month and a half," McQueen said. "It was set up in such a way, if you're a teacher, they want to check the box that teachers are involved, but they don't genuinely want teachers there because if you did you'd do this in the summer."

In any case, McQueen had decided that he opposed Common Core and didn't want to participate in writing its tests anymore – or to provide camouflage for those who were really running the show.

Unprepared Classrooms

McQueen had wanted to prepare his students for an unfamiliar test format and adjust his instruction to what Common Core tests would require. Making this adjustment was a challenge for teachers across the country: many schools were still struggling to adapt to the new standards when the trial tests were being administered and even when the full roll-out began. "We start testing on standards we're not teaching with curriculum we don't have on computers that don't exist," one teacher tweeted.[2] "We're flying the airplane as we're building it," said Karen Lewis, president of the Chicago Teachers Union, in June 2013.[3] Dallas Dance, the superintendent of Baltimore County Public Schools and a Common Core supporter, used the same metaphor later that year.[4] A superintendent in

Ohio did, too.[5] What's worse, the Core-pushers were still building a flying plane *with children inside.*

While writing new tests is a massive undertaking, it pales in comparison with getting millions of teachers and tens of millions of children learning by an entirely new program, said Doug McRae, a retired testing executive. In the 1990s he helped develop California's STAR assessments, which were so well regarded that many states used them until Common Core supplanted them. California did a curriculum overhaul around the same time, and McRae noted that a successful overhaul requires four to six years of switching schools over to the new curriculum before new tests can usefully be applied. But with Common Core, "they implemented the test before they implemented instruction."

McRae faults the federal government for setting the 2015 deadline for full implementation of the tests and signing four-year contracts with the test developers, even though schools and districts would likely not be prepared for a new assessment regime. "The consortia said, 'If you sign up with the consortia you agree to implement the tests in 2015,' all without regard to whether Common Core instruction has been implemented," he noted. In fall 2014, two-thirds of school districts in a national survey said they had not yet worked Common Core into all their schools. A quarter of districts said it would take at least another school year to get the curriculum in all their schools and have all teachers prepared to use it.[6]

Common Core's creators should have known their timeline was unrealistic. In addition to instructional lag time, there were technological hurdles. For example, the plan was to require all schools to administer Common Core tests entirely online by the 2017-18 school year, but setting up the necessary infrastructure is a long and costly operation. The advocacy organization Education SuperHighway noted that 77 percent of public schools did not have fast enough Internet to administer online tests in 2013.[7] In the fall of 2014, a nationally representative survey of school districts slated to use Common Core tests the following spring found that half did not have the technological infrastructure to administer the tests, and three-quarters predicted challenges in getting the needed equipment.[8]

President Obama tried to solve the technology problem in 2013 by proposing unilaterally to increase the federal tax on every phone line by approximately $5 per year to increase technology subsidies to schools.[9] But it takes years to get the technology and IT staff in place, and federal programs don't seem to be efficient at doing so. E-Rate, which is the

Schools and Libraries Program of the Universal Service Fund, was already burning through a cool $2.25 billion per year, half of it on broadband, yet 80 percent of teachers and principals in E-Rate schools said they still didn't have enough broadband in early 2014.[10]

The only independent national estimate of the cost for the technology necessary to implement Common Core arrived at a sum of $6.9 billion.[11] Technology was the largest implementation expense that the study predicted. Obama pushed to boost E-Rate by another $2 billion, nowhere near enough money – even if it were appropriate for the feds to raise taxes to help pay for a "state-led" initiative.[12] States and localities would have to pick up the rest of the tab. Moreover, new research finds that "the more E-Rate funding a school received, the worse its students performed."[13]

The foreseeable technology shortage resulted in the waste of millions of man-hours when schools started using Common Core tests for the first time. Technological glitches with the tests plagued schools nationwide. From 2013 to 2016, two-thirds of states reported extensive testing problems.[14] Ten states had major technical difficulties in 2015: California, Colorado, Florida, Georgia, Indiana, Minnesota, Montana, Nevada, North Dakota, and Wisconsin. Others – including Illinois, Maine, New Jersey, and Rhode Island – experienced more isolated glitches. Many states continued to have technical problems in 2016, including Georgia, Mississippi, New Jersey, Tennessee, and Wisconsin.[15]

"Technical problems" meant children sitting and staring at screens because they couldn't log on to the test, or because the test wouldn't move forward a page, and so forth. Many school districts across the country postponed testing for a few weeks after several wasted days trying to make it work. Things were so bad in Montana and in Clark County, Nevada – the nation's fifth-largest school district, with 328,000 students – that testing was made entirely optional there in 2015. Major concerns about testing accuracy arose from all the crashes, starts and stops, and low numbers of students tested in some districts. How accurate are test results if the test taker had to sit and click for hours while nothing, or the wrong things, happened on the screen?

Writing software for the national Common Core tests is incredibly complex and prone to bugs, said David DeSchryver, vice president of education policy at Whiteboard Advisors, a well-connected D.C. consulting firm. The software must work on a wide variety of computing devices, operating systems, and Internet browsers, and it must operate simply enough for non-techies, like most teachers and principals. That's a tall order, which PARCC and SBAC seem to have left unfilled. It wouldn't matter so much if they were private companies that people could fire for poor performance. But they are *publicly funded* private organizations whose contracts with states effectively empower them to compel millions of American kids to participate in their poorly constructed experiment.

The main reason for the debacle is that Common Core has been run more as a political enterprise than an instructional one, and it was politics that governed the schedule. In effect, Common Core's advocates set their project up to fail by forcing kids to take their experimental tests before teachers had time to adjust their instruction, and before schools could get the technological platforms up and running. They moved quickly because otherwise they would not have been able to stampede the states into Common Core. To achieve a PR success by getting lots of bureaucrats to sign forms and issue reports, they had to undermine the possibility that the project itself would genuinely succeed. They chose feel-good fanfare over any benefit to American children.

The Best Tests in World History

Schools were not ready for the new tests when they launched, and the tests were not ready for the students either, since their reliability as a measure of learning was in doubt. In announcing that his department was funding the creation of the tests, Secretary Duncan said they would provide "valid and reliable assessments that will truly foster better teacher [sic] and college and career readiness." At the same time, he promised "game-changer" assessments that would end boring "fill-in-the-bubble tests of basic skills."[16] These promises are hard to reconcile, because fill-in-the-bubble tests are the most reliable kind. Any experiment with a new testing format puts reliability in question, and it's quite difficult to get both innovation and accuracy in testing, as various states have already found out.

A basic ethical principle in psychological and educational testing is that studies documenting the reliability and validity of standardized tests be available before people use them to measure others, according to standards from the American Educational Research Association, the American Psychological Association, and the National Council on Measurement are allowing an 'opt out' for the field tests." But he maintained that parents may not refuse the official tests or data collection on their kids' behalf, which meant no opt-outs when Common Core tests replaced the state tests.

North Carolina may have the harshest penalty for students who opt out, as sixth grader Zoe Morris found in 2013 when she decided that taking Common Core tests violated her conscience because it pushed teachers to teach from scripts and refuse to answer kids' questions that weren't explicitly part of the curriculum. Charlie Morris, her father, told school officials that he and Zoe had decided she would not take state tests anymore as an act of civil disobedience to protest the state's phase-in of Common Core. The district set its lawyer on him. Ultimately, Zoe sat in front of the screen and didn't enter a thing on the state's annual exam. The school had effectively placed her on time-out for refusing the test.

Charlie and Zoe thought it was over. Later that year, however, they got results for the test that Zoe had not taken. Even though she never touched the test, she was given the lowest possible score, marring her excellent academic record. By North Carolina law, state tests must constitute 20 percent of a student's final grade in the subjects tested.

Students who are absent on testing day and for whom "it is not possible to administer a make-up" can have their final grade calculated without the end-of-course exam, said Tammi Howard, director of accountability for North Carolina's department of education. "This may occur in situations such as a death in a family," she explained, adding that penalties for opting out are "local decisions."

While the Common Core field tests were not mandatory, PARCC and SBAC needed kids to sit for them so the tests they put together could accurately measure student abilities, Howard said. "If enough students opt out, the final test would not represent all students of the population." She also noted that when No Child Left Behind required schools to test 95 percent of their students, it was partly "to be able to say this school didn't just pick 50 percent of the brightest students, so test results reflect the vast majority of their students."

Federal law, however, only requires schools to *give* the test; it doesn't require kids to *take* the test. That distinction is lost on many officials, said Tom Slekar, an education professor at Penn State Altoona and a leader of United Opt Out. Like NCLB before it, the Every Student Succeeds Act (ESSA) requires all public schools to administer tests annually to in Education.[17] "Validity" and "reliablity" are terms with precise meanings in the testing industry. Reliability is essentially a matter of consistency – for example, will similar groups of students show comparable results on the test each time it's administered? Validity is a matter of how closely the test correlates with competency in the tested skill outside the test itself: Does a high score on a math test correlate with high grades in math class? Do the tests accurately predict college performance in those skills?

Testing companies ordinarily make studies of reliability and validity available to states before new tests are administered to any children, said McRae. If the companies get an exclusive contract to develop tests for a state, the state decides when it must receive the reliability data, he said; but tests are always validated before being given to children. At least, they used to be.

Neither the public, nor state lawmakers, nor independent testing professionals who don't work for PARCC or SBAC saw any validity studies on the Common Core tests until they were already operational. So far, Massachusetts has commissioned the only independent study to examine Common Core tests' validity. The study found that PARCC results would not predict college readiness, as promised, any better than the state's previous tests had done.[18] A child psychologist in Utah, Dr. Gary Thompson, offered a $100,000 reward to his state's education department in 2014 if it would provide him the validity studies for its own Common Core tests, which are not the national tests but were written by the same contractor that supplies testing software and consulting to SBAC. The reward went unclaimed.[19] SBAC and PARCC promised the federal government they would create validity studies, but did not provide any such studies to the public or to states that used their tests in 2013, 2014, or 2015, either during or directly after the testing season.

There are no open-records provisions within the consortia's governing documents, and they are technically private organizations so "it's done basically behind closed doors," even though "it's federally funded, so they're using your money," said McRae. He made a public-records request to his home state of California for the validity data on SBAC tests in January 2015, not long before they were to be fully implemented across the state. In response, he got a letter saying, "We've got none of that data and we're not going to go to the consortium to get it for you."

Standardized test makers normally try out their questions on thousands of test takers before using them as a measure of learning. That's why the Graduate Record Exam, a leading graduate-school entrance test, includes an entirely experimental section on every test. The students taking the test don't know which are the experimental questions that don't count toward their score. The test makers can then compare the results on the experimental section with the established part in order to assess the validity and reliability of their new questions. Common Core tests were entirely new from the ground up, so everything was experimental when the consortia began testing the tests on millions of American schoolchildren in 2013.[20]

In November 2014, after the two years of trial testing had passed, a teacher in Louisiana referred on her blog to a report by SBAC admitting that the grading scale for its tests was little more than an educated guess, because no data tied it to college success.[21] Mercedes Schneider quoted a footnote in the report that read: "Additional research will be needed to validate the achievement level descriptors in relation to the actual success rates of students when they enter college and careers." That makes sense, of course. The kids who had taken SBAC tests weren't in college yet. The report said that designations of achievement levels on the tests (such as "novice, developing, proficient, advanced") were meant to "serve only as a starting point for discussion" and "should not be interpreted as infallible predictors of students' futures."[22] This means that Common Core supporters have been pretending – insisting – that these tests can predict "college and career readiness" when they actually have no idea if that's true. They're tying high school diplomas and college entrance possibilities to unproven tests. We'll know whether it worked once (if?) the kids get to college. Bill Gates himself admitted in 2013, "It would be great if our education stuff worked, but that we won't know for probably a decade."[23]

Shortly before the spring 2015 testing season, a report from Missouri found that the SBAC tests to be used there had no external measures of validity or reliability.[24] Asked about the reliability of PARCC tests in May, Derek Briggs of the University of Colorado Boulder, a member of the PARCC Technical Advisory Committee, told the Colorado State Board of Education, "We just don't know yet. It's too soon.... [I]t's really, really important to see PARCC for what it is: an evolving enterprise."[25]

In short, there was really no way of knowing if PARCC and SBAC tests were accurate measures of learning when those tests were implemented nationwide, and their reliability and validity are still not firmly established by either public or independent research. But history suggests the kind of tests that PARCC and SBAC have aimed to create tend to be much less accurate than many of the leading tests.

Generally speaking, the most reliable kind of standardized test is based on multiple-choice questions, for which the answers are either right or wrong and the scoring process is straightforward. But many educators regard a multiple-choice format as an inadequate way of measuring a person's academic skills and learning. Common Core tests therefore include some open-ended questions, where a child writes several sentences, performs a task on a computer, or has to explain his answer, as in this question that appeared on a PARCC test for the fourth grade: "Explain how to find $2 \times {}^5/_{12}$ using the number line."[26] Here's one from New York's third-grade Common Core tests:

> Jimmy's teacher asked him to describe a situation in which the number of objects could be represented by $24 \div 4$.
>
> Jimmy started his description, shown below. Complete the description so that the number of objects can be represented by $24 \div 4$.
>
> [The description begins:] A pet store had a total of 24 fish.
> _____ "[27]

This is followed by a blank space in which children are supposed to write Jimmy's answer.

Questions of this type are meant to elicit "critical thinking," but they also introduce a verbal component into the math section of the test, as Professor Wayne Bishop of Cal State Los Angeles has written. When a math test requires students to "answer follow-up questions and perform a task that shows their research and problem-solving skills," it may sound like a sophisticated kind of testing, but in reality "it makes the mathematics tests far more verbal. Any student with weak reading and writing skills is unfairly assessed. That is especially problematic for English learners."[28]

Open-ended questions are also more difficult to score with precision. Some states have used open-ended test formats before. Kentucky was one of the first to try more "critical thinking" questions, in the 1990s, but the results of those tests were notoriously unreliable. Parents and state lawmakers were deprived of accurate information about how schoolkids were doing for at least a decade, said Richard Innes, an education researcher at the Bluegrass Institute for Public Policy. Similar experiments elsewhere with open-ended questions have had similarly disastrous results, whether a human or a computer grades the tests.

SBAC's chief operating officer, Tony Alpert, said in 2012 that the testing organizations wanted to develop computer algorithms to score open-ended answers, and to create "adaptive" tests that present students with harder questions after correct answers and easier questions after incorrect ones.[29] Computer-adaptive "game-changer" tests of this kind require much larger banks of questions, McRae pointed out. Thus they are quite expensive and time-consuming to create, and this is likely one reason that both consortia scaled back their use of such questions.[30] But there's enough game-changing to create issues of reliability.

Including questions other than multiple-choice on standardized tests isn't necessarily bad, said Ted Rebarber, CEO of AccountabilityWorks, a nonprofit that develops tests and helps teachers learn how to use them. He explained that the movement toward open-ended questions was a reaction against a narrow focus on basic skills and knowledge that are easily measured, such as grammar and vocabulary, while the ability to *use* those skills for any larger purpose is overlooked. "You have kids that could answer these questions but would have trouble putting these together into an essay or a coherent piece of writing," Rebarber said. So there's "some sense" in using open-ended questions and performance tasks for a more "authentic" type of assessment, "because if you're going to have tests for public accountability or reporting, they can't just correlate with what you want, but actually have to model what you want your students to be able to do." In other words, can students apply their skills effectively?

Teachers can formulate good open-ended questions and performance tasks in line with their classroom instruction, and can evaluate the results in a meaningful way. Doing this on a large scale is more challenging. The state of Vermont has successfully used portfolios of students' work for assessments, as the College Board does in its advanced art tests. These assessments do "reach a certain level of reliability, but not as high as a multiple-choice test," Rebarber said. Even when scoring criteria are specified in detail, different people will interpret and apply them differently. (Think the academic version of Olympics figure skating judges.) Moreover, when states tie the results to accountability measures such as high school graduation or school ratings, portfolio graders are incentivized to go easy. "In absolute terms, in just reliability, performance tasks tend to have lower reliability," Rebarber stressed. "But you can get them to an acceptable level if they are part of a larger assessment and they're well-designed, well-defined tasks and you have other short-answer questions."

When the testing format is unfamiliar, or complicated with extra steps such as asking young children to drag-and-drop or cut-and-paste on a computer screen, what is actually being assessed becomes murky. A test question that throws a complex problem at children and asks them to solve it on their own is often "a formula for frustration for a lot of students" if they haven't worked through similar problems in class, Rebarber noted. "A lot of students struggle and you get a lot of special-ed referrals." The students may actually be capable of solving the problem but stumped by the test writer's unfamiliar way of framing it, whereas their own teacher could present essentially the same problem in a way that calls forth a good answer. (Remember what Brad McQueen said about how the PARCC test writers were posing questions: "A teacher doesn't ever write it this way.") Or the test could just be needlessly complicated so it looks fancy for the cameras. In PARCC questions, for example,

> the answer to Part A sets up a question in Part B that compels students to go back to the question in Part A and into the reading passage(s) used for the question in Part A. Parts A and B are designed to move test-takers back and forth through the text and the answer options. Unless readers make the correct choice in Part A, however, their answer in Part B will not be scored as correct, even if they select the right answer in Part B.[31]

Or the test maker might be looking for a particular method of reaching an answer, another situation where an objectively correct response might be considered not good enough – as Heather Crossin's young daughter found out in her math class when she could easily identify the longer of two bridges but didn't show the required formula.

With more complicated test questions, writes Sandra Stotsky, "scores become less a measure of subject matter knowledge and more a measure of ability to discern the logic of the format or the meaning of the instructions." One result is that teachers start teaching the test format as much as the subject. They will "increase time on practice drills to improve the test performance of low-achieving students and spend less time on instruction in subject matter – ultimately a poor trade-off." Stotsky said this explains why "the innovative test items on Common Core-based tests are rare on tests outside the United States."[32]

Spending class time on teaching the test format gets things backward. A math teacher, for example, will spend time coaching students in language formulas they will be expected to follow in answering problems, when that time could have been used for teaching actual math skills. During the several decades McRae spent developing and analyzing tests for McGraw-Hill, among other companies, he kept a little blue index card with a quotation from Henry Dyer (1853): "If you use test exercises as an instrument of teaching, you destroy the usefulness of the test for measuring the effects of teaching."

Rebarber observed that effective performance tasks and open-ended questions actually require students to have a lot of knowledge content. But specific content, as we've seen, is something that the Common Core curriculum mostly eschews. Instead, it emphasizes skill or process, such as "close reading" of a "text," primarily because a focus on knowledge is thought to put the less affluent children at a disadvantage. Likewise, test developers today consider expectations of specific knowledge about a subject to be a source of bias in tests of reading comprehension, because children from wealthier families naturally pick up more knowledge than children from poorer families, said Lisa Hansel, president of the Core Knowledge Foundation.[33] Since Common Core specifies very little content for children to encounter in school, test makers can't predict what they are expected to know, so they have to write more open-ended questions, which are difficult to score with precision. But students perform best on open-ended tests when they've had a more content-rich curriculum than what Common Core outlines. If kids then do poorly on the tests, Common Core supporters say it disproves charges of watered-down standards!

Because the Common Core tests were new and unvalidated, Kentucky made an effort to gauge their reliability when it administered trial versions in 2013, by adding in some questions from its previous test. Researchers could then examine how the same child performed on both sets of questions and calibrate the scores. This calibration gave the public a way to know whether children were objectively doing better or worse from year to year, even when the testing format changed for all children. New York did not do the same kind of transition tests, but instead created its own Common Core-based tests to replace its existing tests, and jumped in with both feet. And New York "got hammered," as McRae put it. "Their test results came out a whole lot lower, and nobody could explain why. They didn't have the information necessary to put an interpretation on the new results." Most other states did not do transition tests either as they switched over to Common Core, although running pilot tests on some students alongside the existing tests would have allowed for some comparison.

Because California is essentially run by its teachers union, which is resistant to providing the public with information about student progress, state officials did not concern themselves with creating transparency by comparing the old and new test results. They decided to administer only the Common Core assessments in 2014. That was flatly illegal, but Secretary Duncan didn't punish California. Instead, he let every state do the same thing, unilaterally suspending a federal law and giving states what he called an exemption from "double testing" for spring 2014.[34] His action lifted any threat of federal consequences from schools or states that had used Common Core pilot tests for accountability purposes in lieu of more reliable state tests. Why did he do it? Because the testing consortium needed the huge contingent of California students to provide data for its second year of trial tests. As McRae explained it, "California is half of Smarter Balanced's students. If Duncan had been tough with California on the waiver, he would have tanked Smarter Balanced." Saving the Common Core testing apparatus (if only temporarily) took priority over continuity in assessments and public accountability.

The result was a break in testing data in the six states that used only the Common Core tests that year.[35] "In 2014, we didn't have accountability here in California," McRae said. "I figure 2018 would be the first year we get it." The state could not compare the results from the Common Core pilot tests administered in 2014 against the results of the state tests used in 2013. The results from the Common Core tests administered in 2015 – supposedly the validated version – could not be meaningfully compared with the pilot tests because they were effectively different tests. Adding another wrinkle; in 2015 the tests were given to students in both electronic and paper format, and the results on the two formats were not comparable, so the 2015 data could not be reliably used as a baseline for 2016, McRae said.[36] So 2017 will be the first year when (theoretically) a direct year-to-year comparison can be made for all students statewide, but it will take until 2018 for trend lines to start emerging.

Another factor in the accountability lapse is that Secretary Duncan also announced in August 2014 that states would have a one-year reprieve from using test results to evaluate teachers, which would resume in 2016.[37] But teachers are evaluated on year-over-year comparisons to avoid unfairly punishing those who teach kids who start further behind. Thus, there's a similar gap in useful data for teacher evaluations.

The upshot is at least four years of essentially no useful public information about how much children are learning in the nation's most populous state, or in the other states that went the same route. And for reasons we have already seen – the lack of validity studies, the differences between pilot tests and the official version – there was effectively a testing gap in every state in the nation that replaced its previous tests with Common Core tests in 2015, which is nearly all of them.

The testing gap nullified state and federal school accountability measures that are contingent on year-to-year tracking of test results. Republicans in particular have called for test-based accountability so taxpayers will have some idea of what they are getting in exchange for the $620 billion or so that goes to K-12 education annually. But many influential Republicans have supported the Common Core experiment that essentially suspended public accountability nationwide for three or four years while it was being phased in. That lack of accountability is most harmful to children who attend the poorest-performing schools.

Big Data Goes to School

If Common Core testing were merely an unproven and unreliable means of delivering useful information about academic achievement, that would be bad enough. What may be of greater concern to parents is that the tests are designed to collect all manner of personal information on their children.

Jenni White is one of many parents who have become deeply concerned about the data collection facilitated by Common Core. She runs Restore Oklahoma Public Education, a grassroots organization that sends representatives to every state department of education meeting just to monitor what's happening. That's how they discovered that the state tracks homeschool students in its database, and pieced together Common Core's corporate and philanthropic networks. (Education is big business, especially after you create a national market.) White and her friends read thousand-page government documents in between shuffling kids to activities and keeping their network informed of quickly shifting state laws and rules.

The conjunction of big data with education is what brought White to oppose Common Core. The national Common Core testing organizations are not just collecting the kind of anonymous, aggregate student information that states have historically submitted to the federal government, but also "student-level data" that goes into national databases. There, the federal government and any person or organization it designates will have "timely and complete access to any and all data collected at the State level," according to the testing organizations' contracts with the federal government.[38]

White, a spunky, spiral-curled woman who often sports cowboy boots and a silver belt buckle, knows just why she doesn't want her children's personal information fed into national databases open to anyone that bureaucrats permit to see them. "I was a horrible child," she explained. Looking at her twinkly eyes, you can believe it. "I didn't mature until after forty. I can't conceive of what my life would be like now if I had a record of 'what Jennifer did as a kid' following me."

U.S. government agencies actually started amassing data collections on citizens long before Common Core. For several decades, the federal government has been giving money to states to build comprehensive data systems, so that forty-six states currently track children from preschool through their careers.[39] The most recent rounds of federal grants are connecting separate state data systems, such as those for education, health care, and social services, to create cradle-to-grave government dossiers on U.S. citizens.[40] The federal government's National Education Data Model suggests that states track personal information about kids (and their parents), such as specific religious affiliation and bus routes.[41] It may sound like a crazy conspiracy theory, or even a communist plot – China maintains similar records on its populace and uses them to ensure social conformity.[42] But it's true, right here in America.

Many politicians are dismissive of her concerns about government spying, White said. "People think you're nuts when you just want to make sure your kids have their childhood – that not everybody in the world knows about your kid, that your kid can be an individual person, and that your child doesn't have a record." But she can joke about it too: "We're going to get outfits wearing fringe and go to our Oklahoma County Republican meeting saying, 'We're the fringe.'" In reality, though, her views are more mainstream than fringe. Pew Research reported in 2015 that 91 percent of American adults think consumers have lost control over their personal information, and 81 percent of parents are somewhat or very concerned about how much information on their kids is collected by advertisers online.[43] Major companies such as Google and Microsoft sell products to schools, and it's unclear how much they leverage these relationships to build data profiles of kids who use their products.[44]

Because the data collection on children had been expanding before Common Core was a gleam in David Coleman's eye, supporters of Common Core often insist that they are completely separate issues. An Obama administration factsheet labels as "myth" the idea that "The two consortia of states developing new assessments aligned to the Common Core State Standards are required to provide individual student data to the Federal government."[45] That statement directly contradicts the administration's own contracts with SBAC and PARCC, which clearly specify the collection of "student-level data" and "complete [federal] access to any and all data collected."

The administration's factsheet acknowledges that it is illegal for the federal government to create a national database on citizens. To get around this prohibition, the feds have used pretty much the same trick as the one employed to get around the laws against imposing a national curriculum: by paying states and nonprofits to create their own data systems, make them interoperable, and give federal agencies access to (but not ownership of) the data. This would effectively establish a national child database without going directly through federal agencies, as an analysis by the Home School Legal Defense Association explains.[46]

PARCC's contract with the federal government promised it would create or plug into "a centralized Interactive Data tool and reporting platform/system that will work in tandem with current state longitudinal data systems. In addition, the Partnership will establish a set of common identity management and data technology standards for member states." It would also assign ID numbers to each student and teacher in PARCC states "to better track students and teachers through the system and allow data to follow individuals across Partnership states."[47] Further into the contract, we find that PARCC would help "leverage the millions of dollars in state and federal investments in next-generation data and reporting systems to ensure that states can easily and quickly receive assessment results." To this end, PARCC promised that its "assessment system will take in and produce a wealth of data, and that information must seamlessly integrate with states' data management systems."[48]

SBAC also pledged to create a comprehensive national database on students and teachers, and to provide information from it directly to the federal government. Its application for federal funds promised it would "work with the [U.S. Department of Education] to develop a strategy to make student-level data available on an ongoing basis for cross-State or cross-consortia research activities." Further, "Each participating State also will be expected to cooperate with the evaluators during all data collection efforts, including cross-State research studies."[49] SBAC described its national student database this way:

> The Consortium plans on developing two key technology systems as part of its assessment system – a computerized assessment delivery platform to deliver the actual computer adapted assessments ($15 million) and a centralized data repository, reporting, and professional development delivery system ($7.5 million) where all student responses and professional development materials will be housed and all test results and other information will be generated and reported.[50]

So while Common Core did not start the trend of federal data collection, the initiative has facilitated its expansion. Yet Common Core supporters continue to treat this issue as unworthy of public discussion. That's likely because what they've done would be widely unpopular if it were more widely known.

In 2013, the founder of the Home School Legal Defense Association, Michael Farris, reported a conversation he had with David Coleman. Farris told him that one of his main concerns about Common Core was "the creation of the database that would track students throughout their educational career." Coleman replied that he didn't especially like the database and that it was not originally intended to be part of Common Core but other people had "seized the opportunity to make a centralized data collection effort through the implementation of the Common Core," as

Farris recalled his remarks.[51] In other words, Common Core's architect has confirmed that this data mining expansion is real, and that it's tied to Common Core.

PARCC, SBAC, the Council of Chief State School Officers, and the State Educational Technology Directors Association are using Common Core to collect and organize very detailed information about each child that encounters it, by breaking down, labeling, and organizing skills like multiplication or solving for X. By design, the curriculum mandates function as a data taxonomy, or a sort of unified filing system for cataloguing what every person knows.[52]

"Standards, like the Common Core, make big data analytics work because they support the creation of more rigorous models of student learning and enable larger big data systems," as Darrell West and Joshua Bleiberg of the Brookings Institution explained. They noted that it is "technically easier to link data from separate states if they use the same test or an assessment aligned to the Common Core."[53]

Common Core enables people to capture detailed information about a child's mind and to plot discrete lessons for him based on his career goals, said Shawn Bay, an app developer who participated in a White House "Education Datapalooza" in October 2012. Common Core, in his description, "is the glue that ties everything together."[54] Or it would be, if anyone had ever tested whether progression through Common Core–defined bits of learning actually prepares a child for any career. Currently, it's just a bunch of powerful people using the minds of American children as their professional sandbox.

While We're Here, Let's Record
How You Share Toys

The U.S. Department of Education reported in 2013 that Common Core's math standards require judging students' "persistence."[55] The department viewed this mandate as an open invitation to recommend that taxpayers fund new kinds of tests that measure far more than what most people would expect in an academic test. The report called for more research on how to record "noncognitive" factors: "behavior," "attitudes," "values," "dispositions," and "beliefs." Ah, yes, American children are reading and computing so well that the government needs to start meddling with their beliefs and values.

In line with that agenda, the testing world has been moving toward combining traditional academic tests with assessments that measure what some call "soft skills." The "performance components" in Common Core tests, such as asking students to add the cost or weight of items on a virtual grocery checkout line, are a step in that direction. But this is "far from what is ultimately needed for either accountability or classroom instructional improvement purposes," according to the Gordon Commission on the Future of Assessment in Education, a private organization that includes several consultants for SBAC and PARCC.[56] The goal is for students to be constantly and imperceptibly monitored through their interactions with iPads and other gadgets. Then there would be no need for an end-of-year test. Everything would be a test.

Researchers are working to embed "soft skill" testing in video-game-like software, said Paul Weeks, vice president for college and career readiness at ACT, which runs the nation's most-taken college entrance exams. ACT also developed its own Common Core test to compete with the federally funded tests from SBAC and PARCC. It's called ACT Aspire, which Alabama and South Carolina are using. Aspire tests kids repeatedly throughout the year to give more continuous feedback. The tests include activities such as a virtual science experiment where students can "grab" flasks and "pour" liquids into a beaker. "This is the way students are learning now – gaming, interacting socially," Weeks said. "It is a more natural environment."

In its application for federal money, SBAC said it would test for "aspects of student performance" that "have traditionally been difficult to measure on standardized assessments, including skills such as the use of relevant evidence and technology, thoughtful critique, and adaptive reasoning."[57] It also wanted to explore tracking "self-management skills" such as "time management," "self-awareness," and "persistence."[58]

ACT is already doing that, too. Another component of ACT's K-12 tests, called Engage, examines "academic behaviors." Students are asked to report whether they can manage their feelings, work well with others, and finish what they have started, for example. Teachers also rate students on subjective dispositions such as "being open and accepting of others," "not letting feelings get in the way of schoolwork," "volunteering to work on additional activities or projects," and "listening to others' points of view."[59] Engage is currently for grades 6–9, but ACT is working to apply it to younger children, too, according to Weeks.

"Take something like self-regulation," he said. "In the workplace, this is working well with others. What does it mean when you back it down to an entering college student? They can manage their time, and things like that. Then back it down into early grades. In early elementary grades, it can be [measured by] observations of how students play with one another, how they share toys."

The U.S. Department of Education itself is directly joining the soft-skills testing revolution by way of its biennial tests called the National Assessment of Educational Progress. The NAEP is one of the oldest and most trusted measures of U.S. student achievement over time. By 2017, it will evaluate "grit" and "desire for learning."[60] It may also include "questions about other noncognitive factors, such as self-efficacy and personal achievement goals."[61] The successor to No Child Left Behind, called the Every Student Succeeds Act (2015), further promotes the collection of data on behavior and emotions by mandating that state accountability metrics include "non-academic measures." Eight states have used this law as a license to begin collecting information such as first exposure to street drugs and parents' views about education.[62]

One justification given for assessing noncognitive attributes in school tests is to warn teachers and parents of potential problems so they can "intervene" before kids are "at risk," Weeks explained. "A lot of parents do this as a matter of course. You observe your teen is spending a lot of time in front of the TV and their grades are suffering. But lots of people don't operate that way, and we can't assume that all students are getting that same level of support."

This may sound like a noble concern, but one wonders whether parents are interested in having the government log and evaluate their kids' personality, beliefs, and behaviors – or even just their play habits. Does that really need to be in a government database? In 2014, the columnist Michelle Malkin documented how Colorado preschools were logging kids' potty habits through a program aligned to Common Core and jump-started with federal funds. The program also instructed teachers to photograph and video children and upload these files to a central database. "Last spring," Malkin wrote, "parent Lauren Coker discovered that TS Gold assessors in her son's Aurora, Colo., public preschool had recorded information about his trips to the bathroom, his hand-washing habits, and his ability to pull up his pants." School officials refused Coker's request to have her son opted out of the data collection, she told Malkin. So she pulled him from preschool. But she still has no idea how to erase the data they already collected on him without her knowledge.[63]

As schools plant increasingly sophisticated technology in classrooms, the opportunities for stealthy, intimate data collection expand, said a Georgia father and computer technician whose employer routinely fulfills tech contracts for local schools. (He requested anonymity to protect his job.) Most people don't realize that the typical smartphone can collect voiceprints and faceprints, he noted. It can track our fingerprints, measure our heart rate and body temperature, and even monitor our facial expressions and eye dilation, among other physical clues to a person's inner dialogue. The same is true of the iPads and Chromebooks that kids use in classrooms.

"If I have access to the network, I can turn those things on and off without you even knowing about it," he said. "As the administrator of the network of all those devices sitting in front of those kids, who are all touching it with their fingers, looking at it with their faces, I can with that same camera look at pupil dilation. There's all kinds of biological data I can collect about you. At the same time, I know what content you're looking at, too. So I can correlate all the biology in relationship to what you're looking at on the screen and I can determine whether you agree or don't agree with that information. This is called profiling."

The Department of Education report mentioned earlier suggested studying children by means of facial-expression cameras, pressure-sensitive chairs and computer mice, and skin sensors.[64] Even if state and federal laws secured students' rights to information on themselves (and the laws don't),[65] the mere fact that it's digital opens up security concerns. Just ask anyone whose education records have been hacked. Since 2005, some 186 million U.S. education records have been hacked or otherwise breached by unauthorized users.[66]

"Once it's digitized and out on the Internet, just as much as there are guys who are whiz-bang at developing code to protect it, there are just as many guys who are whiz-bang working to decode it," the Georgia technician said. "Once it's digital, it's done."

Most parents surely have no idea that this is what they could be plugging Johnny into when they send him off to school. But they deserve what every citizen does in a self-governing society: to be informed of policies that affect them and their children, and to be given the opportunity to participate in deciding whether those policies are acceptable.

Jenni White of Oklahoma, for one, believes that schools have no right to invade the privacy of vulnerable children under their care. "You're going to put a record out there on my kid all the way from preschool," she fumed. "I have one [son] who can't even put his shirt on right every day.... No matter what my kid does, anywhere his data is collected, if anything that is not necessarily glowing or shiny or great goes into that record, how do you expunge that record? Data files are absolutely impossible to erase." Adults may have the maturity and the ability to choose whether to allow tracking of personal information on themselves – such as location, Google searches, and grocery shopping habits – but children do not, as White observed. "So stop that."

As the feds, states, and private companies develop and connect ever larger databases of student information that Common Core helps organize, they have tended to exclude one rather important group: parents. John Eppolito learned this in 2014 when he asked the Nevada Department of Education to let him see the data it had collected about his four children in the Statewide Longitudinal Data System (SLDS). He wanted to know what information might be going from his kids' schools into national Common Core testing databases and if he could opt them out of it.

A public information officer for the department, Judy Osgood, emailed him back saying he would have to send $10,194 for the information, because the SLDS – designed "to support required state and federal reporting, funding of local education agencies, education accountability, and public reporting" – was then "not capable of responding to the type of individual student data request you have presented." She estimated that it would take several months for the department to let Eppolito see what they had on his kids (after he paid the money). And no, he could not refuse to let the state collect data on his kids as long as they remained enrolled in public school. Federal grant records show that Nevada had by then spent at least seven years and $10 million creating databases that included up to eight hundred data points about each child.[67] Yet somehow the state could not answer a simple question like "What information are you collecting on my kids?"

It appears that this data is for everyone but the people it directly concerns, said Jane Robbins, a lawyer who does research on student data privacy. Using a person's property without his informed consent is called exploitation.

"Tested to Death"

Parents who object to the collection of personal data on their children may not necessarily be opposed to standardized testing as a means of holding schools accountable. Polls taken during the congressional debate over reauthorizing or replacing No Child Left Behind in 2015 found that about two-thirds of Americans supported the federal mandate to test children in math and reading annually.[68] But that simple mandate to test kids at the end of the year has led anxious administrators to implement many more "benchmark" tests through the year, in order to make sure their kids are on track to perform well on those all-important end-of-year tests. It isn't surprising, then, that another poll taken in mid-2015 found that more than two in five Americans – an increase from 2014 – thought the schools were spending too much time on testing.[69] A 2016 poll found half of parents saying that Common Core had increased the amount of time their kids spent on testing.[70]

These tests are morphing into something much bigger than a time-suck to provide a modicum of accountability. Given the connection of the tests to large databases of information on students (including beliefs and behaviors), and to teacher evaluations and other aspects of school governance, it's clear that the testing regime forms the basis of a central control system.

In conjunction with its demand that states adopt Common Core to have a better shot at Race to the Top grants and get a dispensation from NCLB's consequences for poorly performing schools, the Obama administration outlined three other education priorities: to create reform plans for each state's lowest-performing schools; to rate teachers on the basis of their students' scores on standardized tests; and to reduce duplicative paperwork.[71] The first two employ test results for leverage: Low test scores give central planners an excuse to take over schools, fire teachers and staff, and require "improvement plans." Research has shown that these "school turnaround" measures don't benefit students, with the exception of closing poor-performing schools, which almost never happens.[72] The prospects do scare educators, though, adding to the top-down pressure on local schools to conform to the central planners' testing mandates.

This pressure has been stoking opposition to the testing regime among teachers and parents. For some years now, educators and scholars have spoken out against the use of standardized tests to evaluate schools and teachers as well as students. Between spring 2012 and early 2013, hundreds signed open letters against "high-stakes" testing in the Chicago area, New York, Georgia, and Massachusetts.[73] Parents rose up in protest when the Common Core pilot tests rolled out in 2013–14, in part because they objected to having their children serve as data generators for the test makes, but also for a variety of other reasons that have carried the resistance beyond the trial-test phase.

Michelle Furtado, the resolute Massachusetts mother we met in the prologue, hounded state and school officials to get them to allow her thirteen-year-old daughter Laurie to opt out of Common Core field tests. She did not want her child to be "a guinea pig" for test makers. School officials informed her that Laurie had been randomly selected for the trial test only two days before the girl was scheduled to start watching videos about how to take the test online. Her twin sister was not selected to take the test. "I do not want my children to participate in any unnecessary testing," Furtado wrote to the principal. "I do wish Laurie had not been informed before I was. Now I have to explain my decision to her." The Furtado children became aware of a power struggle between their parents and the school.

The principal told Furtado that opting out was not possible, based on a letter that school districts had received from Rhoda Schneider, a lawyer for the Massachusetts Department of Elementary and Secondary Education (MDESE). The letter said that "participation in the PARCC assessment field test is mandatory and not subject to opting out," a formulation that seems intentionally worded to confuse the plain letter of the law. The superintendent repeated this line to Furtado. She found it inconclusive, so she checked with MDESE directly.

An associate commissioner, Elizabeth Davis, wrote to Furtado saying that "state law does not provide an opt-out for districts or students. We expect and need all students selected for the PARCC field test to participate so we can build the best possible test." Davis also refused to answer

Furtado with a *yes* or *no* to the question whether opting out was illegal. She would only say "there is no opt-out provision."

Furtado wrote to practically every district and state official she could find with authority or expertise in testing policy. None directly answered whether opting out was illegal – probably because it's not, but they didn't want to tell the truth. Given this silence from higher-ups, the school authorities told Furtado that her daughter must sit for the three-hour duration of the test whether she entered anything on the screen or not. This is called "sit and stare," a common pressure tactic that school authorities have used on children.

In frustration, Furtado sent the principal one last email the day she dropped her daughter off to stare at the test. Laurie, she wrote, "may shed tears from being singled out (and because while she's sitting there doing nothing, she's missing instruction and a test in another subject). Please hand her a tissue. Do not call me to pick her up.... Her attendance is of utmost importance to both of us. I hope she learns from the 'sit and stare' experience, that what doesn't kill her makes her stronger."

The Massachusetts school districts of Worcester, Norwood, Peabody, and Tantasqua bucked the state department of education in spring 2014 by passing resolutions telling parents they were free to opt their children out of the field tests, despite MDESE's deceptive implication to the contrary. None of these districts has faced negative consequences for this stance – because it didn't violate state or federal law.

"I find no reason to waste valuable educational resources, both in time and money, field testing an assessment that is presumably based on inferior educational standards," said Bill Gillmeister, a Tantasqua school board member and father of two daughters. "We already have an assessment that's working perfectly fine. We already did our field tests with the [state test]. And I don't want my kids to participate." He said he was "making a political statement. My kids are being tested to death."

Gillmeister noted that the Massachusetts education commissioner, Mitchell Chester, was chairman of PARCC's governing board and therefore had a vested interest in these tests. The Massachusetts Association of School Committees asked state auditors to determine whether the PARCC tests would constitute an unfunded mandate since many school districts didn't have enough computers or bandwidth to put so many students online for testing. "Local school districts need to allocate their resources the way that they think best," Gillmeister said. "It may be the case that computing resources are not what they think best to spend their money on. But here, if they have to implement the PARCC assessment by computers, they don't have the choice."

Another member of the Tantasqua school board, Mike Valanzola, told the Worcester *Telegram and Gazette*, "Every time you turn around, there are new requirements on our school district but no money to back them up. We are tired of the mandates and, ultimately, we are a School Choice district that believes in choice. Choice should rest with the parents."[74]

Officials at MDESE insisted that Valanzola was wrong. "What we're advising parents or districts is that the law does not provide an opt-out for students from this testing program," said J. C. Considine, the department's chief of staff. "It's important for the state to gain valuable information. We want students to be a part of the development of what could be our next assessment system."

I repeatedly asked Considine whether it is illegal for a parent to opt his child out of Massachusetts tests. He would not answer directly, but instead kept saying: "There is no opt-out provision." That response was "a bluff," said Sandra Stotsky, a former senior associate commissioner for MDESE. It only meant that state law is silent about opt-outs, not that opting out is illegal. "So long as the law does not forbid opt-outs by parents, then parents can opt out – anywhere."

When asked what penalties students would face for opting out, Considine said, "We're not looking at penalties right now." An MDESE senior associate commissioner, Bob Bickerton, stated essentially the same position after questions at a public meeting in March 2014: "We're not going to force the kids to take the test," the *Medford Daily News* reported him saying.[75] At that meeting, parents complained that MDESE was talking out of both sides of its mouth. Education officials wanted to intimidate parents so the opt-out movement didn't keep growing, said Barbara Madeloni, the Massachusetts coordinator for United Opt Out, a national volunteer organization.

Several other state departments of education adopted a similar line. In November 2013, Nevada's state superintendent, Dale Erquiaga, issued a memo saying that state and federal law included no opt-out provisions and required "all" children to be tested.[76] After Christina Leventis, a grassroots leader, asked the state attorney general to review that memo, Erquiaga issued another in March 2014, saying, "state law does not require the expressed participation in field testing.... Indeed, other states

95 percent of their children in the designated grades (third through eighth, and once in high school), but it does not require students to complete the tests put in front of them, since the express purpose is to evaluate the *schools*. No federal law forbids individual opt-outs, and few states have such a law.

"We haven't found any state that has a no opt-out clause," Slekar said. "We ask for [administrators] to put in writing that it's illegal to opt out, and there hasn't been one case where they're willing to put their name to that. It isn't illegal." A 2016 study of the opt-out movement found that state barriers to opting out slightly reduce opt-out numbers, but even in states that prohibit opting out, 73 percent of parents who describe themselves as opt-outers have done so anyway.[77]

When Common Core pilot tests were being administered, Slekar said it was inappropriate to use children that way "to provide data for assessments that don't help kids understand what they need to learn." He was hearing more and more parents say, "Not my child, not my child's data." United Opt Out added four thousand members in the first half of 2014, which more than doubled its size, and it is still active. Parents have called Slekar directly for advice, too. A few days before we spoke, he had spent two hours on the phone counseling a parent about opting out.

The opt-out form posted at Truth in American Education, a nexus for Common Core opponents, was accessed 49,882 times in the 2013-14 school year, said Shane Vander Hart, an Iowa dad who helps run the site. In addition, it was accessed nearly 200,000 times from Box.com, said James Wilson, a Washington dad and teacher (whom we met in Chapter 2) who also helps run Truth in American Education. Wilson said in an email that he was seeing "a noticeable increase in email and voicemail Truth in American Education receives related to opt out questions and issues."

Parents raised an uproar in March 2014 when Chicago officials pulled kids from their classrooms to "interrogate" them about whether teachers had encouraged them to resist mandated tests.[78] Officials have used similar tactics nationwide. In Colorado around the same time, school officials sent police to a family's doorstep after an autistic child's parents opted him out because tests make him so anxious he bites himself.[79] In 2014 and 2015, students opted out in unprecedented numbers in Chicago,[80] Denver,[81] Seattle,[82] Nashville,[83] Maine,[84] Germantown and Madison (Wisconsin),[85] and New York.[86] Parents who pull their kids from tests complain about lost instructional time, test anxiety, lack of relevance to instruction, and the use of tests to push teachers and schools around. Others see opt-outs as a way to protest Common Core.[87]

New York was one of two states to jump straight into Common Core-based tests in 2013, and by 2015 it had the nation's highest opt-out rate: one in five of the state's schoolchildren sat out the tests.[88] Some districts, such as Chateaugay Central School District in northern New York, saw opt-out rates as high as nine in ten students. The district superintendent, Loretta Fowler, told the *New York Times* that losing the approximately $150,000 in federal funds that Chateaugay received for poor kids because of those opt-outs would force her to lay off three of her forty-six teachers. But she still respected parents' decisions concerning their own children: "I would say that is their right as parents. Leadership isn't about telling people what to do."[89]

Many of Fowler's peers were not so defiant. In response to pressure from state officials, many principals and superintendents went to ludicrous lengths to get kids' butts in the testing seats. Many state officials have pushed school districts to crack down, even insisting that opt-outs are illegal. That's debatable. Again, there is no federal law against individual opt-outs, and few if any state laws with any teeth. Yet most state departments of education have attempted to strong-arm parents into having their kids tested anyway.[90] They are most likely doing so in response to federal pressure.

Secretary Duncan personally threatened federal action against states that didn't yank the chain on their schools for high opt-out rates. A spokesman for New York's education department, Jonathan Burman, told reporters in an email in spring 2015 that "the feds *are* discussing the possibility of imposing penalties for failing to hit participation rate targets." The Obama administration was telling states that it expected them to "consider imposing sanctions" on school districts where more than 5 percent of kids refused Common Core tests; the sanctions could include withholding money "in the most egregious cases," Burman said.[91]

The administration went a step further in its 2016 regulations for ESSA, aiming to require "robust action" against states and school districts with high opt-out rates despite a lack of authority for such action in the law itself.[92] The regulations propose sanctions against disobedient schools, including assigning them the state's lowest accountability rating (which may open them up for state and federal action such as school takeovers), and developing "improvement plans that address the reason or reasons for low participation in the school and include interventions to improve participation rates in subsequent years."[93] In other words: Cross us, and we will put your teachers' and principal's jobs on the line and make their desks ache with paperwork.

Not only do these rules run contrary to law, they run contrary to public opinion. A 2016 poll by Achieve, Inc., found that 13 percent of parents had opted their kids out of tests in 2015-16, and 19 percent were planning to do so in the 2016-17 school year.[94] As bureaucrats attempt to clamp down on individual choice, the desire for it only grows.

The Education Solyndra

Common Core's supporters made various promises about the new tests: they would enable comparing all states on the same measuring stick; set a high bar for student performance; provide accurate and reliable information; get useful information into teachers' and families' hands quickly enough to help the kids improve; make results "transparent" so nonspecialists can understand; improve classroom instruction; and represent a big advance over "fill in the bubble" tests. Common Core tests broke all of these promises. We have already examined the issues of reliability and whether the tests actually represent an advance, so let's dissect the other promises.

The tests were supposed to be national tests so we could compare performance across states, even though statisticians don't need all kids across the country to take the same test in order to compare their performance meaningfully.[95] The National Assessment of Educational Progress has allowed cross-state comparisons in a highly reliable format since 2003.[96] Still, the advent of Common Core had NAEP's people thinking their own (better) test was now obsolete.

As it turns out, states have fled PARCC and SBAC in droves.[97] Twenty-six states initially signed up to work with PARCC and thirty-one with SBAC. By the end of 2015, PARCC had declined to six member states, two of which were on the fence. SBAC had shrunk to fifteen states, and three of those were thinking about dropping out.[98] PARCC was so desperate to stay afloat that it began selling pieces of its tests, such as test questions and software, to states.[99] That leaves fewer than half the states still involved in the supposedly national tests. If you count by percentage of the total K–12 population in the United States, only 36 percent are now taking these "national" tests.[100]

We were promised that the tests would set a high bar for performance, something most state tests have not done so far. No Child Left Behind was considered a win for Republicans because the mandate for states to test 95 percent of their students would mean that all schools, for the first time, had to demonstrate what taxpayers were getting for their money. But NCLB did not specify the contents of those tests, because it is illegal for the federal government to do so. States responded by setting low standards, because NCLB also authorized the federal government to use failing scores as a justification for taking control of local schools. The evidence is quite strong that states have been passing forward children who haven't learned what they should in each grade.[101]

Common Core supporters thought the way to fix this problem was not to make local schools once again accountable to parents, but to go the other direction: doubling down on centralizing the school system by establishing national standards and tests. Secretary Duncan insisted that Common Core tests would end the practice of "lying to children and parents" by deeming a poor performance "proficient" to satisfy federal demands.[102] But Common Core states then proceeded to do the same thing with Common Core tests. In the first year (2015), Ohio and Arkansas decided to use lower benchmarks for proficiency than other states using the same tests.[103] Illinois, Massachusetts, California, Florida, and North Carolina quickly followed suit.[104] The reality is that when politicians control tests, they are not going to allow lots of kids to fail them. The politicians get nothing out of it except bad press. Besides, rating a child "proficient" or "failing" is a judgment call, no matter who makes it. Using standardized tests is a way of substituting central planners' judgment for that of teachers and parents, under the veneer of "science" and "data."

Common Core promoters sold their computerized tests with the promise that they would send results back to families and teachers quickly. Duncan promised they would offer "immediate feedback" and "instructionally useful" results instead of "after-the-fact, year-end tests."[105] This too hasn't happened. Illinois, a PARCC state, didn't release its spring 2015 scores until mid-September.[106] New Jersey released its scores in October.[107] In Mississippi, it was December.[108] The picture didn't improve in 2016. Nevada's beleaguered testing contractor withheld the results of

200,000 students' tests, with little explanation.[109] Colorado, a PARCC state, released its spring test results in August.[110] It was the same story in Michigan (which had its own Common Core test using parts of Smarter Balanced testing).[111]

Duncan promised test results that would be "transparent, intelligible, and consumer-friendly."[112] This also didn't seem to happen, as one prominent Common Core advocate has acknowledged. Chester Finn Jr. helped drive states into Common Core, particularly by riding herd on Republican lawmakers from his position as head of the Thomas B. Fordham Institute, a self-described "conservative" education think tank and one of Common Core's most unflagging cheerleaders. As a member of Maryland's board of education in 2015, however, Finn complained about the PARCC test reports for parents: "Most parents [of students with lower scores] receiving this report will not understand that their child is not on track for college or a career. It is not clear."[113] Louisiana's board of education had to issue an open-records request to get essential data on its students from PARCC.[114] So much for transparency!

Common Core tests were supposed to bring classroom instruction into alignment with the standards. "We want teachers to teach to standards," said Duncan in announcing that he would fund the creation of the tests, which were intended to "guide instruction."[115] The tests will "measure students' progress toward those standards," he wrote in the *Washington Post*.[116] According to a talking-points memo from Achieve, "Assessments that measure the full range of the English and mathematics standards will help ensure that the new standards truly reach every classroom."[117]

Teachers are to be judged on whether they are delivering Common Core to kids, and tests are a way to know if that's happening. By using the test results as the basis for teacher evaluations and school funding, the central planners aim to ensure that Common Core effectively controls Miss Smith's third-grade classroom from two thousand miles away in Washington, D.C. Andy Smarick, a former U.S. Department of Education official who is now a consultant at Bellwether Education Partners, said the curriculum mandates "are only meaningful to the extent that teachers and school leaders in districts and state department leaders take seriously the idea of tougher work for kids and rigorous tasks and so forth, and all of that is dependent on assessment. That old saying what gets tested gets taught ... Everything hinges on these assessments."

In July 2009, a year before Common Core had been written, Bill

Gates spoke to the National Conference of State Legislatures about the importance of coordinating tests with the new curriculum: "When the tests are aligned to the common standards, the curriculum will line up as well."[118] Out of all the promises made about these tests, this one has at least come partly true. But if Common Core is not a high-quality set of standards – and we will see more evidence that it is not – changing classroom instruction to align with its tests does not mean a better education for kids.

"There is always a difference in any sector between sales and implementation," as David DeSchryver put it. We all know this. So why didn't those who control education policy exercise an appropriate degree of modesty and caution? Perhaps because people *can* use the power of the state to do what they want with other people's kids and tax dollars. Political rather than parental control of education leads to boondoggles and abuses because politicians only need promises to convince them to use their power for a certain agenda. Parents have a bigger investment, and they tend to demand more substantive proof of effectiveness before they commit to a shiny new scheme.

Think of these tests as one of many education Solyndras: another government-backed, market-destroying taxpayer shakedown that leaves a big empty building behind. It didn't happen bloodlessly, either. In pursuing their ambitious dream for all American schoolchildren – including an intrusive regime of data collection – Common Core supporters blithely created chaos in schools and disrupted the public accountability they had promised to improve. State officials were "betting the farm on PARCC and Smarter Balanced," said Smarick. That means betting with American schoolchildren. And they lost. Not that this caused any of those officials to lose their jobs, or their affinity for command-and-control education.

CHAPTER 4

Backlash — Taking On the System

Parents and teachers who had unpleasant experiences with Common Core as it entered their kids' classrooms looked first to the logical place to get relief from government-inflicted messes: their local representatives. Grassroots activists rose up and started hounding politicians and haunting state capitols around the country, calling for a repeal of this latest education scheme. When Indiana became the first state to reconsider Common Core in 2012, it was largely thanks to the efforts of two mothers from Indianapolis.

Common Core had arrived in this conservative state under a popular Republican governor, Mitch Daniels, and a nationally hailed state superintendent, Tony Bennett. After signing on to Common Core in 2010, they promoted it in 2011 as part of a reform package including statewide vouchers, a streamlined system to generate new charter schools, and teacher evaluations tied to student test scores. It looked like a Republican education policy dream come true. Soon after Mike Pence replaced Daniels as governor in January 2013, however, state politics turned against Common Core, following a grassroots campaign led by Heather Crossin and Erin Tuttle.

Crossin was one of the earliest crusaders against Common Core, beginning in 2011 when her third grader in Catholic school started bringing home math worksheets that she – a college-educated mother with a pre-kids white-collar career – could not decipher. Like other parents, she had three major objections to this new math: it involved a drastic reduction in practicing basic arithmetic; it compelled children to approach problems "in odd ways, unfamiliar to parents"; and it required them to spend an "inordinate amount of time" explaining how they reached their answers in a scripted fashion. (We saw an example in the prologue.) To add multiple-digit numbers, there was no more stacking them up and adding columns from right to left. Children were to break down the numbers into hundreds, tens, and ones; add all the numbers in each category separately, then add the intermediate sums together – as the first graders did with their one-cubes and ten-sticks at Liberty Park Elementary School in Warren Township. It's basically like counting on one's fingers, or returning to ancient tallying techniques such as using notched sticks or clay tablets stamped with pictures.

Crossin and other parents complained to the principal. "We were told how lucky we were, because our students had one of the very first Common Core–aligned textbooks," Crossin said, flipping her red-brown bobbed hair and looking affronted. The principal told the parents, "We have to teach it this way. This is how the math will be on the new Common Core tests." This was a parochial school, but Indiana's voucher program requires participating private schools to measure their students by public school benchmarks through multiple state tests.

This was the first that Crossin heard of Common Core and its federally funded tests. "Suddenly, I realized control of what was being taught to my children in their Catholic school had left the building," she said. "In fact, it had left the state. It now resided with nameless, faceless bureaucrats in Washington, D.C., and was being dictated by standards that were owned and copyrighted by private associations. I had nowhere to go. There was no one in Indiana who could change these standards."

Crossin and Tuttle called their state senator, Scott Schneider, who sat on the senate's education committee. It was nearly two years since the governor had signed on to Common Core, and Schneider hadn't yet heard of it. The duo called education reporters from the state's largest media outlets and found them similarly uninformed. They read the minutes of the meeting at which the state board of education had adopted Common Core and were surprised to learn that the board had not reviewed any related research or conducted a cost analysis. Each new discovery made them feel increasingly betrayed by the very people who were supposed to be looking out for them and their kids.

Next, they would feel betrayed by their own elected representatives. At the ladies' request, Schneider introduced a bill in spring 2012 to repeal Common Core, but it was opposed in the state house of representatives by the speaker, Brian Bosma, and the education committee chairman, Bob Behning. The repeal bill failed.

Tuttle and Crossin then tried taking their cause to the news media. The education reporter for the *Indianapolis Star*, Eric Weddle, kept telling them that Common Core wasn't news because no one knew what it was, Crossin said. (Perhaps that was because Weddle and his colleagues had not been keeping the public informed.) So they printed homemade flyers at Kinko's and started distributing them everywhere they went. They composed a PowerPoint presentation and took it on the road to any Indiana group that would listen to them, which was typically local Tea Parties. That's how I met them in my hometown.

Their presentation took about forty-five minutes, covering the history of efforts to nationalize American education, the difference between European-style vocational training and American education for citizenship, and the lack of public input into Common Core. They cited a series of studies and papers, and were impressively well-spoken and attentive to data. They emphasized a report from the Core-supporting Thomas B. Fordham Institute comparing Common Core and Indiana's previous standards that rated the latter among the top three in the nation and as "clearly superior" to Common Core. It also rated eleven more states' curriculum mandates as comparable to Common Core in overall quality, including high-population states such as California and Texas.[1] This meant that 48 percent of American kids attended schools where Common Core brought no significant improvement.[2] Crossin and Tuttle were appalled to learn that their state had abandoned top-flight academic benchmarks in favor of lower-quality national uniformity.

Schneider again introduced a bill (SB 193) to repeal Common Core in February 2013. This time, Republican leaders hesitated before attempting to steamroll it, because voters had kicked Tony Bennett out of the superintendent's office the previous November and elected in his place a former teachers union president, Glenda Ritz, a Democrat who had criticized Common Core and test-based education policies.

"A lot of people who voted for Glenda Ritz really have no idea who she is and what she might do," said Larry Grau, director of Indiana Democrats for Education Reform, before the new superintendent took office. "It was an anti-Tony Bennett vote as opposed to a pro-Glenda Ritz vote."

Election results showed that Bennett lost largely because many people who voted Republican in other races crossed their tickets to vote Democratic for superintendent. Indiana voters simultaneously elected a new Republican governor, Mike Pence, and Republican majorities in the legislature. "Ritz was able to pick up some Tea Party support over their concerns about Common Core," said Brian Howey, an Indiana pollster and analyst. "But I don't believe it was the key element in Bennett's defeat." He cited teachers' anger at vouchers and standardized testing, and suburban moms' trust in teachers, as larger factors.

That's not how it looked to out-of-state analysts. Jim Stergios of the conservative Pioneer Institute in Boston wrote that "the numbers point to anger among [Bennett's] base over his vocal support for and adoption of the national standards and tests."[3] Rick Hess of the American Enterprise Institute in Washington, D.C., a personal friend of Bennett's, attributed his loss partly to the teachers union and partly to "frustration among Tea Party conservatives that Bennett was championing an initiative that they've come to see as an Obama administration initiative,"[4] meaning Common Core.

Andrew Rotherham, an education blogger and consultant in Virginia, wrote that Bennett was "caught in a pincer between conservatives upset about his friendliness to the Common Core standards and an education establishment upset about … his support for ambitious and disruptive reform." The state's political insiders were "shocked" by the outcome, he added, noting that Common Core supporters "have a political problem that is far deeper than a few activists with email lists."[5]

Bennett especially lost women voters, said Christine Matthews, a pollster who attributed his defeat to the "mom/teacher grassroots network." In spring 2014, conservative activists primaried and defeated two incumbent Republican state representatives who had voted against Indiana's Common Core repeal.

Even after Bennett's political demise, statehouse leaders made Schneider change his bill from a full repeal to a "pause" in order to get it a public hearing and a vote. The House version (HB 1427), passed in late April and signed into law by Governor Pence in May, suspended Common Core for a year while the state board conducted a "comprehensive evaluation." A legislative committee was to study the matter; the budget office was to conduct a fiscal analysis; and the state board was to hold "at least three public meetings" on curriculum mandates before adopting revised standards by July 2014.

The fight was not over for Crossin and Tuttle, but this was a partial victory, and it was anything but easy. Tuttle admits to spending so much time on activism that she began buying packs of freezer lasagna to feed her family, and stopped folding the laundry. She and Crossin attended every statehouse Common Core hearing, which typically ran eight or nine hours. they pounded lawmakers' doors, coordinated rallies that drew hundreds of parents to the statehouse during work and school days, arranged for expert witnesses to testify, fielded and initiated calls with reporters, and held their political opponents' feet to the fire on their blog.

The ladies routinely returned home in the wee hours after yet another drive to another corner of the state. During one hearing, Tuttle's son texted her plaintively: "Dad says if you come home he'll take us to Outback for steak." She held on another twenty minutes, then left – apologizing to her fellow activists – to join her family for dinner. The eight-hour hearing went on until almost 9 p.m.

Crossin marched into hearing rooms on high heels that boosted her bitty frame, lugging giant mom totes and baggie-encased sandwiches. Tuttle once confessed that she was wearing her Easter dress to a hearing because she had gone through her entire professional wardrobe several times in recent months. Both wielded their iPhones like weapons. They scheduled conference calls with contacts around the state and the nation for their kids' carpool times, or during drives out to the family cabin. At hearings, they texted lawmakers furiously, suggesting questions for witnesses and providing play-by-play commentary to allies who weren't in the room.

For using their families' time and resources to keep an eye on what the state's education bureaucrats were doing with their money to their kids, Crossin and Tuttle earned nothing but scorn from those public servants. But their tenacity was inspiring to grassroots activists nationwide.

The passage of Indiana's House Bill 1427 sent ripples across the country. In Pennsylvania soon after, the minority chairman of the state senate's education committee, Andrew Dinneman, said that his state should pause Common Core "like Indiana." The Pennsylvania Democratic Caucus issued a statement calling for a pause on the standards and tests. In Michigan, lawmakers stripped state funding for Common Core that June, pending a fiscal analysis and a series of public hearings.

March of the Moms

The year 2013 brought a wave of Common Core repeal bills, more than doubling the number filed in 2012: from 117 to 293. The number climbed again in 2014, with 427 bills, according to data from the National Conference of State Legislatures. In 2015, the bill count shot up to nearly seven times the number filed in 2012.[6]

National Conference of State Legislatures

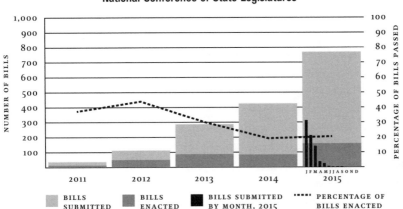

Behind every repeal bill was a little posse of women led by a cantankerous mother bear or two with as much zeal and determination as Heather Crossin and Erin Tuttle. While men typically fill the think tanks and legislatures that hash out Common Core policy, produce white papers, and pen op-eds, women have generally been the iPhone activists swapping articles on Facebook, alerting phone and email chains to upcoming legal action, pestering the snot out of politicos and reporters on Twitter, and hosting public forums.

In Utah, three mothers lit a fiery grassroots opposition to Common Core, taking to blogs and Google chats to discuss what they had uncovered since they began to find confusing worksheets and textbooks in their kids' backpacks. On their joint YouTube videos, one of the three often has to leave the screen to deal with a crying or nagging child, while the other two carry on just like any mothers chatting over coffee.

Alisa Ellis and Renee Braddy were giving a presentation similar to Crossin and Tuttle's at a public forum in April 2012 when Christel Swasey met them. Until that day, nearly two years after Utah had adopted Common Core, Swasey had never heard of it, although she is a Utah-certified teacher who still follows education news after she quit teaching to mother her children. She has also taught at the college level and worked as a grant writer for charter schools. "I think most parents in Utah still don't know what the term means," Swasey said. "Utah adopted the Core before the standards had been published – like getting married without dating."

Ellis had first heard about Common Core when her child's teacher handed her a brochure about it, unable to explain the new curriculum beyond telling her it was "great," Ellis said. "For a year, I couldn't find any answers."

The scourge of Oklahoma's legislature on the issue of Common Core was Jenni White, whose main weapon was also her smartphone. Her family checkbook covered her frequent trips to the statehouse to counter well-paid, seasoned lobbyists and career backroom dealers. She patrolled the statehouse in 2013 and 2014 with a small band of mothers, visiting lawmakers to look them in the eye and remind them that hundreds of Oklahomans had repeatedly swarmed the capitol on their own dime just to get a hearing for their Common Core repeal bill. In their bright green T-shirts, the women were conspicuous in the halls of the state legislature. They sent bouquets of cookies decorated with anti–Common Core slogans to key lawmakers, and created baseball cards depicting legislators as sluggers for having mom-approved voting records.

An activist in Kansas named Kristin George told me over the phone, "I look at my kids and I can't imagine not fighting back for what I see as their whole future in education." Her preschooler could be heard clamoring for her attention in the background, and I was bouncing my own sleeping baby on my chest in a pack as I jotted down her words. "It's so much more to me than just standards," she said. Her biggest concerns are whether she has a say in the policies that affect her family, and whether her children will have the same possibilities that were open to her. "I grew up with parents who said, 'You can do anything you put your mind to,' and that was the beauty of the country we live in," she said. "I don't want to see that changed for my children." She noted the painful irony that her activism in their behalf has cut into family life, which is actually the principal factor in their future prospects: "My son will tell me, 'Mom, I think you've had enough computer time today.' I feel like I'm fighting something because of them, and then taking time from them to do it."

George frequently drove five hours to Topeka, with playpen in tow, to lobby for legislation to suspend or repeal Common Core. She stayed with her in-laws, who watched over her two young sons while she and other mothers spent hours in legislators' offices before crucial hearings and votes. She talked to moms in her library's toddler reading group and held potlucks to tell others about Common Core. And she helped bring me to Kansas to explain Common Core to a Tea Party group, which passed a blue bucket around the room to defray my travel costs.

Grassroots activists in New York used a crowd-funding site to help cover travel expenses for two anti-Common Core speakers. Meanwhile, their opponents' expenses were paid with tax money (as we will see later). Common Core opponents typically don't have a lot of money or status. They don't make high-dollar campaign donations. But they are highly motivated: they feel that their children's and their country's future are at stake.

Arne Duncan, the secretary of education, was not exactly being fair in November 2013 when he disparaged anti-Common Core activists as "white suburban moms who – all of a sudden – their child isn't as brilliant as they thought they were, and their school isn't quite as good as they thought they were."[7] But at least he was correct in pointing to the central role of mothers who worried about what Common Core was doing to their kids' classrooms.

"Even Bubba Can Understand"

In Alabama, the mostly female opposition to Common Core has had a savvy ally in Ken Freeman, a former pilot who is now a rancher on the foothills outside Huntsville. He speaks with his mouth pursed to one side as if he is perpetually gnawing a stalk of hay. His home, which he built himself, sits at the end of a long, daunting gravel driveway, nestled into a valley encircled by rollicking, emerald-green hills.

Freeman's political activism was born of concern for private property rights. He has traveled as far as Australia to give presentations on how so-called "sustainable development" initiatives diminish human prosperity. While representing his statewide property rights group in a visit to the Alabama statehouse, Freeman ran into the anti–Common Core moms, whom he described as "energetic ladies who didn't know how to move a bill."

In Alabama, the Eagle Forum chapter and the Federation of Republican Women adamantly oppose Common Core. Established national political networks such as Eagle Forum, Americans for Prosperity, FreedomWorks, and various Tea Parties have fostered opposition to Common Core, helping activists meet each other, distribute information, and pressure lawmakers more effectively. But the strongest leaders of the movement swung into action long before any organized assistance came their way.

Freeman thought the activist moms could use some help. "It occurred to me it wouldn't be any good to save the ranch but lose the country," he recalled, whizzing his Subaru Outback down Alabama highways lined with honeysuckle and kudzu. So he sold his rare red Angus cattle (save for two, from which he hoped to generate a new herd later), and joined the moms at the statehouse in spring 2013. He would frequently drive the nearly two hundred miles from Huntsville to Montgomery, staying in the capitol late into the evening like lawmakers.

One of his chief assets, said Freeman, is his ability to speak "Bubba talk": to explain the big picture simply and directly rather than getting into complicated details, where grassroots advocates lose the attention of busy lawmakers. "It's a national takeover of education," he said. "Even Bubba can understand that."

In 2013, every Republican on the Alabama senate's education committee initially cosponsored a bill to withdraw the state from Common Core. The bill looked set to fly through, until the state superintendent, Tommy Bice, and board of education members met privately with Republican leaders shortly before the bill's hearing in March. They told lawmakers they would "pull us from Common Core without legislation," Representative Ed Henry (R-Decatur) told me. So the bill's sponsor, Dick Brewbaker (R-Montgomery), chairman of the senate education committee, sabotaged his own hearing.

Each side had been allotted thirty minutes for testimony, which meant room for six people speaking for about five minutes, said Elois Zeanah, president of the Alabama Federation of Republican Women. The organization flew in education experts including Sandra Stotsky and James Milgram to testify. When 120 supporters of the repeal bill arrived at the statehouse, aides shooed them away from the hearing room, saying that only those testifying could enter, and sent them to the gallery, Zeanah recounted.

After one person on each side testified, Brewbaker announced that eighty new people had signed up to speak, so everyone else would have only two minutes each. Those testifying for the bill had to slash their testimony on the spot, while Stotsky and Milgram, among others, could not testify at all, Freeman said. The committee members directed all their questions to Bice and his staff.

"Not once did either chair call one of our experts to give a comment or ask a question to refute the superintendent," Zeanah said. "We were all in disbelief."

Today, contrary to promises by board of education members to lawmakers, Alabama is still a Common Core state.

Critics to the Left, Critics to the Right

Once they started paying attention to the issue, mainstream media outlets routinely characterized Common Core opposition as a Tea Party-driven political movement. One of the first stories in the *New York Times* to mention any opposition, in June 2013, fingered "Legislators and Tea Party critics in states including Indiana and Michigan," and made no mention of liberal critics or even worried mothers.[8] The *Times* might as well have been following a script from Secretary Duncan, who later that month complained to the American Society of News Editors that "Common Core has become a rallying cry for fringe groups that claim it is a scheme for the federal government to usurp state and local control of what students learn." He called on the news editors to investigate "what's true and false, what's a responsible statement and what's not," adding, "Many of you have done fine work on that front."[9]

In October – a few weeks before he apparently decided that mothers were the real problem – Duncan belittled opponents of Common Core by again invoking the Tea Party and claiming that a substantial part of that movement "thinks the president is a Muslim from Kenya. Facts are sort of irrelevant." He vowed to continue advocating for Common Core without addressing citizens' concerns about federal intrusion into education.[10]

Education Week, the most widely read education trade publication, also persisted in locating the source of Common Core opposition in the Tea Party. On October 21, 2013, *EdWeek* reporter Alyson Klein wrote that Common Core and budget battles are both "areas on which the grass-rootsy, tea party, activisty side of the Republican Party doesn't exactly see eye-to-eye with the business community."[11] She, too, failed to mention liberal opposition to Common Core, something the *Washington Post* and the *New York Times* had begun to acknowledge by then. The *Post* ran an article including substantive criticism in December 2012 – the same article that got Jamie Highfill into hot water (as discussed in Chapter 1) – and it portrayed the opposition as rooted entirely in academic concerns rather than politics.[12]

There is something to the Tea Party association, as we have already seen. Many Tea Partiers discovered Common Core when Glenn Beck first mentioned it in late spring 2013, and seized on it as a potentially winnable battle after the Supreme Court gave Obamacare a pass and Obama won re-election. But criticism of Common Core runs across the political spectrum. Professor Diane Ravitch, a former Reagan education official who has grown increasingly critical of Republican education policy and is now typically in sync with teachers unions, came out against Common Core in February 2013.[13] She refers to it as "corporate education reform" on her widely read education blog. A sizeable number of progressives are as troubled by the direction of national education policy as Tea Partiers are.

One outspoken critic of Common Core, Paul Horton, is a history teacher at the University of Chicago Laboratory Schools, which is about as progressive a place as they come. The original school was founded in 1896 by John Dewey, who is credited with converting American public schools into progressive institutions. The Lab Schools have taught a veritable who's who of liberal leaders, including Justice John Paul Stevens, Secretary Duncan and his children, President Obama's daughters, Obama adviser Valerie Jarrett,[14] and the children of Rahm Emanuel, Obama's first chief of staff (subsequently mayor of Chicago). But they don't teach by Common Core, and neither does Sidwell Friends, the prestigious Quaker school that the Obama girls have attended in Washington, D.C. Neither of these schools is required to administer state or Common Core tests.[15] Sidwell does not publicly disclose its students' results on standardized tests such as the SAT, the ACT, and Advanced Placement exams.[16]

Twenty teachers from the Lab Schools were among the signatories of an open letter to Duncan in February 2013 criticizing the heavy emphasis on standardized testing that came with No Child Left Behind and intensified with Common Core. The letter decried the "widespread trend of teaching to the test," the pedagogical effects of reducing the humanities to standardized assessments, and the efforts of "corporate interests" to "control American education."[17]

One of Horton's Lab School colleagues, Wayne Brasler, voiced his opposition to Common Core in a critical documentary on the subject, called *Building the Machine*. Horton observed that the mainstream media were "definitely not reporting" progressive opposition to Common Core. "On this issue, we and Tea Partiers see eye to eye. Then they get into waving the bloody flag, I call it, of the '60s culture wars. That's the only thing that I find gets under my collar a little bit."

While some conservative bloggers have linked Common Core to Bill Ayers, the highly controversial Obama acquaintance and former Weather Underground bomber, personal emails from Ayers show he opposes the project but fears that a public statement would only generate unproductive controversy. Horton, who is acquainted with Ayers, confirmed that the latter opposes Common Core largely because he supports local control and despises standardization and corporate influence in education. In 2012, Ayers wrote a public letter remonstrating against the Obama administration's use of Race to the Top dollars to entrench the national testing regime.[18]

Progressives and Tea Partiers agree on several main points related to Common Core, Horton said, talking quickly on his cell phone during the school day as his students responded to a fire drill. The first point of agreement is concern for "the democratic process." Common Core was created within nongovernmental organizations, which are not subject to open-records and open-meetings laws. Nonprofits are not a legal means by which to create public policy. Second, grassroots progressives and Tea Partiers alike favor local decision making, not centrally mandated and managed programs. Third, both sides are wary of behind-the-scenes corporate and government collusion.

Progressives tend to link Common Core with a basket of other policies that the Obama administration has pushed in concert with it, such as tying teacher evaluations to student test scores, state and federal school takeovers, and data collection on students, Horton said. The authority for federal school takeovers actually began under George W. Bush with the No Child Left Behind law of 2001, and so did a significant expansion of data collection on both student achievement and personal characteristics such as race and family income. But Common Core testing – which is half the initiative, according to its own founding documents – has accelerated those trends.

Labeling Common Core opponents as right-wingers is a deliberate strategy of its supporters, Horton said: "If you get any pushback in a public forum about Common Core, you immediately talk about the right-wing nuts and helicopters coming in." This has the effect of associating anyone who's against Common Core with Glenn Beck and the fringe right, "and you know how that's perceived by Democrats." It also handily averts tough questions. "I think they're worried if they're asked the wrong questions, if they slip up and give any hints, if there's been any kind of federal orchestration of national curriculum, they could incriminate themselves." (The federal government, of course, is prohibited by law from specifying the content of curriculum or tests.)

Horton acknowledges that Republican lawmakers have paid better attention to their constituents than Democratic lawmakers on Common Core. But some key Democratic constituencies have been hesitant to express their reservations about it. Horton has been in leadership positions in several national education organizations, and between the foundations and the unions, he said, "everybody I talk to is against this, but very few people are willing to come out and say this stuff in public." The fear of honesty on this issue echoes the fear of saying anything that crosses the reigning orthodoxies on college campuses today.

Horton attributes the silence on Common Core to worries among politicians and nonprofits that they will lose donations if they speak their minds or listen to the humble grassroots. "They don't want to alienate any income source," he said, with frustration in his voice. "It's ridiculous, because it's like 'Do you believe in democracy or not? How can you teach about civics when you're denying democracy in education?'"

Another self-described liberal teacher, Mercedes Schneider, began snooping into the financial documents of the businesses and nonprofit organizations that underwrote and benefited from Common Core after being told at a faculty meeting in 2010: "It's not finished, but it's going to be great." Schneider, who has a doctoral degree in statistics, keeps a prolific blog revealing what she finds in those hundreds of pages of legalese. We met when she emailed me to ask how I had found the IRS 990 forms of Common Core–related nonprofits after reading some of my early reporting. In her view, money is obviously more important to Common Core's creators than any progressive ideals they might profess, such as democracy and social justice.

"Anybody on the outside of this would realize these are major conflicts of interest and it's all about making money," she said in an interview. "I see all of this fiscal incest…. Wherever this is present there is also the hiding of facts, the hiding of allegiances, all of these things are going together, but there is the byline and the public word in the media of promoting transparency and accountability."

Kris Nielsen is a self-described progressive who left his job teaching middle school science in North Carolina after only five years, in fall 2012. He objected to the already heavy emphasis on standardized testing and test-based evaluations, even though his students had posted higher scores than their peers. He chafed under the tightening controls on how he conducted his classes as the Common Core mandates were going into place.

Nielsen said that opposition to Common Core by teachers and others on the left arises mostly from the same objections to micromanagement of their classrooms through curriculum mandates, and to high-stakes, standardized tests. Many teachers prefer to use assessments that align with their own methods of instruction, not those designed by faraway bureaucrats who may never have taught children. Many believe that Common Core tests put unrealistic expectations on children, seemingly with the goal of failing more of them and thus building pressure for altering public education by means such as charter schools or federal school takeovers.

State and national teachers unions generally support Common Core, Nielsen acknowledged, but many locals do not, because the bosses are closer to the rank and file, and they're concerned about restrictions on professional freedom. Union leaders also worry that a teacher evaluation system based on standardized test results may create a rationale for removing low-performing teachers, which upsets the union employment model. The result is some internal strife for unions, as national leaders – notably including Randi Weingarten, president of the American Federation of Teachers – attempt to keep their rank and file happy while presenting a reform-friendly image to politicians and the media.

Nielsen, like Horton, suggested a political calculation in the silence about opposition from the left in media coverage of Common Core: "If you can make somebody sound crazy or fringe, then you can basically shut down the whole thing, and if you're not giving a voice to the people who have other arguments that the public might consider – forgive me for saying – more legitimate, then you can discredit the entire movement."

Horton sees broader implications in the political range of opposition to Common Core. "We're entering an age when there might be a new politics," he speculated. "There are issues that are common to left and right. They both have a problem with the way parties are controlled." Common Core is a bipartisan issue, as are crony capitalism and crony philanthropy. It is one of many issues that have been realigning politics lately: the opposing camps don't always sort out into right versus left, but sometimes into the ruled versus arrogant, out-of-touch rulers. The national elections of 2016 have provided further indications of such a realignment.

Get Thee Behind Me, Parents

Parents and teachers across the political spectrum have voiced legitimate concerns about Common Core once they were allowed to learn about it, but they have routinely been treated with contempt by their own elected officials and a cabal of unelected Core-pushers. Consider this sampling.

Before a hearing in October 2013 on a bill to reconsider Common Core in Ohio, the chairman of the state's house education committee, Gerald Stebelton (R-Lancaster), told reporters that Common Core critics "don't make sense" and have bought into a "conspiracy theory."[19] In the same month, a Wisconsin state senator, John Lehman (D-Racine), told a packed audience that state hearings on the subject were "crazy" and merely "a show."[20] When Michigan's legislature reinstated Common Core funding after several hearings, one state representative, Tim Kelly (R-Saginaw County), remarked triumphantly that they had "marginalized, quite frankly, the anti-crowd into a very minute number."[21] Delaware's governor, Jack Markell (D), called opponents a distracting "fringe movement."[22] In November 2015, Governor Bill Haslam of Tennessee mocked Common Core critics while discussing his state's ostensible review of the mandates:

"Are they a Communist plot or are they the world's greatest thing ever?" he asked, purporting to sum up the two sides of the debate.[23]

These officials' dismissive comments are not just rude, they're factually wrong. The most trustworthy polls have shown that a majority of the public was against Common Core as early as 2013, and opposition has only grown since then.[24]

Thousands of New York parents and teachers have attended public forums to protest Common Core. In the fall of 2013, at the first of sixteen state-sponsored town halls scheduled on the topic, the audience roundly booed the state education commissioner, John B. King Jr., when he talked over parents repeatedly and gave the large, angry crowd only twenty minutes to ask questions after a two-hour presentation supporting Common Core.[25] Afterward, King declared that the parent-packed forum had been "co-opted by special interests whose stated goal is to 'dominate' the questions and manipulate the forum."[26] So he canceled the other fifteen forums. Amid calls for his resignation, he announced a new series of invitation-only forums. Despite being entirely out of touch with constituents from his own back yard, King failed upward, becoming a deputy secretary in the U.S. Department of Education in January 2015, and then the acting secretary a year later.

Then there's Florida, where Jeb Bush, the former governor, said in 2013 that people who objected to Common Core were relying on "conspiracy theories."[27] At a conference that year held by Bush's Foundation for Excellence in Education, the political strategist Mike Murphy noted that most of the public wasn't yet familiar with Common Core, according to polls. The opposition, he said, came mainly from Republican primary voters who "think it's a secret plot controlled by red Chinese robots in the basement of the White House."[28] The president of Florida's senate, Don Gaetz, ridiculed opponents of Common Core by saying, "You can't dip [the mandates] in milk and hold them over a candle and see the United Nations flag or Barack Obama's face. They're not some federal conspiracy."[29] (Gaetz, a Republican, hails from Niceville. Really.)

When opponents in Utah met with Governor Gary Herbert (R) to discuss their substantive concerns, he asked derisively, "Is Common Core going to teach gay sex or communism?" according to three people who attended the meeting.

Going beyond insults, Common Core-niks have been comfortable using government force to get the plebs in line. In Baltimore, a dad was arrested after standing up at an informational public meeting, attended by the state superintendent, to complain that Common Core had dumbed down his kids' instruction. A smartphone video shows Robert Small standing up, saying in a calm voice, "I want to know how many parents here are aware that the goal of the Common Core standards isn't to prepare kids for full-fledged universities, it's to prepare them for community college."[30] That is the plain truth, as one of Common Core's lead writers acknowledged in public testimony.[31]

Small raised his voice a little when people applauded, and he continued. Thirty seconds in, an official interrupted him and demanded that he ask a question, but Small kept talking – still in a calm but emphatic voice. Another thirty seconds later, a security guard walked over, touched his arm, and said, "Let's go." The guard, who was an off-duty police officer, showed his badge, at which point Small told the audience, "Don't stand for this. You're sitting here like cattle."

The guard yanked Small's arm, throwing him off balance, and tugged him out of the auditorium, while he shouted: "Is this America? Parents, you need to question these people. Do the research." While the guard brandished handcuffs, the official with the microphone said, "I do want to be very respectful to everyone who asks questions, and so the next question really is ..."

After being pushed out of the auditorium, Small was arrested and charged with second-degree assault of a police officer and disrupting a school function.[32] The video of the incident netted a million views on YouTube – and then the charges were dropped.[33]

A father in New Hampshire was arrested after going over his allotted two minutes while complaining to his local school board about his daughter's sexually graphic literature assignments, which came from the recommended list in the Common Core standards' appendix. This too was caught on video and posted on YouTube: William Baer's voice was agitated, and he interrupted a school board member who talked over him and tried to shut him down, but he didn't shout or even stand up or show any physical aggression. He just expressed his annoyance in an annoyed tone, and then he got arrested.[34] So much for "local control" and "government of the people, by the people, and for the people."

Combined with other tactics of crowd control and intimidation, these scattered arrests for constitutionally protected speech underscore that Common Core has been imposed upon an unwilling citizenry. When people object, they are treated like subjects rather than citizens. Common Core is soft coercion, occasionally reinforced by harder coercion. It reveals the truth that police power – the power to punish and imprison – is ultimately behind every single government regulation, even those that seem innocuous, such as the ones dictating what kids will read in school. If citizens think it's wrong to force someone to do a particular thing at the point of a gun, they ought to rethink making it a government mandate in the first place.

Lobbying Voters with Their Own Money

As citizens began to put their lawmakers on the spot over Common Core, numerous state education agencies and the federal government used another soft-coercion technique: spending tax dollars in an effort to convince the taxpayers to lay down their arms.

"This has turned into a pitchforks-versus-elites conversation that is dangerous politically," an education policy director for a prominent Republican governor told me in August 2013, when that governor was pondering whether to continue supporting Common Core. "There are a lot of states, specifically red states, that are very, very scared right now.... Legislators are getting beaten up by constituents."

A constellation of government agencies and private foundations responded to the disgruntled citizens by launching expensive public relations initiatives. *Politico* reported that the Business Roundtable and the Chamber of Commerce bought pricey ads on Fox News and mobilized their state chapters to keep legislators in line. The Fox ads featured teachers, because focus groups have found them to be the most persuasive advocates for Common Core.

State departments of education are especially attuned to federal interests, since a large proportion of their funding comes from federal mandates, and so does much of their reason for being. The more federal mandates, the more money and staff will go to state education agencies.[35] That's why state education bureaucrats are naturally inclined to support centralizing policies such as No Child Left Behind and Common Core.

In January 2014, Idaho's education department received a $200,000 grant from the GE Foundation via the Foundation for Excellence in Education.[36] The latter has received $3,179 million from GE through its Chiefs for Change program to "maintain community support and advocate" for Common Core across the country.[37]

"Most Americans don't know much about the standards," said Rod Gramer, chairman of Idahoans for Excellence in Education, which managed the grant. He cited polls showing that approximately two-thirds of Americans hadn't yet heard of Common Core. "And there's a lot of misinformation out there on the standards, so we feel it's important to get good, accurate information out to parents and the public." (That's the nice way of saying that Common Core opponents don't know what they're talking about.) After schools began teaching by the Common Core mandates, Gramer noted, parents started asking for more information, and "they're picking up this bad information in the media or from those people who are not supportive of the standards." For example, he said that Common Core is a state initiative, not a federal one, and that "the standards are not related to data collection. If they were canceled tomorrow, the state would continue to collect the same data it has for several years."

Aiming to counter what Gramer described as misinformation, the Idaho coalition launched ads on TV and local newspaper websites. They also used marketing in social media, particularly Facebook and Twitter – because that's where people are, said Melissa McGrath, spokeswoman for the state department of education. "We talk to legislators, but getting information into parents' hands is extremely difficult," she said. "We don't have email addresses for every parent, but even if we did, it's hard to get them to read about [Common Core] because it's a more in-depth issue. Parents do care about their children's education and if we can put something out there on Facebook where they already are, they can access that and hopefully share it with their friends."

In November 2013, Connecticut's education department requested proposals for a multimedia communications push on Common Core, to include public events, advertising, "marketing materials," and "earned media opportunities," which meant generating free visibility in newspapers and on TV.[38] A spokeswoman, Kelly Donnelly, said the department had initiated "discussions with philanthropic organizations to start a public awareness campaign."

Soon afterward, however, Governor Dan Malloy abruptly canceled the planned communications efforts. At the same time, he called for delaying teacher evaluations tied to Common Core tests and for reviewing the implementation of the standards. Malloy was facing a close re-election race, and the standards had become a sticking point with educators, who previously backed him.[39]

Arizona's department of education released a "communications toolkit" that included an "elevator speech," "talking points," and messaging specifically tailored to parents, business leaders, and students. There was also a template for a letter that school leaders could send to parents.[40] Two nonprofits, the Rodel Foundation of Arizona and Expect More Arizona, launched a public relations campaign based on teachers giving model Common Core lessons.

One of the campaign's first actions was to commission a poll of five hundred likely Arizona voters, which came out in January 2014. It found that 71 percent favored Common Core after hearing this description: "These new standards have been set to internationally competitive levels in English and math. This means that students may be more challenged by the material they study, and the tests they take will measure more advanced concepts and require students to show their work."[41] Again, all the independent experts have concluded that Common Core is *not* internationally competitive;[42] unless the competitors are low-ranking countries like Chile.[43] But that's not what respondents hear in the poll question. Fifty-eight percent of those surveyed previously had little or no idea what Common Core is. Releasing polls like this could shape public perceptions by making opponents seem like a marginal group – although, of course, people can't have an informed opinion on something without ready access to all the pertinent facts.

A committee convened in Nevada by Governor Brian Sandoval (R) in December 2013 recommended "a comprehensive public communications plan" to push Common Core, in the face of opposition from some residents. The committee reported that "parents and the business community are generally unaware of the effort to increase rigor. An apparently small but very vocal group of Nevadans is significantly more organized in opposing the Common Core than the Department or any school district has been to date."[44]

Nevada's PR committee recommended first using teachers and an existing federally funded Educator Leader Cadre in the state: "Teachers are the most credible and compelling messengers of education information; therefore, teachers and an organized 'Teacher Cadre' will become the primary spokespersons for this communication campaign."[45] The plan called for raising private money to pay for a contract with a communications company, but also listed a raft of state employees to incorporate into a communications team, including the governor, communications staff from the state department of education and several school districts, state legislators, and the higher education chancellor. It recommended enlisting the communications expertise of the state and Clark County teachers unions, whose employees are paid with tax dollars.[46]

The plan said that most Nevadans didn't know about Common Core and should hear about its benefits. It recommended targeting the "moveable middle," with teachers, legislators, and education administrators being "the most critical 'A Level' audiences" to be reached first. The Nevada State Education Association would use a $15,000 grant "to identify and train 20-25 teachers ... to discuss issues and concerns about implementation of the new standards." The teachers would be available "to assist with communication efforts." The Clark County Education Association would use a national grant "to create a cadre of teachers to cover the southern region of the state," and would coordinate this and other efforts with the state department of education.

The Feds' Common Core PR

The federal government has also spent millions in tax dollars on promoting Common Core. Topping the list of its strategies has been training teachers to express their support for Common Core publicly, and hiring professional communications teams to get those teachers' voices into as many media outlets as possible in order to give the false impression that Common Core is popular.

The budgets that PARCC and Smarter Balanced submitted to the federal government in return for their Race to the Top grants indicated they would jointly spend almost $5.5 million in tax dollars to convince taxpayers that their money was being well spent, and that it should continue coming in after the grants ran out in September 2014. Later documents showed that PARCC and SBAC upped that amount to at least $9.9 million.

PARCC planned to spend $400,000 for "a retainer with a communications firm" to provide "public and targeted outreach materials tailored to Partnership state needs." Those materials included "toolkits" and "policy briefs." PARCC also budgeted $3,453,719 to "develop a leadership cadre of content experts."[47] That cadre is known in PARCC states across the country as the PARCC Educator Leader Cadre (PELC). More than a thousand teachers and education staff have participated, according to a PowerPoint presentation by Lynn Brabender, a PARCC program associate.

SBAC budgeted $1.5 million "to work with an outside communications firm" in order to reach "key stakeholders and legislatures about the assessment system and for building support for the system from the public and those stakeholders."[48] A request for proposals from SBAC in December 2013 allowed up to $5.2 million for a communications contract.[49]

There was additional spending on PR activities, such as paying for representatives of the testing organizations to deliver what amounted to marketing presentations to state officials. In fall 2013, for example, after Indiana's legislature had voted to suspend Common Core for a year and subject it to a review, both PARCC and SBAC sent employees to Indiana in an effort to convince lawmakers to keep Common Core and its national tests. So they were using tax dollars to influence state officials to keep sending them tax dollars — a classic example of cronyism. The testing organizations increased their federally sponsored PR push just as parents and teachers across the country began objecting to the national initiative and pressuring their state representatives to withdraw. It was a crucial moment for the consortia, as their federal contracts ended in fall 2014 and the federal money would have to be replaced by state-collected tax dollars for them to survive.

PARCC spent federal funds on two in-person meetings of PELC members per year, according to consortium documents: "PARCC will cover travel and lodging costs for all participants. This includes airfare, meals, ground transportation and hotel room costs."[50] PARCC contracted with the National Math and Science Initiative to create and lead the cadres nationally.[51] NMSI is a nonprofit that has received donations from Common Core supporters including the Bill and Melinda Gates Foundation, the Carnegie Corporation, the College Board, and Exxon-Mobil. NMSI has also received federal funds from the Department of Defense Education Activity, the U.S. Department of Education, and the Office of Naval Research.[52] PARCC's contract with NMSI was worth $4.3 million in redirected federal funds.[53]

Teachers, curriculum directors, and other administrators who participated in the cadres performed a variety of duties, such as reviewing test items for PARCC, attending meetings and webinars, helping PARCC write curriculum,[54] and training other teachers in adapting their methods to Common Core. Illinois PELC members gave workshops on Common Core and PARCC "in many venues," and sent a newsletter on those topics to all teachers in the state's southern region, said Mary Fergus, a spokeswoman for the Illinois State Board of Education.

"They have also served as local liaisons for schools and districts for new standards and PARCC," Fergus told me by email. A request for more information yielded this: "A liaison serves as a bridge, passing on the flow of information, resources, training opportunities around the standards and upcoming assessments. They may not always be the ones leading professional development but could be involved in the planning and support of PD sessions."

I repeatedly contacted officials in five state departments of education for comment on PELC. Some did not return my call; others promised to, but didn't, and ignored follow-up messages. I also contacted at least half a dozen cadre participants in several states. None would discuss the initiative. For example, Char Shryock, a curriculum director and PELC member near Cleveland, Ohio, asked for my questions in writing, which I provided the same afternoon. She never answered, however, despite a follow-up phone call and email three weeks later. PARCC's spokesman also did not respond to a request for comment.

PELC members were expected to promote Common Core to teachers and the public. "The cadres are intended to be an integral part of each state's strategy for engaging educators in the CCSS [Common Core State Standards] and PARCC," according to materials from Arizona's education department. PARCC recommended that cadre members "have a broad professional network that can be leveraged to reach an ever expanding number of educators."[55]

A document from Ohio's education department describes PELC members as "Distributors/messengers/ambassadors" for Common Core; as "strategists, editors, listeners, and messengers"; and as something like a "focus group." They would be "in a great position to push out messages and materials and to ensure benefit from the widest possible circulation," the document says. "At a minimum, they all have e-mail lists of colleagues and ideally are part of broader professional networks."[56]

State departments of education selected the PELC participants, but PARCC "provided recommendations indicating the qualifications states should look for in nominating individuals for Educator Leader Cadres," according to its May 2013 report to the federal government. The cadres were a central component of PARCC's communications strategy, which the consortium intended to expand in "scope and reach" in 2013-14. They were to "develop a group of educators who can serve as ambassadors for the consortium in their state." As the Common Core tests began getting public attention, the twice-annual conventions and the webinars would help cadre members "become even more active in sharing information with their own communities."[57]

A guide for states from PARCC highlights the cadres in Louisiana, Massachusetts, New Jersey, and New Mexico, most of which have made dozens of presentations on Common Core to fellow teachers. It also says that PELC members might be expected to advocate for Common Core to state legislators, to write "op-ed columns for local newspapers and opinion blogs," and to provide "informational briefings with community organizations and education-reform advocacy groups."[58] This means that many of the teachers who appeared to be spontaneously defending Common Core may have been preselected and groomed for it.

When Oklahoma had already pulled out of PARCC and state legislators were considering bills to repeal Common Core entirely (2013-14), the state department of education kept convening its PARCC cadres, according to an employee who requested anonymity for fear of reprisal. "We're still doing work with it here in Oklahoma," he said. "We're just doing it within our state, because we found it so beneficial." Then he stopped talking and said he needed permission to speak with reporters and would call back if he got it. Two weeks later, he returned a follow-up call with a phone message saying, "I'm not really able to talk about the PARCC Educator Leader Cadres," and directing questions to the department's communications office. That office did not return repeated phone calls.

In its May 2013 report to the federal government, SBAC acknowledged that it "faced challenges" in communications.[59] The consortium wanted to remedy the problem with a full-court communications press as its pilot tests began to be administered in the fall. SBAC sought "a comprehensive Communication Plan to enable adoption and widespread acceptance of common college- and career-ready performance standards for the Smarter Balanced summative assessments across all member states."[60]

For $5.2 million, SBAC wanted "compelling messages" aimed at education decision makers – such as state superintendents, legislators, and state board of education members – before key votes on what a passing score would be on its tests. It also wanted materials aimed at "grasstop" people like the media and business leaders, and at "grassroot" people like parents and teachers. Other communications targets included governors, superintendents, teachers union leaders, college and university officials and faculty, and community leaders. The organization that won the contract had to develop a communication plan that involved, among other things:

- "A sustained, proactive media strategy that includes background meetings with reporters, press releases and media advisories, press teleconferences, and on-the-record interviews"

- "A rapid-response capacity to identify and respond to opposition when and where advantageous"

- "Web and social-media strategies"

- "Identification, training, and use of effective spokespeople"

- "Turnkey resources for state use (presentations, sample web pages, op-eds, etc.)"

- "Contingency planning for crisis communications"[61]

A plethora of private foundations and advocacy groups have participated in multimillion-dollar PR initiatives of this kind, with full-time publicity flacks funded by money taken from taxpayers – while many of those taxpayers have attempted to counter this propaganda with smartphones and Facebook groups, relying entirely on their own money and time.

Foundations Spend Millions on Common Core PR

On top of all those tax-funded PR initiatives, a coalition of private foundations spent approximately $2.5 million to promote Common Core, first by training teachers in public messaging techniques. The foundations set up a Common Core Communications Collaborative (CCCC, later called the Collaborative for Student Success)[62] with the goal of "enabling strategic communications efforts nationally and across states in support of the implementation of the Common Core Standards," according to grants channeled through the New Venture Fund, an organization that helps manage nonprofit projects. (The fund did not return repeated requests for comment.)

The founding nonprofits were the Bill and Melinda Gates Foundation, the Carnegie Corporation of New York, the Helios Education Foundation, the Leona M. and Harry B. Helmsley Charitable Trust, the William and Flora Hewlett Foundation, the Lumina Foundation, and the Charles and Lynn Schusterman Family Foundation. Helios and Schusterman did not publicly report their contributions to CCCC, but the other four did. Their gifts totaled $2.35 million. The Gates Foundation was the largest contributor, at $1.15 million, and the Helmsley Foundation was second, with a $600,000 donation. The Gates grant said that CCCC aimed to reach "K-12 educators, parents, policy makers, higher education leaders and other key audiences."

Leaders of the Collaborative representing five of its founding nonprofits did not return calls for comment. Among them was Joanne Weiss, former chief of staff for Secretary Duncan and former director of Race to the Top, now an independent consultant. In 2014 her website said that she represented the Charles and Lynn Schusterman Family Foundation on "the Common Core Communications Collaborative, the Common Core Assessment Implementation Network, and the Common Core Funders Working Group."[63]

Matt Gandal, another independent consultant working in CCCC, asked me "How did you hear about this?" when I reached him by phone. He said he would "try to get back" to me. He neither called back nor responded to three follow-up calls.

Gandal is a former teachers union official and former executive vice president of Achieve, Inc. (which managed the creation of Common Core and oversees one of its tests); he also led Race to the Top implementation for the Obama administration.[64] He helped lead at least one of several two-day conferences that CCCC sponsored for hand-selected teachers who supported Common Core. The first conference of Teacher Voices Convening (TVC) was held in Tennessee in September 2013, and the second was in Arizona in January 2014.

At TVC, teachers and employees of state-focused education nonprofits participated in mock legislative hearings on Common Core and responded to brusque, role-playing "legislators." They thought about how to illustrate their support for Common Core with personal stories, and heard presentations on Common Core "myths."

> CCSS myth: small group wrote standards behind closed doors with no input. FALSE, I know this because I was asked to give input! #TVC14
> — Patty Stephens (@pattystephens) January 11, 2014

Conference leaders encouraged teachers to get active on social media, to meet with civic groups and parents, and to speak up in public forums, said Jerry Boyd, superintendent of Putnam County Schools in Tennessee, who attended the September 2013 conference. Another participant was Charles "C.R." McLeod, communications director for the Rodel Foundation of Delaware. They focused particularly on "the landscape in our state," he said. "We had a chance to work for several hours as the Delaware team on 'How can we be using teacher voices to communicate this to parents,' alleviate the fears about it, instill confidence this is really going to benefit children in the long run." McLeod said the conferences were a way "to make sure teachers don't feel left out from the conversation."

> Messages supporting CCSS not making it through digitally. 80% of online posts negative. Be the + voice. #TVC14
> — Cindy Parker (@cindyjp65) January 11, 2014

Delegates from nine states attended the Arizona TVC in January 2014, and CCCC covered expenses for most of the teachers who attended. State departments of education typically selected the teachers, often through state teachers unions and education reform nonprofits. One of the teachers at this conference was Andrew Vega, an eighth-grade literature teacher in Boston. A big focus, he said, was "how to work with people who aren't 100 percent in favor of Common Core or don't see it's necessary."

Vega grew up in California and taught there before moving to Massachusetts. The difference he saw in the quality of instruction between the two states made him a Common Core supporter. "In a way, I feel like I was cheated because I went to public school in California," he said. "In Massachusetts, I was asking eighth graders to do the same things I had been asking juniors and seniors to do in California." He described the conference as a way to share "best practices" among states "so it can be not just Massachusetts is top ten in the world, it can be the United States is top ten in the world."

California actually had among the nation's best curricular standards before Common Core. Vega's experience says something about how good the Massachusetts standards were, but other factors also influence educational quality and student achievement, including the tougher criteria for hiring teachers that Massachusetts had instituted along with its excellent curriculum. Yet Common Core supporters have maintained an almost cultlike belief in the ability of new standards to revitalize American education. In that spirit, the state teams that attended TVC planned to continue working together on Common Core messaging and be prepared for crucial moments such as state legislative hearings.

In June 2013, Boyd helped start Leading Innovation for Tennessee Education (LIFT), a coalition of eight Tennessee superintendents who supported Common Core as well as merit pay for teachers and tying teacher license renewal to student test scores. One of their goals was to "have a unified voice on the policy level," Boyd said. He and the other superintendents found they were "likeminded" on education policy, so they wanted to give themselves an official name and "gain legitimacy." They wrote a public letter to Tennessee leaders in support of Common Core.[65] LIFT also met just to "bounce ideas off," Boyd said. For superintendents, "every meeting we walk in we want solutions, but sometimes they turn into discussions of compliance, all the woes of bureaucracy," he said. LIFT "is more 'What can we do with this,' solutions we can bring back."

With all the recent education reform efforts, Boyd said, it's hard to sift through them to determine what's best for students. But he's convinced that Common Core does "raise expectations." He also thinks it's important for teachers and administrators to join the policy conversation, and he appreciated that aspect of TVC. Teachers are mainly focused on their own students, and they often "don't have the time to get their voice out" in the way that administrators and business leaders and politicians do. But what's ultimately important in education, Boyd emphasized, is "the day in, day out influence teachers have on kids."

Vega said that teachers deserve to have a say in policies that deeply affect their lives. "If there is a flaw in the Common Core, it is that it did not have a lot of input from the field, but it's still a good document," he said. Like many other teachers, he worried about the tests that would soon be launched in pilot versions. "If the test doesn't go well, it's not going to be on the policymaker. I will hopefully still have a job. At the field level the stakes are highest, and we are the ones who feel the pressure of these changes on a daily basis."

The trial tests did not go particularly well, as we know. They stirred up a public outcry and a large opt-out movement, in some cases encouraged by teachers. This was gasoline on the brushfire of opposition to Common Core that had started quietly with teachers dismayed by the micromanaging of their classrooms and parents befuddled by their children's new homework. Officials were roused into action to tamp down the fury over public policies cooked up behind closed doors. Again, it happened first in Indiana.

Indiana Repeals Common Core ... or Does It?

We left Indiana earlier in this chapter with the legislature voting in spring 2013 to suspend Common Core implementation for a year and submit it to a review and revision. Governor Pence's mistake was delegating the revision to career education bureaucrats instead of teachers and college-level content experts. Those bureaucrats may hold master's or doctoral degrees in education, but the typical education degree, at whatever level, appears to bring little or no value to students in the classroom.

Teachers with education degrees do not have higher-performing students than teachers with subject-related degrees, such as biology or literature.[66] In fact, college graduates with degrees in other fields perform better on teacher licensure tests than those with education degrees.[67] The quality of academic research in education is so low that a mere 0.13 percent of education studies have ever been replicated.[68] This means that much of what "education experts" say just ain't so. But they firmly believe it when their careers depend upon it. And the only people who believe that Indiana's rewritten standards have merit are those who benefit professionally from saying so.

The state education agency directly under Governor Pence, called the Center for Education and Career Innovation (CECI), steered the writing of new standards, and the hands on the wheel belonged to basically the same types of people who wrote Common Core. A spokeswoman for the agency, Lou Ann Baker, said they included professors from schools of education and members of "the workforce" representing various demographics: urban, rural, suburban, and different levels of "socioeconomic status."[69] In essence, those "workforce" appointments were political rather than merit-based.

Many of those involved in the rewrite had been open supporters of Common Core. The education agency appointed two panels of about thirty members each, one panel to select grade-by-grade benchmarks and another to review those selections. One-half to one-third of each panel's members had publicly advocated for Common Core, as Heather Crossin and Erin Tuttle discovered. Moreover, eight people sat on both panels, which meant they evaluated their own work.[70] Several panel members had testified in favor of Common Core when a rewrite bill was before the legislature because they considered it superior to Indiana's previous standards, said Brad Oliver, a state board of education member.

As Oliver noted, there are "two very different competing philosophies about standards right now." One of them provides outlines of the actual content that children should learn in each grade: Multiplication. Major American poets. How to write a topic sentence. This is what parents and the public generally expect from their schools, and it has demonstrably resulted in high achievement in Massachusetts and other states. The other philosophy is the kind that ed-school graduates and bureaucrats favor. It leads to vague and abstract requirements like this: "By the end of the year, read and comprehend literature, including stories and poetry, in the grades 2–3 complexity band proficiently, with scaffolding as needed at the high end of the range."[71] This example from Common Core's English mandates is incomprehensible not because it represents deep expertise, but because the people who wrote it don't know what they're talking about. As Albert Einstein said, "If you can't explain it simply, you don't understand it well enough." The low quality of the curriculum in education schools has produced a huge cadre of "education experts" who get to run schools and make education policy, but wouldn't know a quality curriculum if it smacked them between the eyeballs. And that's the kind of "experts" who were entrusted with providing something better than Common Core for Indiana's schoolchildren.

When a first draft of new standards came out in February 2014, the governor's education agency (CECI) solicited comments from several subject-matter experts. Among them was Sandra Stotsky, who had helped write Indiana's well-regarded former curriculum benchmarks and had written the bulk of the English language arts (ELA) standards for Massachusetts. She has taught in classrooms at all levels and has published peer-reviewed studies demonstrating that education degrees do not indicate subject-matter knowledge.

Stotsky had also published a detailed comparison between Common Core's English standards and those implemented by Massachusetts in 2001 as well as the state's 2010 draft standards. For example, Common Core gives more attention to "informational reading" than to "imaginative literature" at all grade levels, while Massachusetts standards did the opposite.[72] Common Core does not promote the study of American literature until grades 11 and 12; the document doesn't mention it in earlier grades where it would be appropriate, such as when young children could well learn American folk tales. The Massachusetts standards give explicit direction to teachers on which authors and works to assign.[73] In Common Core, "Although vocabulary standards highlight specific figures of speech and rhetorical devices, they do not teach dictionary skills through the grades [or] use of glossaries for discipline-specific terms." In one key standard, Stotsky found "an inaccurate description and examples of the difference between the connotative and denotative meaning of a word." Massachusetts standards, in contrast, "develop dictionary skills through the grades, pay attention to many different kinds of vocabulary groups at each educational level, and teach ways to use context" for understanding new words.[74]

After seeing drafts of Indiana's new ELA standards that looked very much like Common Core, Stotsky wrote in an email to Claire Fiddian-Green, the head of CECI: "There is no point in my evaluating the future work of a committee, bereft of a sufficient number of academically qualified high school English teachers, that cut-and-pasted Common Core's ELA standards for grades 6–12 thinking they were better than Indiana's own standards." She wanted to work with high school English teachers and literary scholars from in-state colleges or universities to formulate better standards.

Fiddian-Green replied, "[W]e remain confident in the qualifications" of the language arts panels. "Therefore, we will not be reconstituting the panels."

At that, Stotsky refused to provide a written review of the standards. In an interview, she said the panels had discredited themselves by putting out a low-quality draft of supposedly new academic benchmarks, demonstrating that they didn't know why Indiana's old standards were better than Common Core, or how to improve upon either. People who can't find flaws in Common Core are not qualified to write something better, she said.

In fact, no independent reviewers — not even those who supported Common Core — gave good marks to the panels' work. Kathleen Porter-Magee, who had testified in favor of Common Core in Indiana for the Fordham Institute (and did a stint at the College Board under David Coleman, the lead writer of Common Core), found the first draft of the English standards to be "less specific, less coherent, and harder to navigate than either Indiana's previous standards or the Common Core." The draft, she wrote, "fails even to address some of [the] most vocal criticisms of the [Common Core] literacy standards."[75]

The math standards basically overlaid Common Core with a pile of extra mandates, according to an analysis by Ze'ev Wurman, a former U.S. Department of Education official and one of the experts the governor asked for comment. The draft "did not focus strongly enough on improving the glaring weaknesses of Common Core standards but instead made minor (and sometime negative) changes, and piled a whole lot of new content on top of already massive Common Core," wrote Wurman in a review requested by Hoosiers Against Common Core.[76]

While the panels of experts scurried about copying and pasting chunks of Common Core into another draft of the "new" standards, members of the state board of education conducted the three public forums required by the repeal law. At these hearings around the state in late February, school administrators and teachers complained that all the mandates in the ninety-eight-page draft could not realistically be covered in a school year. Approving those standards would crowd the curriculum, "making it virtually impossible to properly teach or learn," said Derek Redelman, a vice president of the Indiana Chamber of Commerce, in a press release announcing the chamber's analysis of the draft.[77] The chamber had opposed all efforts to replace Common Core until replacement became inevitable.

Terrence Moore, an Indiana resident who had run one of the highest-ranked public schools in the nation and whose evaluation of the state's draft standards the governor also requested, called them essentially "a cut-and-paste job from the Common Core," full of "circumlocutory edu-speak." When he asked state board members a basic question about teaching phonics, none gave any indication of understanding how to teach kids to read, Moore said. "Either the state school board and the committee they have appointed are in over their heads and unable to outline how students learn to read, write, and do math, or they are deliberately fighting a war of attrition in order to hold onto the Common Core, albeit without the name, hoping that the troublesome parents of Indiana will eventually lose interest in the issue and go away," he concluded.[78]

At the very end of a public hearing in Plymouth, Indiana, a second-grade teacher stood up and said, "I sat here for hours and didn't think I would speak, but I have to." When Common Core went into place at her school, she said, it was so overwhelming that she couldn't "truly care" about her students and their families. "We just run all day long," she said, her voice trembling. "I feel Common Core is really beating up our children." The board members listened to her with quiet faces for the two minutes allotted, then politely thanked her for her comments and called up the next number.

More than two thousand Hoosiers submitted online comments on the draft standards by the March 12 deadline. "That's a lot," said Lou Ann Baker. Typically, just a few citizens comment on proposals for state standards, in Indiana as elsewhere.

While the review was proceeding, Governor Pence called for "uncommonly high" education standards "written by Hoosiers, for Hoosiers." Andrea Neal, a middle school English and history teacher who had criticized Common Core before the governor appointed her to the board of education, met with him in early March to discuss the first draft of new standards. She told him she was deeply concerned that Indiana would approve subpar academic requirements, and she called the draft a "fiasco." The rewrite had produced an even worse version of Common Core, she said, citing reviews by the same experts his own education agency had asked for comments. She asked Pence to make good on his promise of "uncommonly high" curriculum and testing benchmarks.

On March 24, the governor signed legislation formally voiding Common Core in Indiana and requiring new standards. The whole review and revision process had been delayed by months of partisan bickering between the Democratic state superintendent, Glenda Ritz, and the Republican majority on the board of education. The original schedule had the board voting on a set of standards at its April 9 meeting, but the final version didn't come out until April 15. So the board would vote on

April 28, with not quite two weeks to examine the standards. But before that, they had to be approved by the state's Education Roundtable at its next quarterly meeting, on April 21.

The now-defunct Roundtable was a committee of people appointed by the governor, the legislature, and the superintendent; they were selected to represent various constituencies including businesses, Catholic schools, teachers unions, state universities, ethnic minorities, and so on. It's another political committee, but without public accountability. Among the "partners" it listed were Achieve, the Bill and Melinda Gates Foundation, the National Governors Association, and the Council of Chief State School Officers — the organizations that were central to building Common Core.[79]

As the final votes by the Education Roundtable and the board of education approached, Heather Crossin was trying to keep faith with the governor. The "million-dollar question" in her mind was: Did Pence "want standards that are uncommonly high, or did he want to run Common Core through an Indiana-run process?" As Crossin saw it, "All things are on track for the latter."

The final set of standards was little better than the earlier drafts, said Wurman; it merely streamlined the lengthy mandates, or reverted to Common Core language. According to Michael Cohen, then the president of Achieve, Indiana could still use Common Core assessments with its supposedly different standards.[80] Lawmakers later justified the deception to angry constituents by saying that Indiana needed to have Common Core in substance, if not in name, as a condition of retaining its federal waiver of No Child Left Behind sanctions.

When the Education Roundtable was voting on the standards, hundreds of parents and grandparents again rallied with protest signs, hoping to push the members to reject the new standards. The Roundtable could have voted to restore Indiana's previous, highly regarded curriculum benchmarks. But instead, in the presence of more constituents than had ever before attended one of their meetings, and amid a chorus of boos, they voted for lower academic standards. Then they celebrated their decision in media interviews afterward.

Shortly after Governor Pence had joined with the other Roundtable members in voting mediocre academic benchmarks back into Indiana, Andrea Neal requested that he replace her on the board of education. Crossin remarked ruefully that the small grassroots army of Hoosiers who pushed the state to reconsider Common Core hadn't spent countless hours attending legislative sessions, hearings, and rallies just to get it back into classrooms in disguise. Yet that's what happened.

Let's Put Lipstick on This Pig

While the Indiana saga rolled on, officials in other states tried their own sleight-of-hand tactics. In fall 2013, the governors of Maine and Iowa issued do-nothing executive orders blustering that states could still control their own education policies – despite being effectively under contract with the federal government to implement Common Core or risk the loss of federal education funds and other sanctions.[81] Alabama's board of education voted to withdraw a nonbinding letter of support for the initiative that the state superintendent had signed in 2009. Louisiana's elected board of education undertook a review to appease the public, but made little substantive change.

Florida's state board of education received nineteen thousand public comments on Common Core in fall 2013. The day before the comment period closed, the state's deputy K–12 chancellor, Mary Jane Tappen, said in a webinar, "We are moving forward with the new more rigorous [Common Core] standards. So, if anyone is hesitating or worried about next year, the timeline has not changed."[82] Apparently, the invitation for public comment was merely for show. The board of education did, however, approve a motion allowing school districts to ignore appendices to Common Core that were already optional.

Arizona renamed Common Core. That's it. The state superintendent, John Huppenthal, explained that "the Common Core brand has become devalued by curriculum issues not associated with the Arizona standards."[83] In other words, the critics weren't really complaining about Common Core, but they weren't savvy enough to know it. A majority of Common Core states took the same tack: twenty-five of the forty-two states that use the standards now refer to them by a name that does not include the phrase "Common Core."[84]

In some states, repackaging Common Core involved more than sending government interns to do search-and-replace commands on state documents. There were Indiana-like shenanigans in Missouri, where two mothers, Gretchen Logue and Anne Gassel, cornered their state legislature into passing a bill to repeal Common Core in 2014. The eventual result was basically repackaged Common Core, just as it was in other states where legislators called for revision or repeal.

Hundreds of Oklahoma citizens repeatedly descended upon their statehouse in 2013 and 2014 to protest Common Core. "This is a parents' issue, it is not a special-interest issue. The parents are the ones dealing with the fallout of this, not the special interests, not the Chamber of Commerce," said Jenni White, the activist mom we met earlier in the chapter. She was speaking to me from the statehouse, where she had been haunting legislators' offices all day.

Oklahoma's governor at the time was Mary Fallin, a Republican who chaired the National Governors Association. Along with the state superintendent, Janet Barresi, she championed Common Core both in Oklahoma and nationwide. Fallin and the Oklahoma Chamber of Commerce worked overtime trying to keep a Common Core repeal bill from getting a hearing or a vote. Eyewitnesses said the governor pulled senators off the statehouse floor to lobby them to kill the bill.

On May 23, 2014, the last day of the session, the Oklahoma legislature passed a repeal by a vote of 71-18 in the house of representatives and 31-10 in the senate. White initially believed that her state had learned a lesson from Indiana. "House Bill 3399 would be the most thorough removal of Common Core from any state of adoption in the nation to date," she said shortly after Fallin signed the bill in the face of polls showing that Oklahomans disliked Common Core. Fallin was then campaigning for re-election, running neck-and-neck with an opponent who supported the repeal.

The new law required schools to use Oklahoma's previous academic benchmarks for two years while the state created new standards. It mandated a comparison of the new standards with Common Core to ensure that they were not basically the same, and legislative approval before the new standards could be implemented. It also said the replacement standards must require children to master basic algorithms in math, a weakness of Common Core.

Soon after the bill became law, the state board of education sued in an attempt to avoid following it, arguing that the legislature had overstepped its authority because setting curriculum and tests was the board's job.

Oklahoma's supreme court rejected that assertion four hours after oral arguments were presented in July, in an 8-1 vote affirming the legislature's constitutional authority to oversee curriculum.

Even though the repeal law in Oklahoma was stronger than Indiana's law, state bureaucrats managed to sabotage the curriculum revision in pretty much the same way, White found. The same state board that had sued to prevent this process now oversaw it. The bill's sponsor, Republican state senator Josh Brecheen, told White that he could not get the bill passed if he didn't have the state department of education handle the rewrite. But the department stood to benefit from leading Common Core professional development and seeking grants for Common Core curriculum and teacher training.

Two of three national consultants brought in to assist the rewrite blasted the ultimate product as a low-quality curriculum.[85] The new standards came to be regarded as "warmed-over Common Core," said White. "It has been a very closed process with a lot of this 'transparent' talk. As if you say it's transparent and that automatically makes it transparent. It's the magician's trick, where one hand is busy and the other hand is doing something else."

While touting "transparency," the department of education gave state legislators literally three hours to review hundreds of pages of curriculum benchmarks. An email sent to all state lawmakers from the superintendent, Joy Hofmeister, informed them that the department had "scheduled several time blocks for legislators to review the standards" on October 16, 2015: "House members are invited to reviews at 9-10:30 a.m. and 2-3:30 p.m. Senate members are invited to reviews at 10:30-12 p.m. and 3:30-5 p.m." The "review" was more of a promo session, with analyses and endorsements of the rewrite also available – in actual English, not standardese – for representatives to peruse.

White found this approach to curriculum and testing decisions unacceptable. "We have got to get this away from the bureaucrats, and away from the people who are influenced by the federal government," she said. "It's the same people saying the same things to the same people."

Lawmakers in at least twenty-three states proposed amending or repealing Common Core in 2014. Similar proposals were made in at least nineteen states in 2015.[86] Such bills have passed in only four states: Indiana, Missouri, Oklahoma, and South Carolina. The legislatures of North Carolina and Tennessee commissioned reviews that concluded with reinstating Common Core with slight modifications. So far, every state that has reconsidered Common Core has essentially relabeled it and called it good. Common Core has proved more powerful than representative government, because it operates through a bureaucratic superstructure that neuters government of, by, and for the people.

CHAPTER 5

Disillusionment — Teachers Need a Voice, Too

C YNTHIA JONES SAYS she is "an odd teacher." For a lesson on heredity, to give an example, her third graders created their own pretend baby by rolling dice to determine what color of hair and eyes it would have, which parent's eyebrows it would get, and so forth. After filling out the card with its genetic characteristics, her students named their "babies" and wrote birth announcements. Jones had set up various displays around the classroom to explain how genes work.

A lesson like that takes hours of planning and preparation. For consistently throwing her heart into her work, Jones was named Tennessee's Teacher of the Year in 2003. A decade later, Jones quit teaching long before retirement age, and what happened during that heredity lesson in 2012 is part of the reason.

Her principal was in the classroom that day, observing her as part of state-mandated teacher evaluations. Jones recounted what happened: "My principal, halfway through the lesson, jumped off and started joining in. When we got done she said, 'This is one of the best lessons I have seen in many, many years, but come out in the hall.' She said, 'Don't be upset when you get the [evaluation back] because it doesn't fit.' She said, 'I didn't see oral and written feedback during the lesson on everyone's paper.'"

According to the evaluation rubric that Jones's school used, a good teacher provides both oral and written feedback to students during every

150

lesson. Teachers who didn't do that would lose points. Those evaluations would become part of a teacher's file, and a Tennessee law passed in 2010 made such evaluations one of two major factors in hiring and firing decisions. That law also committed the state to the Common Core curriculum mandates and the tests that would eventually enforce them. Starting in 2014-15, student results from Common Core tests would determine the other half of a teacher's evaluation.

Tying Common Core test results to teacher evaluations is another ratchet welded into the Obama administration's Race to the Top initiative, intended to make teachers get their instruction in line with Common Core, as Secretary Duncan and Bill Gates have said. Before Race to the Top, only fifteen states required schools to use "objective measures," i.e. student test scores, in teacher evaluations. In 2015, as a direct result of RTT and the administration's waivers of No Child Left Behind requirements, forty-three states had the same requirement, according to a report by the National Council on Teacher Quality.[1]

"I put a triangle or circle or star [on their desks] to show what group they're going to go to," Jones said. "But my principal said, 'That's not feedback.' I said, you know, 'Poop on the rubric, you said it was a good lesson.'"

A few years later, although she loved her profession and her students, the former Fulbright scholar quit teaching because the steadily increasing mandates and bureaucracy destroyed her joy. "I couldn't fit the mold of everybody doing the same thing," she said, with her characteristic energy.

Many people have lamented how an education system sorted by ZIP code limits opportunities for children in poorer neighborhoods, but fewer have spoken of how a standardized, monolithic education system frustrates good teachers. Those teachers can either put up quietly with being cogs in a Big Education machine that's controlled from afar, or they can ask for something better and put their livelihood at risk. Either way, they lose out, and so do the children they could be serving.

Jones brought other unusual experiences to her students. One time, her husband had found some turkey eggs, so she brought them into her classroom and the children incubated them. When the eggs started to hatch, the kids noticed that baby turkeys "imprint on the first thing they see." So the class all stood back to let the babies bond with their classmate Yancey, who then brought them to his family's farm. "Tell me, did we not learn a tremendous amount of things?" asks Jones. "But you can't do that because some other teachers don't teach that way." Not everyone *can* work the same way, though. "You have to have what things make you tick as a teacher and see what makes you curious and excited."

Jones also kept an albino snake and a Tennessee corn snake in her classroom. Her students would feed them dead mice from her freezer. "All the wildness was totally out" of the children when they fed the snakes, she said. For Thanksgiving, the whole class dressed up as Indians and Pilgrims.

With a master's degree in cognitive psychology, Jones knew that hyperactive and anxious children need structure, so she tried to provide it without boring them. Spelling time was 8:30 every day, but how they practiced words could vary. Some days they would make a karate chop in the air for each letter as they spelled the words out loud, or they would close their eyes and write in the air. Sometimes they wrote the letters in different colors.

After reading a book together, Jones would draw pictures to illustrate the story as students narrated the plot back to her. "Then I would say ... 'Your homework, I'm sorry to break this news, it's going to be awful' – that was a sign that it would be awesome," Jones said. "I would compose myself and say, 'You have to color [a story illustration] and display it to your parents!'" She regularly brought the arts into her lessons because they "cement and move the basics along."

Jones was known for her Earth Day "dirt blobs." She and her students would mix dirt with glue to make a globe. When it dried, students would paint on the continents. Younger students who heard about this project hoped they would be assigned to Jones's class in third grade so they could make a dirt blob.

In her last year of teaching, Jones's boss forbade the dirt blobs because other teachers didn't like the way it made Jones popular, she said. When new students came to her class the next fall, "They would say, 'We heard that you make dirt blobs,' and I'd say, 'We can't do it this year.'"

Despite her zany lesson plans – or perhaps because of them – her students' achievement soared. Several times, she was called to the office because administrators thought the high test scores could only be explained by cheating. But one year, her class's science scores dipped, and administrators then forbade her from continuing the class gardens. "I was told to stop all the things that made my classroom exciting," she said.

Jones decided that she couldn't take giving up anything else, so now she tutors special-needs children privately. She also trains student teachers, aiming to help them work within the new system but still bring engaging lessons to their classes. "I tell them I will evaluate them two ways," she said, with a note of irony. One is "the committee's opinion," using the same rubrics that had stymied her; the other is "their lesson's quality." In effect, "I'm teaching my teachers subversively."

May I Run My Own Classroom, Please?

For teachers, Common Core is "like a paint by numbers," said Scott Schneider, the Indiana legislator who first introduced a repeal bill in his state: "They draw the lines, a teacher fills them in, and they tell us we made the painting." Many effective teachers, like Cynthia Jones, find this stifling.

Polls showing widespread dissatisfaction among teachers and studies finding high turnover rates in the profession have been cited by teachers unions to argue for higher pay and more comfortable working conditions. The same findings have been used to oppose various education reforms, from teacher evaluations to school choice, on the ground that such policies increase staff turnover and destabilize classrooms. A survey of teachers by the National Education Association in 2014 found that 45 percent had thought about quitting solely because of frustration with standardized testing, while 72 percent reported feeling "moderate" or "extreme" pressure to improve test scores.[2] So how many teachers around the country have actually quit on account of the increasing micromanagement of their classrooms?

In Chapter 1, we saw how Jamie Highfill left her job teaching middle school English in Arkansas because Common Core mandates required her to water down the rich literary diet she had been giving her students. In Chapter 4, we met Kris Nielsen, a middle school science teacher in North Carolina who quit after only a few years when Common Core was starting to control classrooms. His resignation letter, dated October 25, 2012, quickly went viral online. It read, in part:

I refuse to be led by a top-down hierarchy that is completely detached from the classrooms for which it is supposed to be responsible. I will not spend another day under the expectations that I prepare every student for the increasing numbers of meaningless tests. I refuse to be an unpaid administrator of field tests that take advantage of children for the sake of profit.... I totally object and refuse to have my performance as an educator rely on "Standard 6." It is unfair, biased, and does not reflect anything about the teaching practices of proven educators.

Nielsen related his experience in his book *Children of the Core*. When he talks publicly about why he opposes Common Core, he tells his personal story. "I didn't know what I wanted to do until I was twenty-seven – and that's okay," he said. "In America, it was up to me what I wanted to be, and it was up to me how I wanted to get there." But his freedom to develop his talents and nurture those of his students was increasingly shackled by a test-based control system, with Common Core mandates adding another layer of bureaucratic control.

A report published by the Center for American Progress in January 2014 claimed to show that Common Core and the new federally mandated teacher evaluations were not pushing teachers out of the classroom or reducing their happiness.[3] But Richard Ingersoll, a University of Pennsylvania researcher who has spent his career tracking the teaching profession, called the CAP report "a terrible analysis of the data." He explained, "I work with those same data. I've been meaning to write [CAP] and say maybe you need to run a retraction because you misinterpreted the data." Ingersoll said the authors didn't look at changes over time, or differences between schools, or the larger decisions that teachers cannot influence.

Statistics that might shed light on whether Common Core has caused an unusual number of teachers to leave the profession are sparse because such data typically take several years to collect and publish. But we do have some data on teachers' opinions of Common Core. For example, a Scholastic poll of teachers in October 2014 found that 47 percent thought Common Core would be good for their students, a figure that was nearly ten points lower than the previous year.[4] A poll conducted by scholars at the Harvard Kennedy School in 2013 found that 76 percent of teachers registered support for Common Core, but in the same poll two years later, only 40 percent did so.[5] According to a poll by *Education Next* in 2016, teacher support for Common Core had plummeted from 87 percent to 44 percent since 2013.[6]

Ingersoll believes the growing burden of state and federal regulation on the classroom is a central reason that teachers decide to quit. The restrictive atmosphere often leads the best teachers to leave in favor of professions where they can gain more satisfaction from professional freedom. Those who stay in the classroom are more willing to bear with mind-numbing regulations in order to keep a safe job.

Despite relatively high job security, teaching has a higher turnover rate than other professions that require a college degree, such as law, architecture, and engineering, Ingersoll said. Some researchers have said it's an inappropriate comparison because teachers tend to come from the bottom half of college graduates, so they have fewer better job options.[7] But Ingersoll pointed out that teaching also has a higher turnover rate than other high-stress occupations with good job security, such as police officer. One reason for the turnover is disciplinary problems and inadequate support in dealing with them, but another one that's increasingly common is "the amount of classroom discretion and autonomy teachers are allowed," as Ingersoll said. A report using federal data found statistically significant declines in teacher autonomy between 2003 and 2012. One of the study's authors said the data suggested that the growth in federal mandates was contributing to this trend.[8] A government survey found that 58 percent of those who had left the teaching field in 2012-13 reported that their influence over workplace policies and practices increased in their new occupation.[9]

At the time of my conversation with Ingersoll in 2014, the most recent data available on teachers' job satisfaction concerned math teachers. Dissatisfaction with limited classroom autonomy is now the leading factor in turnover among math teachers, he said, and the trend has been particularly noticeable since the federal government began forcing schools to test kids in reading and math under the No Child Left Behind law. Math and English, of course, are also the subjects expressly covered by Common Core. Math is "a heavily tested subject and often it's getting into this standardized curriculum where it's 'We want you on this page and this chapter this week,'" as Ingersoll said. But kids have different needs, "and teachers need some discretion and some autonomy to make it work for their kids."

A certain amount of turnover is a good thing, he acknowledged, because some people just aren't meant to be teachers — as is the case in any vocation. People sometimes choose the wrong course for themselves.

But his data indicate that high turnover in the teaching profession is more than the typical job churn, and it has negative consequences for kids and the nation. For one thing, "the real story behind the so-called math and science teacher shortage is turnover.... It's not that we make too few [math and science] teachers, it's that we lose too many." Classroom autonomy is more important to departing math teachers than salary, which is a striking fact considering that they could often earn higher salaries in the private sector, where a math degree is worth more than, say, an elementary education degree. Those departing math teachers are likely to make valuable contributions in their new workplace, but the national economy suffers from the loss of high-quality math and science instruction.

There's also a personal loss to children when they never have the chance to be in a truly stimulating classroom. Anyone who has ever had a favorite teacher – and that's most of us – can understand how much poorer our lives and minds would be if we had never sat in his or her classroom. If Common Core deepens the feeling of powerlessness among teachers, fewer kids will be blessed to learn from someone like Cynthia Jones or Jamie Highfill. And that adds up to a cultural loss for whole communities, and for the nation.

Common Core Is "Beside the Point"

Like many social experiments, Common Core may be the least beneficial to those who are most in need. Despite myriad promises that it will help disadvantaged children, Common Core is "entirely beside the point" in the Baltimore public high school where she teaches, said Dana Casey. The students regularly curse at, talk over, ignore, and even shove her. They wander in and out of class to chat with their friends, ignoring her efforts to get them to pay attention to a lesson. "All of these discussions about Common Core are useless unless our students learn basic things like you actually have to do work to earn a grade and you actually have to stop talking on occasion," Casey said.

Of the ninety students who take her high school English classes in this inner-city school, thirty are designated as special needs. "Some of those students have reading levels of second grade, but they're sitting in my SAT prep class," she said. "Of course those kids are going to cause problems.

They can't do the work. But I can't adjust SAT prep down to a second-grade level."

Casey's school puts these students in classes that are way above their heads because of pressure to funnel everyone into college-prep coursework, which Common Core encourages. Teachers and administrators keep telling the kids they will go to college, "but if you have a second-grade reading level, you are not going to college," Casey said. "And there is no alternative for you" in the Common Core scheme.

Casey is another excellent teacher who is frustrated by administrators' and politicians' zeal for imposing one-size-fits-none programs on all, without considering the different needs of individual kids or diverse neighborhoods. While affluent parents may be concerned that Common Core skimps on their children's intellectual formation in its narrow focus on "career readiness," Casey worries that it doesn't equip disadvantaged students with the skills to build a livelihood. She wishes her school would shift resources away from unrealistic ideas that mainly provide campaign boasts for politicians, such as college prep for everyone, and into things that would truly benefit her students, such as vocational training.

"If you tell these kids they are going to college when they know they're not, they will have no hope," Casey said. "Instead, we could be training these kids to become an electrician, a plumber, a food services manager, and many of them could do very well and make a lot more money than I do." She once asked a radiator technician who visited her school what he earns in a year. He said $150,000, with six months of training. Casey makes approximately $60,000 per year. "Many of our kids could be doing this," she said. "They want us to get kids Common Core college-ready, but I think being able to buy a house and feed your family is really powerful."

Turtles All the Way Up

Some administrators may want to allow teachers freedom in their classrooms, but they often feel constrained by bureaucrats and ignored by politicians, as Joe Rella told me. I met with the superintendent of the Comsewogue School District on Long Island on a midwinter day in 2014. Snow softly blanketed the turf surrounding his 1950s-style brick offices, with multicolored window headers lending the air of an elementary school. Rella became an unlikely overnight celebrity in spring 2013 when he sent his students' parents a robocall urging them to fight Common Core, and his recorded message went viral online.

The state of New York had jumped straight into the Common Core tests that year, ahead of every other state except Kentucky. A dramatic drop in test scores over the previous year provoked an angry reaction among parents and teachers, so New York came to be on the leading edge of opposition to Common Core, too. It has been the nation's leader in test opt-outs (as noted earlier), and Rella has played a big part in building that resistance. Many of his fellow superintendents agreed with him but were scared to stand up themselves, he said: "I think they're betting with the house."

When we spoke, he looked more like an NPR correspondent than a revolutionary, in his navy blue cardigan and rimless glasses. Above him hung a sign: "Kindergarten shouldn't be rigorous." His office displayed pictures of his five grandbabies alongside leather-bound reams of state regulations. He had been working in the Comsewogue district for some eighteen years, four as a teacher, eight as a principal, and six as superintendent. Regular robocalls to parents are a part of his open-door policy, along with office hours every Tuesday and Thursday evening. He began the robocall practice in his first year as superintendent, with this message: "Every year we start fresh. Say your prayers, eat your Wheaties, and see you in the morning." Parents liked it, so he kept doing the calls.

"One of the goals I had when I got here was to make sure info got out," he said, leaning back in his burgundy leather chair behind a dinner-table-sized desk. "My experience was that everything was spun, info got out two weeks late. Insiders always had the advantage because they had the information. But if you have a case of the whooping cough, parents need to know that. I gotta tell you how much time it saved me, fixing things early."

He got flooded with anxious queries from parents when the first Common Core test results came out, so he made that famous robocall. "We need your help," he told the parents, saying that the new tests were "part of a bigger plan to destroy public education, and tell kids they're failures and losers."

Rella told me the new tests were unfair to schools because "students and teachers hadn't been prepared, and the curriculum was incomplete." On top of that, he said, the state department of education had decided arbitrarily that only about one-third of the kids would pass the test, so in three years the pass rate on mandatory standardized tests dropped from 90 percent to 30 percent. Rella tossed his head: "Does that mean all the kids got dumber over the summer?"

Like many other New Yorkers, he suspected that the low scores were part of a political ploy to justify a "corporate takeover" of schools — a popular theory among teachers unions. In fact, there are special interests that stand to benefit from chaotic public schools, including charter school companies, curriculum and media companies, and test makers. Politicians might want to use a crisis as an opportunity to award government contracts to companies run by their campaign donors, and that idea colored Rella's view of the Common Core tests.

In his robocall about the tests, he urged parents to stampede the state legislature. They did. Their complaints led to legislative hearings on Common Core in 2014 and a series of bills and promises that have garnered lots of media attention but have not as yet materialized into substantive changes. Thousands of Rella's students refused to take the tests in 2014 and 2015. When one of his teachers publicly refused to administer the tests in 2015, Rella backed her up.

During my visit, he also talked about issues he has with the curriculum mandates and with the dismissive attitude of state officials to his questions about them. He asked his state representatives for the research showing that Common Core was internationally benchmarked as promised. The lawmakers threw up their hands and told him it was the education department's deal. He asked representatives of the education department for the information. He got nothing from them, either. In a public meeting held by the department, he had to submit his question beforehand and was limited to two minutes of testimony. That irked him, especially given his own practice of extending his office hours as long as parents want, so they will feel satisfied that their concerns are heard.

State officials told Rella and newspaper reporters that teachers had been allowed to help write the Common Core standards. That was only technically true, he said: "Teachers were handpicked, and changes they suggested mostly ignored." (That's the same experience that Brad McQueen from Arizona had when he was invited to participate in writing PARCC's tests.) It was nothing like the way New York educators had previously managed curriculum changes, meeting across districts and writing curriculum together.

Rella describes Common Core as an unfunded mandate – something that lawmakers are quite fond of. Regulations, of course, are a form of hidden taxation. The government requires you to put your own time and resources into achieving the government's purposes, without having to tax you openly or compensate you for your time. Education regulations are a tax on the school districts that must cover associated expenses, and on the teachers, administrators, and families who have to spend time on compliance. And the government uses your own money to claim your time.

The state of New York received $700 million in federal Race to the Top funds in 2010, but that's only about 1.2 percent of the approximately $53 billion the state was spending on K-12 at the time.[10] That "gift" from the nation's taxpayers came with conditions. "It's like dealing with the Mafia," Rella said. "Whether they buy you or force you, they own you. That's the federal government." He has a particular beef with the teacher evaluation system mandated by Race to the Top and designed to work together with the Common Core tests. Some of his "brilliant master teachers" received low marks, which demoralized them, he said. Moreover, the test results were not as detailed as promised and were released far too late in the year to help teachers focus on areas where kids needed more attention. That trend has continued every year since, with 2016's test results coming out at the end of July, well after school let out for the summer.[11]

Rella sees hope for addressing Common Core's problems, based on the kind of complaints he has heard from parents in his district. They have not been like the helicopter-parent gripes that Johnny didn't get his fiftieth participation trophy or an easy A. Parents have told him they want their kids to be challenged in school, but Common Core only frustrates them instead. "You've angered the mothers of New York State," Rella said. "God help them. The mothers of New York State will not be quelled."

"I'm Just Keeping My Mouth Shut"

Administrators like Joe Rella might be willing to defy the pressure to conform, but it's riskier for teachers to speak up and stand out if they don't have a supportive administration. Christina Leventis, an activist mom in Nevada, has been asking teachers what they think about Common Core, and the answers are revealing even when they are guarded. Here's a sampling from Clark County:

"I've got two years to go [until retirement]. I'm just keeping my mouth shut and counting the days," said a first-grade teacher.

"It's so bad for teachers. I'm looking to get out," said a high school teacher.

Leventis asked an eleventh-grade English teacher if she would publicly voice her objections to Common Core, and the teacher replied, "I'd better not. I have to feed and clothe my children."

When Leventis asked a fourth-grade teacher how she felt about Common Core, the teacher's eyes widened and she started backing away, looking left and right. "At first I thought she was being silly," Leventis said. "She wasn't. She was actually afraid to say a word, and we were in a movie theater — nowhere near her school. So sad that she was so afraid she might be overheard. She continued to back away from me, smiling and looking around. 'Good to see you,' was all she said."

A ninth-grade teacher in the district told his students, "I don't know what I'm allowed to teach you anymore. I have to check."

An eleventh-grade English teacher told Leventis, "I used to love my job, I used to love teaching. Now I don't even want to get out of bed in the morning. I can't do anything without getting permission."

An elementary school teacher said, "The problem with common core [is] it is changing the way we teach math and it doesn't make any logical sense and we are seeing non-age-appropriate skills being taught."

A fifth-grade teacher told Leventis, "The testing is constant, so much so that my [students] have extreme test anxiety. I've had countless kids in tears over the tests."

Teachers' professional training does not prepare them to deal with this new reality of test-based "accountability," nor does it encourage them to challenge what they might regard as counterproductive mandates. In a 2010 survey, only 24 percent of professors in teaching colleges thought it was "absolutely essential" for them to cultivate "teachers who understand how to work with the state's standards, tests and accountability systems," while 68 percent said that preparing their students "to be change agents who will reshape education" was important.[12] But the operative definition of "change agents" is not teachers who speak up about what they privately say is hurting their students and destroying their own careers.

Instead, teachers are conditioned to embrace group thinking and "we-feeling" in order to advance a preapproved "change process," as the education historian Diane Ravitch explains:

> Specialists advised state and local school leaders how to use group dynamics to build consensus among teachers. Getting teachers to abandon their traditional ideas and adopt progressive ideas was known as "the change process." The change process involved organizing group discussions run by trained leaders; encouraging group members to express their feelings freely; guiding the group to a consensus about the need for change; and building a sense of group solidarity. Techniques such as role playing, the specialists suggested, helped to develop participation and the group's "we-feeling." Individualism should be discouraged, as it would create too many problems. Carefully planned exercises in which all staff members identified common problems and eventually came to share common goals would produce group thinking. The successful group would adopt common norms and values, which subtly pressured dissident individuals to conform.[13]

Ravitch describes the techniques that progressive education reformers have developed for pressuring teachers into accepting curriculum changes. These include inviting "impartial experts" to conduct training activities that put teachers in a submissive, learning posture; holding workshops in which teachers discuss common problems and are guided by a facilitator into "consensus"; and creating committee upon committee to occupy teachers with busywork.[14] Schools are also coached to use many of the same techniques on parents.[15]

Teachers' professional training seems almost designed to make them submissive to micromanagement, because it does not center on building knowledge-based confidence or professional responsibility. Most professors at teachers colleges think a teacher should be a "facilitator of learning" (84 percent), rather than a "conveyor of knowledge" (11 percent). Accordingly, the curriculum at those institutions focuses more on psychology and therapeutic-style instruction than on academic content.[16] For thirty years, E. D. Hirsch has documented the prevalence of empty platitudes in teacher training at the expense of content knowledge and instructional strategies supported by research. His most recent book, *Why Knowledge Matters* (2016), finds no decrease in this trend. To the contrary, Common Core reinforces it.[17] The de-emphasis of subject-matter knowledge hinders the ability of teachers to make their own informed judgments about how best to conduct their classes.

This may help explain why teachers, according to some research, tend to be more risk-averse than other white-collar professionals, such as businesspeople and lawyers.[18] So it isn't surprising that teachers have told Leventis they're afraid to speak up in public. It might endanger their jobs, as it did for Brad McQueen in Arizona.

McQueen, as we saw earlier, had been invited to participate in writing Common Core test questions for PARCC, but he became disillusioned by the growing awareness that his presence there was mostly for show. Then he began to speak out on the subject. He wrote an op-ed for the *Arizona Capitol Times*, and a few days later he got a phone call from Sarah Gardner, the state's Common Core testing director. She left him a message on his classroom phone.

With trepidation, he called her back during his lunch break. "I'm like, 'Hi, it's Brad McQueen, you called me,'" McQueen recounted. "Silence, for like ten seconds. I'm like, 'Hello? Yes. You're there. Yes.' It's funny now, but at the time, I'm like what is going on?" Finally, Gardner said to him, "I hear you have some problems with Common Core and PARCC." Then she asked whether McQueen was teaching Common Core in his classroom.

He sensed a trap. "I felt like she was setting me up for something, because my contract clearly says I will implement all policies of the school. Luckily, my kids were coming into the classroom. I said, 'Sarah, I got to go, my kids are coming into the classroom.' Silence. Then, 'We will continue this conversation,' and she hung up."

After McQueen mentioned this to a reporter at the *Arizona Daily Independent*, the pair used open-records laws to get a copy of emails regarding McQueen from the state department of education. Those emails revealed that department officials began retaliating against him professionally after his op-ed opposing Common Core appeared in the *Capitol Times*.[19] In one email, for example, Kathy Hrabluk, an associate superintendent, wrote to Irene Hunting, a deputy associate superintendent, saying: "Just thought you might want to check your list of teacher teams (from which teachers are selected to work on tests at the Dept of Education)." Hunting replied: "Thank you. We have made a note in his record."

McQueen believes those emails explain why he stopped getting invitations from the state education department to do summer work, which had provided him supplemental income for years. "I was like, okay, maybe they blackballed me," he said. "I didn't know for sure, because I didn't get the emails yet, but now I know that's exactly what they did." He no longer wanted to serve as window dressing for a test-writing process controlled by bureaucrats, but they froze him out of other opportunities as well, and it had all the appearance of retaliation. McQueen saw it as an infringement on his free-speech rights, so he filed a legal complaint with assistance from Goldwater Institute attorneys.[20] He dropped the suit in August 2015, after Arizona voters had ousted John Huppenthal from the state superintendent's office and installed a new superintendent, Diane Douglas, who publicly supported McQueen's right to free speech and herself criticized Common Core.

While federal and state education initiatives have advertised a focus on "teacher accountability," their designers and promoters reject the input of experienced and competent teachers. "Accountability" in bureaucratese is a euphemism for testing, but standardized tests are often a poor measure of students' knowledge. They are used more for political ends than to provide useful information to students and their parents and teachers. The testing apparatus tied to Common Core is set up mainly to serve bureaucrats, while it leaves teachers feeling controlled, disrespected, and powerless.

Many good teachers are responding by bowing out. That isn't good for kids, or for our society at large. Common Core exacerbates a classroom culture of anxiety and submission that is good for nobody except paper-pushers. This is not what Americans want. But it's what we get when our representatives keep deferring to an out-of-control education bureaucracy.

CHAPTER 6

Alternatives – Parents Find a Way for Their Kids

As you enter Ridgeview Classical Schools' newest building, a marble inscription challenges you: "What will justify your life?" Just inside, a former Louisiana State University professor is overseeing study hall. Between sharp rebukes of tittering students, Dr. Robert McMahon explains that he's come up here to Fort Collins, Colorado, to teach high school literature because he "got sick of the hatred for undergrad teaching" that prevailed at the university.

Teaching is what McMahon loves. He's the author of four books, one on teaching high school literature, and he's won a bevy of teaching awards. That might be somewhat surprising at first glance, considering his exacting manner toward the fourteen-year-olds who are reading under his watch. But talk to him a bit and you'll find that this bespectacled man who has never owned a television and disdains modern teaching methods can pierce your soul in just a few minutes of conversation.

"The discipline I teach is reading carefully and understanding what you read," he said. "You can either understand what the words mean and map it onto the bigger issues in the work, or you can't."

McMahon laments that even "Advanced Placement teachers don't assign whole books. It's a preparation with no intellectual integrity whatsoever." Another problem with current instruction methods is the demand that students apply what they learn to "the real world" before they have fully digested it. Students never learn the art of full and sustained attention, and their character development suffers as much as their intellectual growth. "The capacity to pay attention to someone is directly proportional to your capacity to love," he said. There's that soul-piercing: his comment lands right between my ribs as I ponder what it says about my habit of fiddling with my smartphone when my husband is trying to converse.

Observations that make a full meal for mind and soul abound here at Ridgeview. Try this one on for size, from the principal, Derek Anderson: "We're not training [students] for a job, but for life. Your life is divided into thirds: sleep, work, leisure. Sometimes your work does define you. But so does your leisure, and if you don't use that well, a third of your life will be destitute.... Americans fill leisure with escapism or more work because they don't know what to fill it with."

Ridgeview is a K-12 classical school, where children learn phonics, traditional math and science, Latin, and the Western and American heritage. They study the great books and receive instruction in art and music. They get an education in the real liberal arts: what centuries of Western leaders, including America's founders, have considered essential knowledge for free men who govern themselves.

Because it's a public charter school started and managed by a board of local parents, students attend for free – if they can get in. There is a perpetual waiting list of some 900 children hoping for a place at the 780-student campus. *U.S. News and World Report* consistently ranks Ridgeview's high school among the best in the nation. Peggy Schunk, a mother who helped found the school and now runs its admissions and human resources, explained that they "went the charter route" instead of starting a private school "because we believed everybody should have access to a good public education, and is capable of it."

As the true liberal arts are uprooted from college campuses, they are blooming in new soil. Terrence Moore, Ridgeview's founding principal, now travels the nation starting other schools modeled after it for an initiative spearheaded by Hillsdale College (my alma mater) when he is not performing his duties as principal of Atlanta Classical School, another charter in this new network. The newly released third edition of *Classical Education: The Movement Sweeping America* documents the recent boom in classical education in the Hillsdale-supported charters and others such as the Great Hearts Academies and the National Heritage Academies, as well as a growth in classical private schools and home schools.[1]

"Classical education is always inclined, by nature, toward decentralization, toward localism, toward connecting authority with responsibility," said Andrew Kern, a coauthor of the book and founder of the CiRCE Institute, which publishes curriculum and holds seminars for classical educators. "You're not self-governing if you can't rule yourself. Classical education is the means to freedom, the *sine qua non* of a free people, because it trains people in self-governance, in perceiving and living with the truth."

Classical educators like Kern, Anderson, and Moore draw a sharp distinction between what they offer and the kind of progressive education that has ruled U.S. schools since the 1900s, and is today embodied in Common Core. The aim of Common Core is job preparation, or "college and career readiness," a formula that Congress endorsed by making it the defining characteristic of acceptable state K-12 goals in the Every Student Succeeds Act of 2015, replacing No Child Left Behind. But enthusiasts for classical education hope their students achieve far more than entry-level job skills. Like America's founders, they believe that education should cultivate the public and private virtues necessary to sustain America's unique form of constitutional, limited government.

"We don't know what [students] are going to be — lawyer, garbage man," Anderson said, with a characteristically direct look. "But you will be an American, and can determine our fate through voting. They will all be humans. Se we want them to be good at it."

Educating for liberty, through the tradition that began with Moses and Plato and persisted in the Western world until a hundred years ago, is antithetical to the progressive agenda in government and in education. This practically guarantees a conflict between classical education and what is now the prevailing approach. Common Core is "an existential threat" to his school's mission, Anderson said, because doing what it demands means betraying Ridgeview's academic philosophy.

Ridgeview's board was one of the first to oppose Common Core publicly in Colorado, releasing a resolution in 2013 that presented two major objections. The first was that the state law authorizing charter schools specifically provides that they offer innovative alternatives to general public education in the state and not be required to follow the same academic program. The second objection was that the Common Core standards " do not accurately assess the rich curriculum that has been conveyed to Ridgeview's students, nor does it value any of the intangibles that make up much of a liberal arts curriculum." The board said that Ridgeview was offering its students an education "more rigorous, less costly, less intrusive, and more accountable" than what Common Core requires.

Judging Ridgeview by Common Core metrics puts the school at an unfair disadvantage, Anderson said, because its model is so deliberately different: "It's like asking 'How orange does your apple taste?' Not very."

To get a sense of the difference, let's take a look at the Ridgeview philosophy in action. You'll be blown away by what the kids can do.

Classical Education in Action

In a corner of every Ridgeview classroom sit two or three bright blue padded, stackable chairs. Those are for visitors, who range from parents checking out Ridgeview for their kids, to new school headmasters hoping to gain some tips.

As I enter Tim Smith's Western Civ classroom, a freshman named Grace with blond hair and swoopy bangs walks over and hands me her study questions along with a copy of the book under discussion – Plutarch's biography of Julius Caesar. Students will repeat this gesture of hospitality in about half the classrooms I visit, automatically and without disrupting class.

The sixteen students are discussing the freshman thesis due soon. "Write so your parents who have not read the book can understand," Smith tells them. A few students take two minutes to summarize the assigned reading, then dive into a discussion of Caesar's marriages and the savvy political alliances they built. "Caesar is genius at doing what piety demands and getting popularity for it," Smith tells the class. In this context, piety means not just fulfilling religious obligations but also meeting civic expectations. Smith compares Caesar getting his father-in-law elected consul to presidents hurrying through a series of executive orders just before they leave office.

Later, Smith likens an ancient Greek election to how Ross Perot split the U.S. presidential vote in 1992. A young man lights up, noting the similarity to the elections of 1860, when Abraham Lincoln became president despite receiving only 40 percent of the popular vote. Students call out comments and rejoinders energetically, with Smith occasionally drawing the quieter folks into the discussion. They all have arguments about what Caesar is doing, why, and how. "He is slippery," one student remarks after another has marveled at Caesar's political genius.

When the class is over, Smith stands beside one of his bookshelves, where the ancient Roman poets Horace and Catullus sit alongside the early English poet Chaucer, the Russian novelist Leo Tolstoy, binders of madrigals, and John Milton's *Paradise Lost*. Smith himself has translated the *Aeneid*, taking a decade to work through nearly ten thousand lines of Latin dactylic hexameter. He was named Teacher of the Year by the Colorado League of Charter Schools in 2013.

"If we want to save or prolong human lives, to what end?" he asks. "What kind of world have we saved them for?" These questions are part of his explanation of why studying ancient history is important. He is introducing young people to their cultural heritage and asking them, "So, how are you going to contribute?" Under Smith's guidance, they "study great men to analyze their character and form our own, and inspire similar acts."

On the wall is a framed quotation from Heraclitus, an ancient Greek philosopher: "Character is destiny."

Downstairs, second graders are working on their science writing with Kyle Luttman, an energetic young teacher who sports a scruffy beard, black-rimmed glasses, and a school T-shirt. "We need a topic sentence for our paragraph," Luttman says, pointing to a diagram the class has generated on the whiteboard. "A butterfly life cycle is a ..." A little boy pipes up: "a complete metamorphosis."

"Next sentence? Jeremiah?" Luttman asks. Jeremiah spits out a tumble of words. "You've got a good idea, but try rephrasing it," Luttman coaches. Jeremiah thinks for a moment. "A complete metamorphosis is when an invertebrate goes through a complete life cycle," he says finally.

Remember, these kids are seven years old. But they have help. Earlier in the class, they mapped what their paragraph will say. Luttman calls it a "web of thoughts." The children use it as a reference while Luttman guides them through each sentence of a paragraph to serve as an example. Then he sets the children free to write their own paragraphs, giving them approximately ten minutes before dismissing them to math class.

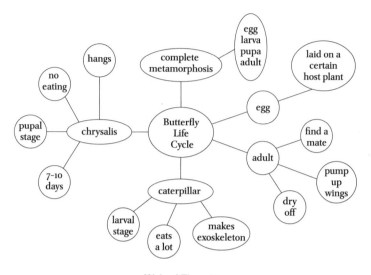

Web of Thoughts

Ridgeview uses no bells to mark the end of class periods – it's too disruptive. Instead, every classroom has an atomic clock so that teachers can synchronize their dismissal times. The children then walk themselves to different math classes, because each child attends math at his ability level rather than with his age mates.

Upstairs again, off in a corner classroom approached by a maze of irregular hallways (Ridgeview's main building was previously a church, and an oddly designed one at that), Mr. Collins is perched on his desk, dramatically reading Alexandre Dumas's *The Count of Monte Cristo* with his sixth graders. His face alternately grimaces and pops with excitement as he reads.

The walls are decked with portraits of presidents, a Rembrandt print, and a bust of Lincoln on a ledge. A neat stack of abacuses rests on a side table.

Collins pauses after the passage in which the count sews himself into his cellmate's body bag, and asks: "What happened?" Eleven hands rise, representing almost half the class of twenty-six. After he calls on a student, Collins asks: "What do you predict is going to happen next? Can Edmund survive in icy waters?" The students discuss this question briefly, then Collins goes on reading, wondering aloud if what's to come will make their predictions true or false.

At points, he pauses before a large word and the class automatically chimes in, reading the word aloud. The young people are on the edge of their seats, gasping audibly when they learn that the count had been in prison for fourteen years. When Edmund is rescued by sailors and pretends to be a sailor himself, Collins asks: "Is this the first disguise, class?" "No," they chorus. "Let's keep a list of Dante's disguises," he responds.

Then he switches to having each student read a few pages in turn. He interjects occasionally, again calling their attention to salient points: "Remember Shakespeare's seven ages of life? Dante is probably now on, what, the fourth one?" He's referencing a famous monologue from Shakespeare's *As You Like It*, in which a man's fourth stage of life is living like a soldier.

Down a hall that smells of hairspray, filled with young people switching classes and talking about prom, is Kurt Mueller's Latin class. The seventh-grade students take turns putting Latin sentences on the whiteboard and correcting them. The class parses the sentences as they go. They use words like "pluperfect," "subjunctive," and "declension" with ease, but wrestle with getting the sentences entirely right.

Mueller ties the grammar lessons into geography and history, telling students, "You need to know the location of Rome like you know *puella* means 'girl.' Rome is where more things happen than anywhere else."

Downstairs again, several classes of elementary students have gotten together for a Colonial Day party, the boys sporting black tricorn hats and the girls in beribboned mobcaps. They're snacking on popcorn and clutching cornhusk dolls they've made.

Liberal Arts and Core Knowledge

Ridgeview's classical curriculum in K–8 is organized around the Core Knowledge Sequence, which originated with E. D. Hirsch's research into why U.S. schools perform so poorly. Hirsch "sought to resurrect elements of the 19th-century common school, which instructed students in the knowledge and values necessary to participate in a democracy," explains an American Enterprise Institute review of how his principles work at Ridgeview. "The Hirschean idea that Americans are defined by certain shared ideas and ideals, and that a school is the main vehicle for passing on those ideas, is central to Ridgeview's understanding of civic education."[2]

The Core Knowledge Sequence begins with a list of major ideas that several hundred scholars have identified as forming the heart of what educated Americans should know. The list is arranged into a sequence of concepts to be learned at each grade level, so children can move seamlessly between schools that use the curriculum. (That's how state standards are supposed to work within each state.) While large portions of Common Core focus on content-empty skills, a Core Knowledge curriculum is based on research showing that knowledge builds on knowledge, and so do academic skills.

The sequence is quite specific. Kindergarteners, for example, learn the seven continents, counting by fives and tens, and classic stories and parables such as "Little Red Riding Hood" and "The Grasshopper and the Ant." The schedule for learning particular concepts is accelerated over other curricula. For example, while Common Core introduces money in grade 2, Core Knowledge recommends that children begin learning about money in kindergarten. Common Core introduces fractions in grade 3; Core Knowledge does so in the first grade. Common Core expects children to be proficient in multiplication and division by fifth and sixth grade; Core Knowledge expects these skills by third and fourth grade, as high-achieving nations do.

Although Hirsch and his Core Knowledge Foundation endorsed Common Core, they also said that the 640-page document does not sufficiently outline the "content-rich curriculum" mentioned in its introduction. Initially, Hirsch hoped that one little clause would prompt more schools to reach beyond Common Core into Core Knowledge. As a political liberal, he has no objection to nationalizing curriculum mandates, despite the lack of authority for such in the U.S. Constitution. To him, the possibility of getting transformative curriculum into all the nation's schools – for the benefit of the nation's disadvantaged children in particular – justified the means.

Hirsch was enthusiastic when his organization was asked for input on the Common Core benchmarks. But he found they "were already written when we were called in," and the writers "did not pay any attention to what I said about what they had written," he told me in an email in 2013. I asked how he could hope for good things to result from Common Core when those things are not mandatory or explicit in its text. "Gegen Dummheit kämpfen Götter selbst vergebens," he replied. Against stupidity, the gods themselves contend in vain.

By 2016, Hirsch had begun to criticize Common Core and its tests, gently but publicly, because his hopes for it had not materialized. On the contrary, he thought the initiative had diverted money, effort, and attention into a broadly ineffective program. "The Common Core language arts emphasize skills such as finding the main idea, managing complex texts, and reading closely," he wrote in *Why Knowledge Matters*. "Yet real improvement in students' verbal abilities will not depend on practicing these skills; it will depend on how much students know and how big their vocabularies are."[3] In other words, Common Core is kind of beside the point.

That's why a number of Core Knowledge schools have rejected Common Core. Ridgeview essentially ignores it, and focuses on what works: a curriculum from Hirsch's foundation. It is rigorous and precise, yet teachers are not micromanaged in how they present the required material. "Education has to do with human beings trying to grow as moral and intellectual beings, and if you regiment it you denigrate the ideals of education," said Florian Hild, who served as principal for a year and now teaches English, German, and history to upper-school students. "We don't worry about the state tests and the Colorado state standards or the Common Core standards. We worry about the integrity of our curriculum and the implementation of a serious classical education." Ridgeview's leaders have generally thought of state standards and tests as things not to worry about, because the school aims higher anyway. But Anderson, the current principal, sees Common Core as something more damaging, and it does worry him.

Hild and Anderson agreed that the most important task of a principal is finding and cultivating excellent teachers who know and love their subject. In Massachusetts, Sandra Stotsky pushed for higher academic standards in teacher education as a necessary complement to a high-quality curriculum.[4] It may actually be the biggest part of the equation. There is very strong research indicating that the caliber of teachers is the most important thing a school can control that contributes to high student achievement. Good teachers even have an effect on teen pregnancy rates, college attendance rates, and saving for retirement.[5] The benefits of government-imposed education standards are more dubious, judging from state-by-state as well as international comparisons.[6] Poorly designed standards and curriculum mandates may actually hobble good teachers.

Enticing talented people into teaching and keeping them there

173

requires offering them things they want, including freedom to choose their own classroom methods. A lack of professional autonomy, as we have seen, is a major reason that teachers give for switching to another occupation. Conversely, teachers are more likely to stay in their job and express satisfaction when they believe they have greater control of what happens in their classroom.[7] Hild understands that this factor is crucial for providing students with a quality education. "We have a curriculum which we will teach, but we want to hire adults who are self-respecting intellectuals," he told me, "and you can't tell a self-respecting individual that the Colorado state standards will determine how we teach the American Revolution." All the teachers at Ridgeview "will cover the same material, but they have to *own* it."

In a nearby classroom, Stephanie Jhones demonstrates her ownership of the material that the curriculum assigns to the first grade. Each youngster has a large map depicting the Louisiana Purchase. The kids are coloring the map while Jhones walks around the room asking questions: "What president wanted to buy New Orleans? Why? What did he get on top of New Orleans?" The children answer each question in a singsong chant. Jhones has to leave class early for her daughter's medical appointment, but her aide smoothly continues the questions.

Ridgeview, like most charter schools, gets less tax money per pupil than traditional district schools. In 2014, the average charter school received about $7,300 per student, approximately $3,000 less than district schools.[8] So Ridgeview has only recently been able to afford teacher's aides. Parent volunteers run the morning reading groups, where children read books at their individual level out loud for about twenty minutes. The school does not offer lunch or busing, but what it does offer is more than adequate compensation, as a ninth grader named Audrey suggests when I speak with her outside the school in the spring sunshine.

In her magenta polo shirt and khakis (the school uniform), Audrey is humming "I'm Gonna Wash That Man Right Outta My Hair," the song she's learning in choir, while she waits for her ride home. Parking space is limited at Ridgeview, so the drop-off and pick-up of students are highly choreographed, with the youngest students let out earliest. A silver Mercedes sits behind a battered light blue Saturn Relay minivan in the pick-up line.

Audrey has been at Ridgeview since the second grade. In the fall semester this year, she tried out another high school to "see what it was like," and quickly decided to come back. Here, teachers "don't just throw facts at you," she says. "They give you the tools and let you figure it out." Audrey adds: "It's very challenging. I didn't realize how easy other schools are. Here, it's more like a conversation, like we're learning with teachers."

Families who leave Ridgeview often complain that the curriculum is too demanding, Peggy Schunk said over dinner at a classy downtown Fort Collins restaurant the evening before my school visit. "We're not here to babysit," she said, with a little shake of her sandy long bob. "We're here to educate."

The students do their part to make it all work, too. Anderson told me, with a chuckle, that it took five years for Moore to persuade him to teach at Ridgeview, and what finally sold him was the students. "Our students are not robots. They take seriously ideas, virtue, and struggling with these serious things." For him, "Ridgeview is being able to continue the graduate school experience." Faculty hold book clubs among themselves and with parents and students. Ridgeview also holds a weekly colloquy, with an academic talk by a teacher or a student. Each graduating senior writes and presents a thesis encapsulating his or her vision of the good life, then defends it before the school community in the spring.

It's challenging, certainly, but the rewards are great. "Children always choose the path of least resistance, but that's not life," said Kristina Menon, the president of Ridgeview's five-member board. "When they persevere and push through, the confidence it builds – they're proud."

A "Type A" District

Two hours south of Ridgeview, another top-rated Colorado school system is also defying Common Core, but its education style is completely different. The Douglas County School District, between Denver and Colorado Springs, is known for outstanding performance and relative wealth, with many executives and other high-flyers living there. The district is retooling itself to cultivate the next generation of ladder-climbers by listening to what business leaders say about the skills they need in the workplace.

The principal of Rocky Heights Middle School, Mike Loitz, had business management books on his bookshelf and on his football-shaped desk. He pointed out his favorites and said they guide how he manages his 1,400 students and 95 teachers. This is noteworthy because academia may be the arena where business and free enterprise are most despised. Teacher blogs and trade publications routinely feature invective against "for-profit" ventures and "treating education like a business." But that isn't the spirit in Douglas County. Here, business leaders have a strong presence in the schools, as well as on the school board (which has been majority Republican since 2009).

On a typical school board, roughly half the members have an advanced degree and most have a substantially higher household income than the American average.[9] The Douglas County board is a step beyond. At the time of my visit, the board members included a Johns Hopkins graduate with three degrees who formerly advised a U.S. senator, a trauma surgeon, a retired Navy commander who has advanced degrees from Princeton and Stanford and worked in several U.S. embassies, and an aerospace engineer who works for the Department of Defense. Even the full-time mom on the board has a master's degree.

The district is full of overachievers. They don't want to be merely above average. They want to be the best. "A majority of our parents have advanced degrees and place a high value on education," said Andy Abner, the principal of Rocky Mountain High School, which has two thousand students. He's built like a football player, with a chiseled jaw and refrigerator shoulders. "Other schools suspend a kid and receive no contact from parents. Here, you call a parent and they show up immediately."

Douglas County has gotten national attention for proposing the first district-run voucher program – which is one reason that *National Review* dubbed it "the most interesting school district in America" in 2013.[10] District leaders say their path-breaking effort to pay teachers at market rates has been far more divisive. Its teachers are also experimenting with entirely new curriculum and tests they created themselves, and the district wants the state to give them the freedom to use these without also having to layer on Common Core, which district leaders say is a better fit for the industrial age, or for today's low-performing schools.

"These suburban districts think they're doing a great job because they compare themselves to urban districts," said John Carson, the former school board president who looks like a rancher even in a business suit. "But we need to compare ourselves to the rest of the world. That is frightening."

He's not kidding. The average student from the best school districts in the United States performs worse than his international peers (i.e. those from similar economic circumstances, family structure, and so on), according to the Global Report Card.[11] When our top students can't hold a candle to top students from similar demographics worldwide, it suggests a problem with instruction, not with spending. The Global Report Card also says the average Douglas County student performs better in math than 65 percent of her peers from the top 25 industrialized nations, and better in reading than 72 percent of her international peers. Using the National Assessment of Educational Progress, the report card determined that in both math and reading an average Douglas County student scores better than three-quarters of her American peers.[12] That puts Douglas County students in the company of those in top-flight countries such as Canada, Finland, Singapore, and Switzerland.

Douglas County is Colorado's third-largest school district, with 63,000 students and 7,000 employees. Like many other school districts, it is the largest local employer. If it were a business, the district would be in a category with the biggest 0.02 percent of U.S. employers.[13] Its annual budget is more than $500 million.

In 2012, the school board majority refused to bargain with the local teachers union, and those board members retained their seats in a tough election the following year. Afterward, along with then-superintendent Liz Fagan, they rethought all the fundamental policies that define a school district: teacher roles and pay, organizational structure, school funding, curriculum and testing design ... You name it, Douglas County does it differently.

The district wants freedom to pursue its own priorities in its own way. Its mantra might be: "We can handle it ourselves. Let us." That attitude has brought Douglas County into conflict with state and federal policies, not least with the Common Core curriculum mandates and tests that Colorado requires all public schools to administer. Fagan, a woman with direct eyes who stands a head shorter than most people, jokingly calls it "Common Floor." In 2013, the board unanimously affirmed a resolution opposing the mandates on the grounds that Common Core is less academically challenging than their own curriculum and that it reduces their freedom to run their own affairs with the approval of local voters.[14]

While the district is no friend of unions, it found common ground with the Colorado Education Association in 2014 on a bill to exempt high-performing school districts from several state testing mandates. District leaders asked the local state representative, Ray Scott, to introduce

House Bill 1202.[15] By the time the governor signed it, though, the bill only created a taskforce to study whether state testing mandates were too onerous. The taskforce recommended a few test cutbacks that made their way into law by summer 2015, including confirming the right of parents to pull kids from tests and reducing the number of mandatory tests in high school. But the state refused to let Douglas County use its own tests unless the U.S. Department of Education allows it.[16]

"We want freedom from the regression-to-the-mean model," said Judy Reynolds, a school board member. "We understand there are districts for which Common Core is a step up, but that's not us.... They're killing us and our teachers with their average or below-average assessments."

Fagan said the choice for Douglas County teachers is to use one of the state education department's "crummy tests approved by their buddies in the testing world, or to double-test," meaning to give students the state tests that don't measure what the district wants, plus another set of tests that do. "We believe in, we expect accountability," Fagan stressed. "We would have it with no laws whatsoever. But bad tests become bad curriculum, and send a message to teachers that 'all we care about is this low-level stuff; if you focus on this, you will be rewarded.'"

Recall that the national Common Core tests were supposed to be "game-changer" assessments, with open-ended questions to measure skills in a more meaningful way. Because of concerns about reliability, however, they ended up being mostly multiple-choice along with some more open-ended questions (although a formulaic response may actually be sought). That's not good enough, Fagan says. "For the pinnacle of English [class] to be compare and contrast, that's laughable." Students should instead strive to understand an author's intent, and create their own literary work. Instead of vocabulary-based tests that measure command of a specific core of cultural knowledge, Fagan wants completely open-ended performance tests. This puts her in company with Stanford University's Linda Darling-Hammond, an adviser to one of the national Common Core test groups who regards those tests as only a step toward her portfolio-based ideal.

The kind of tests and curriculum that Fagan and her staff prefer are not what you might expect in a relatively conservative school district. Paradoxically, Douglas County's "Guaranteed Viable Curriculum" is as pedagogically progressive as its name sounds, with a focus on process more than content. This model is often called "twenty-first-century learning" and summarized as the Four C's: collaboration, communication, creativity, and critical thinking.

"I don't want to see a lecture and a worksheet. Students should be running the school, not adults," said Mike Loitz. He enthusiastically displayed a product of this approach: a YouTube video. Every one of Loitz's 1,500 students participated in making the six-minute "lip dub," where a camera follows a series of students walking backward through the halls of their school, lip-synching Carly Rae Jepson's "Good Time" while their classmates bebop along the camera route.[17] They filmed it in one shot.

As Loitz sees it, Common Core and other federal education initiatives have been based on a faulty diagnosis of the problem: "Common Core, No Child Left Behind, and whatever came before that are predicated on a few things: that all schools are failing, and on ranking — schools, staff, and kids. The third assumption is that all kids should be on a factory model, that a seventh grader in Iowa is the same as a seventh grader in Colorado. But when you engage them on a passion of theirs, you'd be amazed at what they can do." *Passion* may be Loitz's highest-frequency word.

His middle school students recently revamped the school yearbook and won three awards in competition with high schoolers. "Photography isn't in Common Core," he said. If he had been in a district that pushed him to follow Common Core, he "would have made those kids take another writing class."

Loitz leaned forward over the table so far his purple tie flopped onto it. "The world is full of a lot of people, and they don't all need a multiplication table to do their jobs," he said, gesturing firmly. Although he thinks textbooks are old-school, he finally broke down and bought a set for math because parents wanted to know if their kids were on track for second-level Advanced Placement calculus in high school so they would have a chance to get into the Colorado School of Mines, a prestigious engineering school.

In the district's curriculum, "Content is the vehicle for the skills business wants," Fagan said. "Business has been clear with us on that." But what about the more traditional concept of public education as an institution that helps cultivate the self-governing citizens of a republic, or an institution by which society passes down its culture and its moral values? "The bottom line is, twenty-first-century skills are what employers want," Fagan emphasized, adding, "Of course we also want people to be good citizens."

———————

The Primary Innovation Studio

To see what twenty-first-century education looks like in action, let's visit a Douglas County classroom. Mammoth Heights Elementary School appears brand-new. Much of the Douglas County area is either new or under construction, and census projections say the population will continue to grow. The streets and highways teem with bulldozers clearing the way for yet more subdivisions of large homes with three-car garages, small yards, and nearly identical rock and vinyl siding, connected by winding roads that feel mazelike to an outsider.

Mammoth Heights sits in such a subdivision, in a dip of earth beneath the refulgent Colorado sky. A high proportion of the teachers here support the district's changes, said Ben DeGrow, an education analyst at the Independence Institute, a free-market think tank.

Just inside the double doors, an eight-foot-tall fuzzy mammoth sculpture greets visitors. He's covered in artwork, and so are the walls. Upstairs is Mary Lisa Harper's Primary Innovation Studio – or, her second-grade classroom. Harper said of course she teaches the curriculum benchmarks that the state requires, but she aims far higher than that. Her motto is: "Students first, standards second."

"Students first" means putting them at the center of the classroom – sometimes literally. In the studio, which Harper redesigned with funding from a private grant, students have no assigned seats. In fact, there are no desks. The room has a large, round orange rug, where students sit or dance during group time; several roughly triangular tables beside the "Maker's Space," which is basically a glorified craft table; a few plush black beanbag chairs; and, in front of a neon green wall, a stage with a retractable projector screen. Behind it, tacked to an orange wall, is a Plexiglas panel on which children have written vocabulary words in dry-erase marker: "bayou," "deforestation," "Hernando de Soto." It also includes an outline of how to structure a short piece of writing.

As the students wander into the classroom, Harper calls them to the orange rug. It's productive free time, she says. Kids will get twenty minutes to work on their "quality products." Many of them immediately scurry to curl spots to gaze lovingly at their iPad screens. Some head to the Maker's Space and pull out supplies from colorful bins labeled "markers," "clay," "paper," and so on. They are supposed to demonstrate their learning by making something creative, and Harper has given them a book full of ideas, along with grading rubrics. Here's a sample:

A girl decked out in purple, with a bow in her shiny straight bob, comes over to show me the "quality product" she has been working on. She opens an app on her iPad, and a virtual bookshelf pops up. She touches the screen to pull out one of the "books" she has created in response to things she found interesting. This one is about birds. Each "page" has a picture of a colorful bird at the top, and below it a sentence in a seven-year-old's print: "Sum birds migrate each year." "Many birds feathers fall out. It is called molting." She reads each sentence out loud, slowly but correctly. Harper notes that this is exemplary work for a seven-year-old.

Harper walks about the room, in khaki shorts and hair in a scrunch-ied ponytail. She checks what the children are doing, her face probing and approving in turns, and directs or questions them in a low voice. About a third of the class appear to be engrossed in their iPads, and it's

Primary Innovation Studio Quality Product Rubric

	One Star	Two Star	Three Star
iPad presentation	· messing around · no planning · too many students working on one presentation · embarrassed to share, know it is not a great choice	· some connection to learning but mostly messing around · some planning, but lost control · 3–4 students · somewhat proud to share	· takes a few days to complete · same team worked on it the whole time · 1–2 students · proud to share
Hand-written story	· no planning · doesn't connect to learning · not edited or revised · not able to read · takes one day	· a small plan · some editing but not much · doesn't really connect to learning · takes a couple days	· a solid plan · edits and revisions · rewritten for neatness · has detailed illustration · takes many days
Maker's Space item	· doesn't connect to learning · done very quickly · does not clean up · no name, just thrown back with supplies	· some connection to learning but mostly not · only some clean up · only has a name	· clear connection to learning · obviously took some time · cleans up completely · labeled with a description

not clear whether they're creating "quality products" or poking around on YouTube.

Presently, she turns on a CD player, and childish pop music fills the room. She walks over to the orange rug and begins dancing. Some kids run over immediately to join her, while others spend the rest of the song cleaning up their projects. After the song and dance concludes, most of the kids sit down.

"Who has a quality product they want to share?" Harper asks. A few hands go up, and the kids take turns (with some routing through conversational detours) telling about what they've been creating. After that, the bell rings and they stream out.

Harper has been teaching this way for less than a year, and she says it was a "huge challenge" to change from textbooks and structured lesson plans to iPads, mixed media, and short lessons driven by student interests. It looks a little like group unschooling (a style of homeschooling). The idea is to foster kids' initiative and ability to solve problems for themselves, two character traits that employers frequently complain are lacking in employees.

"I try to figure out how one can limit the 'telling and doing' to kids and maximize kids' natural explorer instincts," Harper says. "We are no longer creating dutiful factory workers as we did in the last century."

The Nail That Sticks Up

Douglas County's version of college and career readiness clashes with how the state and the federal government understand the concept. In eduspeak, "college and career readiness" is a synonym for "Common Core." When states (such as Indiana and Oklahoma) have attempted to bow out of Common Core, their education officials have made it clear they had heard from the feds that differing substantially from Common Core would make them ineligible for federal funds and favors.

Many schools are sick of the battery of tests they're forced to give kids every year, both by states and by the federal government. Every time a kid takes a test that has nothing to do with her teacher's or her parents' learning goals, she has lost time that she could have used more productively under attentive guidance. It's like a tax on her time. A number of states – including New York, Florida, Michigan, Pennsylvania, Tennessee, and

Massachusetts — have been debating the testing mandates. In Texas, the result was a reduction in the number of state-mandated high school exit exams from fifteen to five.

Colorado's legislature too is debating the testing regime. "I don't think anybody is against assessment and accountability per se," said Ben DeGrow of the Independence Institute, "but the big issue that kept coming up over and over is that PARCC [Common Core testing] is eating away at instructional time more than our current state tests.... People are looking for ways to give districts and charters more flexibility to serve their needs, but nobody knows how to get to that. Denver schools testified on how they love PARCC. So let them use PARCC. But what about everybody else who doesn't?"

Some states have been rethinking the locked-in approach. A cluster of four New Hampshire school districts won a federal exemption from state tests, allowing them to use their own internally developed tests to satisfy federal accountability mandates.[18] Colorado's education officials refused to help several of the state's districts apply for such a waiver. This kind of freedom, however, shouldn't require playing time-consuming and expensive Mother, May I games with bureaucrats. It should be baked into state and federal law.

Despite the state legislature's reluctance to give up curriculum control, Douglas County is developing its own tests along with a number of like-minded school districts across the nation. "We want to demonstrate we're not the guys in the balcony of the Muppet Show," Fagan said. "We're putting our money where our mouth is."

Pressure to perform well has to come from somewhere, whether it's the federal government, the state, or parents, said Steve Cook, principal of Cimarron Middle School. The district gets plenty of pressure from parents, and their purposes are different from the federal government's. The mandates that states and the feds place on all schools are typically aimed at the low performers, so the high performers have to slow down. Cook acknowledged that Common Core and other federal education initiatives were born of a need for improvement, but Douglas County schools were already meeting the community's expectations when district leaders decided to push them even higher. "We're willing to do it without external demand, because it's right for kids," said Cook.

He and Loitz both said they enjoy their jobs because the challenge is rewarding. Their drive to do well comes from within, augmented by pressure from their local customers. Their hard work pays off, and they don't see why someone else's priorities should keep getting in their way. They want their students to have a similar attitude about learning – to learn because they love it, not because of grades or test scores. They want children to act on their inner drives and learn how to direct them productively through trial and error.

For the most part, Douglas County is able to do what it wants *and* what the state wants. The district begins with premises similar to those of Common Core – education as career preparation – but goes further, faster. District leaders also talk a lot about inspiring and fostering kids' "passions." This is diametrically opposed to the foundational principles of classical schools like Ridgeview in Fort Collins. Derek Anderson, the principal of Ridgeview, believes that "the point of this is not for you to be happy, it's for you to become an adult. If you've got a fourteen-year-old hormonally charged teenager and you tell them to follow their passions, I question your prudence." But Anderson shares Loitz's objection to schemes concocted by faraway bureaucrats who have no real understanding of what their students need. At Ridgeview as in Douglas County, the people who deal directly with schoolchildren want the freedom to decide what works best for them and what satisfies their local communities.

While the carefully considered approaches to learning at these top-performing schools are widely different, both models are at odds with Common Core, partly because both are reaching for higher levels of intellectual and personal development. Here again is Andrew Kern, a leader in classical education: "We value human beings above their marketing value, their economic value, for the creativity and love they can show to each other, the way they can make their little part of the world a beautiful spot."

Some of the Douglas County principals that the district's communications team assembled to chat with me sounded similar. Patti Magby, the principal of Meadow View Elementary School, told me a story about a boy in one of her classes when she was teaching in a high-poverty, traditional public school. One year, when she had helped the school win a grant to support arts instruction, there was a school play and "Bad Tommy" was cast as the lead. After that, "he was no longer Tommy, but Thomas," Magby said, smiling quietly. But the arts program depended on the special grant, so it ended when the funding did, and other bad Tommys lost their opportunity to transform.

Today, Magby is pulling Meadow View into an educational style called

Artful Learning, which blends the arts — dance, theater, visual arts — into all subjects. Magby learned about it when Fagan authorized a fair with booths displaying a variety of education brands and styles, and told her principals, "We can do this if you're interested." Artful Learning has four phases: Experience, where children encounter a "masterwork," from the *Mona Lisa* to a Lego brick and the possibilities it represents; Inquire, where children learn more about the item and its context through activity centers; Create, where the children make their own artwork in response to the masterwork; and Reflect, where they talk and write about what has happened. First graders in Magby's school, for example, created art related to baby animals and their communities as a way of exploring the concept of "connections."

The school principals I spoke with prize working in Douglas County because of the latitude they're given to do their jobs. As long as the kids are learning, they can experiment with ways to make it happen. They can have second graders create a "quality product," or middle schoolers redesign the school yearbook. But we don't know how to reduce a child's photography skills — much less his civic virtue or ability to collaborate — down to a neat, standardized test score. Math and reading are relatively easy to measure, so politicians and bureaucrats have boiled education down to these basic skills, though most parents and teachers want kids to receive far more than those rudiments. It's as if the federal government reduced our nutritional needs to the average vitamin intake and insisted that we get it through a predetermined mix of pills. That way, you know, we're ensuring nutritional equality.

But as Loitz noted, the world is full of a variety of people. The business-conscious progressive teachers in Douglas County consider a "factory model" inadequate for educating human beings, and so do proponents of classical education. "When we had the industrial revolution," said Kern, "it tried to make education efficient, and you can't. It's like making a farm field efficient. You can't. You have to wait years for some crops to grow. Part of the transition from the agrarian craftsman mindset to the industrial mindset said if we have an industrial economy, we need industrial schools. But we don't. When we think about education, we need to remember that we're educating human beings, not economic units, not technicians, not soldiers."

Top Schools Demand More than Common Core

High-achieving public schools – including those with large numbers of poor and minority kids – demand more from students than state standards or Common Core does. These top schools generally take one of two approaches to producing outstanding results, said Florian Hild of Ridgeview. "You can be top by playing the testing game better than all of the other public schools," he said, or you can regard testing proficiency as "a side effect of a serious education. So if our students, our ninth graders can read Thucydides and Homer and Virgil, whatever the state test asks them to do, they can do." A look at what some of America's best public schools are teaching children suggests that Common Core may often be superfluous at best.

Consider the BASIS charter schools, for example. This network began in Arizona, where its first two schools consistently rate among the top ten schools on several national rankings. (Charter schools in Arizona operate on $6,500 per pupil, approximately half the national public school average.) Children attending a BASIS school encounter math books two or three levels above their grade – so fifth graders take seventh-grade pre-algebra, for example. To graduate, students must take a minimum of six Advanced Placement exams, four in core subjects. These are typically on the level of an introductory college class and can earn college credit. Every student takes AP calculus. The average student takes *ten* AP exams, and the overall pass rate is 90 percent.

"I would describe our curriculum as competitive with the best schools in the world," said Mary Riner, a mother in Washington, D.C., who lobbied to bring BASIS to her city. She is now its director of external relations. "We really are looking to close the global achievement gap." In the United States, Riner noted ruefully, "we call a school high-performing if 80 percent of kids can read at grade level. Our kids are years behind kids in Canada and Finland and Shanghai."

Riner sought BASIS for her children because she was annoyed over "the crap thrown into school to make it fun." Her fifth-grade daughter's Latin homework, for example, was coloring Latin words. School can be exciting and serious at the same time, Riner believes. "It excites students to know more than their parents, and to have this knowledge and be able to think about it.... That is rewarding. And that is fun. And that is what we're trying to achieve, not this therapy kind of fake, shallow, immediate gratification," she said passionately.

To create a challenging academic environment, BASIS hires teachers who are experts in their field, usually with a content-based master's degree — not an education degree, as most American teachers have. BASIS teachers work together to create a multigrade syllabus, then have freedom to teach the material in their own style.

"We don't even look at state standards," Riner said. "That's the last thing we do. State standards are there because we have to be in compliance. We finish the Common Core by the ninth grade.... Literally what we are using are world standards."

BASIS schools have been criticized for offering a curriculum that many children can't keep up with, particularly those from disadvantaged circumstances. But like most charters, BASIS schools must accept all comers, and they don't hide their difficulty or cajole people to stay. One-third of their students in the District of Columbia are eligible for federal free and reduced-price lunch. Other charter school brands specifically target hard-to-educate children from broken homes, and they too hold their students to higher standards than typical public schools do.

Knowledge Is Power Program (KIPP) charter schools are renowned for doing what many say is impossible. More than 86 percent of KIPP students live in poverty, and 95 percent are African American or Latino. More than 93 percent of KIPP middle school students have graduated high school, and more than 83 percent of KIPP alumni have gone to college.

"The state sets the academic objectives for the children, and [KIPP schools] extend those objectives because our job is not just to take them to college but to get them through college so they are successful and happy," said Alma Salman, principal of KIPP's Houston elementary school. To prepare for being a KIPP principal, Salman visited top public and private schools around the country, where expectations are higher than most state standards. She wanted her own students to have the best, too.

"The state says by the end of the school year the kindergarteners should be reading on level four, for example. We want our children to be reading at level six," she said. "We read a lot more books to them and expose them to a lot more literature and phonics." Texas expects kindergarteners to be able to count from 1 to 20, but KIPP Houston teaches kindergarteners to count to 100. Common Core asks the same, but it does not introduce kindergarteners to ordinal numbers (first, second, etc.), time and calendars, or graphs. KIPP Houston does.

KIPP teachers, like those at BASIS schools, meet together across grade levels each year to plan lessons and make sure that each subject in one grade connects with the next grade's courses.

Also in Houston, eleven YES Prep charter schools likewise aim to lift disadvantaged children. Two of the high schools rank in the top hundred nationally and in the top twenty statewide, according to *U.S. News and World Report*. YES Prep students are 97 percent Latino and African American, and 79 percent low-income. All the students graduate and attend college.

Teachers write the curriculum and thrice-yearly internal exams, said Jason Bernal, YES Prep's president. In hiring teachers, YES Prep does not rely on formal certification, which has little or no effect on student performance.[19] It does administer a behavior assessment to see if prospective teachers will fit the school culture. Then, candidates give a sample lesson in front of the principal and the school leader they would work with. New teachers participate in a two-week intensive training regimen, and all receive personal coaching and group professional development every week. The school bases salaries on performance rather than seniority.

"It took fifteen years to develop the curriculum and tests the schools use now," said Jennifer Hines, a YES Prep senior vice president. "The schools' curriculum development team started with AP exams and worked backwards to define what students will learn in each grade. We built 100 percent of our curriculum." Each summer, they revisit the curriculum to keep improving it. "We're using AP as a proxy for what kids should know, and it's admittedly a blunt instrument but we've found it to be at least consistent and fairly good."

State education standards are "somewhat helpful" but not very specific on what should be introduced in each grade, especially in language arts, Hines said, and likewise when it comes to "skills, not content, in science and social studies. So if we are teaching a rigorous set of expectations and ensuring students are mastering them, we do not need to teach explicitly to the state assessments. And we will ensure we cover state standards, but that's a small proportion of what we're doing." In short, education standards imposed from outside are only a "starting point" for YES Prep, even in a non–Common Core state. The best schools pay little attention to state standards, period.

Parents Take a Leap

There are indications that Common Core is motivating many parents to seek better options for their children's education. One of those options is homeschooling, and the numbers are soaring in many states. Local home-school leaders attribute the increase, in part, to parents' dislike of Common Core.

North Carolina saw a 14 percent jump in homeschooling from the 2012-13 school year to 2013-14.[20] "I have met people almost on a daily basis who are escaping Common Core Standards via home education because the traditional system is failing their families," said Lynne Taylor to School Reform News. She has homeschooled her own kids in North Carolina for more than a decade.

For Danielle Widney, a New Yorker, Common Core meant "too many tests and too many people telling me what is good for my children," as she told USA Today not long after she started homeschooling. "The Common Core math doesn't make any sense — and I have a master's in electrical engineering."[21]

Florida had a 10 percent jump in homeschool enrollment from the 2013-14 school year to 2014-15.[22] In the first four years after South Dakota began using Common Core, homeschooling doubled in Sioux Falls and also increased statewide.[23] "We are seeing a lot of this as of late," said William Estrada, director of federal relations for the Home School Legal Defense Association. For large numbers of parents, he told Fox News, Common Core is "the final straw after many concerns about the education of their children."[24]

While many parents are going solo to provide a high-quality education for their children, others are joining forces to establish new schools. In 2014, a Catholic couple, a Protestant couple, and a Mormon couple dug into their savings to shell out a down payment on a vacated public school building in Marietta, Ohio, just across the border from West Virginia. There they opened a new private academy for their own kids and others who wanted to escape Common Core.

One of the founders, Khadine Ritter, is a lawyer who speaks five languages. She had expected that she wouldn't have to worry about Common Core because her kids attended the Catholic school in Marietta, which is run by the local parish. She was wrong. In February 2013, she learned that Common Core would arrive in her children's school. "We went through all the proper channels at church, with the principal, local school board meetings, on and on and on," Ritter said. "The decision was made: we were going to stick with Common Core."

Ritter and her husband began meeting with other parents in Marietta. They decided to create a competitor to the Catholic school. That was the hardest part, Ritter said, because it has meant dealing with gossip and strained relationships, even though their priest wished them well. But the Ritters placed a high value on giving their children something better than Common Core.

As for most parents, the math was the worst. "My daughter would come home crying because her teacher wanted her to do [math] one way and I wanted her to do it another," Ritter said. "I don't know how to help my kids. It takes me a long time to figure out what they want me to do, and that's by design. I don't mean to be cheeky, but it was offensive. I'm not stupid. Just teach my kid how to multiply, don't teach them the underlying theory in the third grade. She needs to master the subject, not analyze it to death."

The Common Core approach to language arts was dismaying in its own way. Instead of classic literature, the children were reading social justice tracts where evil landlords ran cozy little bookstores out of business with exorbitant rent. Ritter found that demeaning. "It bothers me when I hear, 'This kid is going to vocational school to be a plumber, so he doesn't need to read Mark Twain.' Why shouldn't he read Mark Twain?" she asked. "You want to talk about class warfare, why is the plumber not entitled to read Shakespeare? Is he not a person just like the doctor? My kids aren't human capital, they're little people."

I met Ritter at her new school, called the Veritas Classical Academy, just a few weeks before it opened for the first time. The founding families were painting the gym and setting up the library. The building was not particularly pretty – typical Soviet-style cinderblock. It needed new carpet and a real playground. But inside those concrete walls, children are now reading the original Mother Goose, poems by Robert Louis Stevenson, *Little House on the Prairie*, and Twain's *The Prince and the Pauper*. First graders learn Latin. Students stay at least a year ahead of most peers in math. In the winter, they sled behind the school during recess. They host an annual Dickens dinner and enjoy live musical performances by period performers.

The Veritas Classical Academy is doing well. From its first year, 2014-15, to its second, enrollment nearly doubled, to seventy-three students. "Probably the best support has been from the business community," Ritter said, "because they realize that your town may have a lot of amenities, but if you don't have good schools it's that much harder to recruit professionals."

Five hundred miles away, in St. Louis, a father pulled his kids from Catholic school when Common Core arrived there, too. The children were taking hours to do math homework every night, and they were only in the third and first grades. "We were spending hours on stuff that doesn't make sense," said Ed Martin.

The Martins live one block away from St. Gabriel the Archangel Catholic Church and School. It's the kind of neighborhood that people move into just so their children can attend the school, as Ed and his wife Carol did. "In the city of St. Louis, this is the best school, best parish, where all the politicians live, and it's considered a nice place with lots of good people there," Ed Martin said. But they decided it was not good enough for their children when Common Core moved in. "It's not worth paying serious tuition when you're not getting something that's better than what you're getting in a public school."

Leaving the parish school in favor of a classical school was difficult for the Martins, as it was for the Ritters. "Most of our neighbors think we're moving because they say, 'If you don't go to school here, what's the use of living here?'" Martin said. His kids have continued to play sports with their old classmates on parish teams, as is customary in the neighborhood. That's been awkward, but their father doesn't mind being upfront when people ask what happened.

Still, because of their neighborhood ties, the Martins initially "chickened out" after a year of classical school and re-enrolled their children in the Catholic school. By September 15, they were already so fed up again with Common Core that they immediately moved the kids to the St. Austin School, a classical school with approximately a hundred students.

Now, like the children at Veritas, the Martin kids memorize poems, passages from the Bible, and portions of the U.S. Constitution. They're learning Latin and Spanish. St. Austin's is "intellectually and pedagogically safe, not just physically safe, and that changed our life," said Martin. It's worth the twenty-minute drive every morning instead of a short walk down the street, he added. Since making the switch, they've been "so much happier."

CHAPTER 7

Reboot – Educating Free Citizens

AFTER I HAD begun to obsess about Common Core – creating Google alerts on the term back when very few articles included it and questioning every person I could find who seemed to be an informed but independent analyst – I started looking into the history of education standards. Why did we have unelected bureaucrats assuming they know what every child needs to learn in every subject and every grade? Where did they get the idea that they're entitled to impose their schemes on other people's children? What kind of political and cultural atmosphere makes that seem reasonable?

At the time, I was running *School Reform News*, the education newspaper of the Heartland Institute, a state-focused, national libertarian think tank. One of the previous editors of that paper, Robert Holland, is a Heartland research fellow. I found he'd written a book in 1995 about something called outcome-based education (OBE).[1] I ordered a used copy of *Not with My Child You Don't* off Amazon for less than a dollar plus shipping. When it arrived, I read the whole thing in one gulp.

It was eerie. Twenty years ago, Bob was reporting events that sounded identical to what has been happening with Common Core: A cabal of big-money business and nonprofit groups scheming with bureaucrats to impose a rotten curriculum on the nation's schoolkids. Closed-door votes.

Teachers having to perform from a prewritten script. Mystifying math problems. Criminally unreliable tests. Intrusive data collection. Angry parents flooding public meetings. Citizens digging into their own pocketbooks to finance a grassroots pushback. Educrats insisting that it was not a political project but simply "what's best for children." In 1992, outcome-based education was even called "the Common Core of Learning" in Virginia. Déjà vu all over again.

Common Core surprised a lot of people when it began popping up in their children's schools. As I've shown, that's partly because its supporters deliberately imposed it by stealth. But it shouldn't have been such a surprise. It's just the next logical step in America's century-long progression toward a nationalized education system.

"People have a short memory. It's also a short cycle of masochism," said Lil Tuttle, a mother of three who served as vice president of the Virginia Board of Education during the OBE battles. She is now with the Clare Boothe Luce Policy Institute. "The parents I know that have gone through OBE, as soon as their kids were out of public schools it was like 'Thank God that's over.' If your child is in the system, you're afraid to be too outspoken, and if your child leaves you're so tired you don't want to deal with it anymore. Every twelve years or so they come up with something new to fool the next generation of parents."

The cycle is repeating with Common Core. States that basically rebrand it may defuse the political tension temporarily. But even getting rid of Common Core would not solve the underlying problem, which boils down to competing visions of what education should be, and more fundamentally still, who should control it.

Peg Luksik was also in the thick of the OBE and school-to-work wars – an earlier round of cultural conflict over education – providing testimony to a variety of government bodies and speaking extensively to parent groups. She's been working in education for thirty-five years and has taught every age group from preschool to college. She has dissected the innards of standardized tests, written curriculum, and worked in policy for the U.S. Department of Education. Luksik said the ongoing education wars can be distilled into "a constant battle between those who see schools as academic delivery systems – in other words, parents send their children to school to learn knowledge, and to become able to read and write and count – and those who see schools as social engineering

mechanisms, to create the citizens that some would want us to be."
Emphasis on *some* – because parents have differing ideas about the citizenship lessons our schools ought to be teaching.

Knowledge versus Social Engineering

American education was planted in the classical tradition of sustaining our country's distinct cultural heritage and passing it on to the next generation, as well as teaching important practical skills. That's what most parents today still want for their children: to read fluently, encounter classic literature, understand major events of history, know something about the natural world, and be able to solve concrete math problems at a respectable level. They see these basics as having practical benefits, such as helping give children a foundation for financially supporting themselves and their families, promoting civic engagement and community service, and fostering virtues that are good for their own sake, such as courage and love.

The American founders thought a broad education was essential for citizens of a self-governing nation, as they noted in the Northwest Ordinance of 1787, the first federal document to mention education (and one of the four "organic laws" setting out the foundations of the United States): "Religion, morality, and knowledge, being necessary to good government and the happiness of mankind, schools and the means of education shall forever be encouraged."[2] The founders' conception of a public education deserving of the name was one that instilled civic virtues and the habits of self-government, such as respecting the liberties of others, assembling peaceably to petition the government for redress of grievances, and taking responsibility for one's local community. This, too, is something that nearly all American parents still want for their children.

That was not flashy enough for the "education reformers" of the late nineteenth century, most notably John Dewey. Applying Darwin's scientific theories to child psychology, Dewey said it is not possible to know truth since our minds and bodies are constantly evolving. Instead, we learn to adapt to our changing environment.[3] He also believed that social engineers could advance human evolution and improve the world by manipulating children's behavior.

Dewey's philosophy has driven the case for curricular change since the beginning of the twentieth century, as Diane Ravitch detailed in *Left*

Back: A Century of Failed School Reforms, a history of U.S. education policy. Throughout the past century, "progressives claimed that the schools had the power and responsibility to reconstruct society. They took their cue from John Dewey, who in 1897 had proclaimed that the school was the primary means of social reform and the teacher was 'the prophet of the true God and the usherer in of the true kingdom of God.'"[4] We hear echoes of this secular messianic language today from self-described education reformers today who endow education with essentially salvific effects. One has to replace God with something.

For Dewey, schools needed to change as society evolved, but they also needed to steer social change, in part by taking on some parental functions. "Society is changing," the argument goes, "and the schools must change too; the family and the community have become weaker, and the schools must now do what the family and community used to do; the best way of addressing the social and economic problems of society is to change the curriculum...."[5] Ravitch chronicles the long tug-of-war between progressive "reformers" who regard schools as instruments of social engineering, and American families who think of schools as institutions to which they delegate some of their authority for the purpose of passing along the accumulated wisdom of generations and advancing Americans' cultural heritage into the future.

Before the 1950s, American schools tended to reflect the expectations and values of local communities. At the same time, across the country, "teachers and parents had a broadly shared understanding about what children should learn in school," Ravitch notes.

> Virtually all communities wanted their children to learn reading, writing, arithmetic, history, geography, and nature study in the common schools, and they wanted the high schools to teach Latin, a modern foreign language or two, mathematics, literature, grammar, the sciences, ancient history, English history, American history, drawing, music, and practical courses such as bookkeeping and woodworking. Local school boards and educators had a keen sense of what their own communities expected.[6]

Curriculum was fairly consistent nationwide because Americans generally had the same ideas about what children should learn, not because any central authority had homogenized the schools.

Progressives disliked the traditional American curriculum with its focus on subject knowledge. They wanted to free children from their parents' "antiquated" views, such as belief in God and in objective truth – the better to advance their own central-planning agenda. Their "modern" methods of education focused more on behavior and "socialization" than on knowledge. Ravitch quotes John Franklin Bobbit, a contemporary of Dewey, saying that the "abilities, habits, appreciations, and forms of knowledge" that people need should be determined by "scientific" curriculum designers.[7] Another progressive education reformer, Ellwood Patterson Cubberly, "portrayed the public school as a powerful tool that the state must use to assimilate immigrants and train workers for their place in the social order." His brave new education world would be "paternalistic, perhaps even socialistic," with children "coming to belong more and more to the state, and less and less to the parent."[8] Cubberly's books on education were widely used for generations.

While local schools were still teaching in traditional ways, progressives targeted teachers colleges and expanded the reach of these institutions, so that now almost everyone involved in education must filter through one of them. That is how their philosophy came to dominate the field. Progressives established the new discipline of "curriculum studies," insisting that curriculum development was a science, "too esoteric and complex to be entrusted to teachers and laymen," writes Ravitch. Applying this notion brought about "an extraordinary shift of power away from teachers, parents, and local communities to professional experts."[9]

Progressive reformers had gained control of teacher training by the time of World War II, and their methods began taking over classrooms. Instead of conveying a specific body of knowledge directly to students, the progressive teacher facilitates "student-led" projects and group activities, in a technique variously called "cooperative," "inquiry-based," or "discovery" learning. An *Atlantic* article in 2016 described this method as applied in a preschool class, where "bulletin boards displayed the questions children brainstormed to prepare for a classroom visit from a plumber. How do pipes connect? How do the workers cut the pipes? How does the pipe get the water to the part in the sink? How did that pipe get black?"[10]

It may appear that the little tots are already developing impressive thinking skills. But did four-year-olds come up with those questions themselves? No, the teacher coaxed them out with leading questions and answer-shaping. Instead of directly telling the children what they should know, the teacher implicitly conveyed what she thought they should know, in a vague and manipulative way. This subtle and somewhat deceptive form of implicit communication is harder for children to understand and learn from if they live in a home not filled with complex English, both spoken and print – typically poor, minority, or immigrant children. Such techniques "are not supported by a consensus of research psychologists," according to Williamson Evers.[11]

How does a small child know what he needs to know? He doesn't. To think he can is folly. The idea that a child should direct his own learning teaches him one thing effectively: that he is the measure of human experience, of right and wrong. People who hold this belief do not thereby become confident and self-reliant; rather, they are likely to be led by ego and emotion, and thus more easily manipulated. Furthermore, as Lil Tuttle asked, how can you hold teachers responsible for what children learn if teachers are regarded as merely facilitators of their students' self-direction and subjective choice?

Progressive pedagogy destroys the idea of learning altogether, write Andrew Kern and Gene Edward Veith: "If there is no objectively true content, what will there be to teach? If there are no intellectual standards, how can children be assessed? If there are no moral absolutes, how can children be disciplined and educated to be responsible citizens?" In the progressive model, students "can learn methods to cultivate their subjectivity and to explore and share their feelings. They can also be taught to establish new social and political identities as members of (usually victimized) groups. But processes such as learning how to read, write, and calculate are neglected in favor of such postmodern values as entertainment, group interaction, and consciousness-raising."[12]

Progressives deliberately rejected the principles of education that had produced generations of self-reliant citizens – in particular, the principle of handing down a coherent body of knowledge tied to the robust virtues necessary for life in a republic. They aimed instead to mold children into a new kind of citizen, fit for a relativistic age in which feeling takes precedence over thinking. This elevation of subjectivity deprives children of the solid knowledge with which to make informed decisions, leaving them more susceptible to social control. It also separates children from the traditions of their parents and their country. It assumes that tradition and history have little to say to children.

The use of vague, jargon-laden language to prescribe what children must learn is another way to distance parents from their children's education and weaken public oversight. You can't evaluate something you don't understand — or something you're not informed about. This is what has frustrated many parents about Common Core. Selise Chiddister told me her six-year-old son, in first grade, "refuses to talk to me about math" because it's full of procedures she has never used. She said he refers to a certain exercise as "the dots of doom," and she wasn't laughing when she told me. His school's decision to migrate exercises and homework onto iPads also puts distance between them, because it's harder for her to review his homework and see what's going on. Her son is possessive of his device, and he can always claim he "has homework" when he wants access to it, which makes it difficult for her to enforce rules about its use.

Once during an interview for a story, an education researcher told me teachers "raise our kids," then giggled and stuttered, "Well, not entirely, but you know what I mean." Yes, I do. A family member once told me that an acquaintance had advised her to put her children in public preschool so the teacher would train her toddlers to listen attentively and follow orders, relieving my relative of this responsibility. My relative did not take that advice, which she considered appalling. Schools should be seeking to reinforce family bonds, not break them down, since engaged parents are a child's best advantage in life.

The Federal "Reform" Train

Progressive ideas and methods reign in education today, despite research amply demonstrating that they diminish academic achievement.[13] After gaining control of teacher training, progressive educators have continuously sought to expand and leverage the federal role in education. The federal government is their preferred vehicle for reshaping schools and society because it allows a small group of people to control the rest.

As early as the 1950s, Congress began disregarding its lack of legal authority to meddle with education, by giving out grants for model curriculum. In 1959, President Eisenhower called for national education goals, and subsequent presidents of both parties have promoted the idea.[14] When student achievement took a nosedive in the 1960s, it added urgency to the calls for federal involvement in K-12 education — just as the Great Depression had invited more federal control of the economy. Keep in mind that this decline in academic performance followed the spread of progressive teaching methods across the country, and E. D. Hirsch among others makes a convincing case that the two are linked.[15]

The College Board announced in 1975 that SAT scores had been dropping relentlessly since 1963, and a similar decline was found in every other standardized test. Education standards became a national issue.[16] Later research by Hirsch, Richard J. Herrnstein, and Charles Murray confirmed the slide in test scores. The College Board subsequently watered down the SAT to hide the decline, but the trend has not reversed.

The researchers who first documented the SAT decline concluded that "curricular changes" were the culprit: "Our gross data indicate a considerable enrollment decline in academic courses," which had actually been a progressive goal for decades. But instead of telling the progressives to skip town and take their brain-maiming ideas with them, national and state lawmakers began giving them money to "solve" the problem their theories had caused.

The National Science Foundation set the pattern. Congress had created the NSF in 1950, and almost immediately it began using federal money to write science curriculum and train K–12 teachers,[17] even though all the governing federal education laws prohibit federal involvement in curriculum.[18] Like all the other federally supported curriculum initiatives since then, the NSF's curriculum was progressive to the hilt. An analysis of NSF curriculum activities by Michael McKeown, a biologist, along with other working scientists in 2000 found they "tended to reduce academic standards for instruction in math and 'weaken' the educational basis on which American science necessarily rests." Nationwide NSF programs were "riddled with errors and relied on 'post-modernist' research, in which 'what is generally called a scientific fact' is instead 'taken to be merely a belief system.'"[19] NSF's federally funded curriculum initiatives provided a minuscule amount of money to recipient districts, but it was enough to enable the federal government "to shape or reshape state and local educational policies and direct use of their resources even though local and state taxpayers are paying most of the bills."[20] This, you may recall, is also how the Obama administration leveraged the relatively small Race to the Top grants into nationwide adoption of Common Core.

The argument for federal involvement in education intensified when the Reagan administration released its blockbuster report titled "A Nation at Risk" in 1983.[21] The report ominously warned that "the educational foundations of our society are presently being eroded by a rising tide of mediocrity that threatens our very future.... If an unfriendly foreign power had attempted to impose on America the mediocre educational performance that exists today, we might well have viewed it as an act of war."[22] Among its recommendations was for states and localities to administer and publish the results of standardized tests, an idea that most Americans still support.[23] But standardized tests have little-known adverse effects, such as crowding out subjects other than math and reading.[24] They also remove control of education from local communities, i.e. from parents.

The "Nation at Risk" report launched a raft of reform efforts. That same year, the National Council of Teachers of Mathematics created the first set of national academic standards, but it, too, was rife with ineffective progressive notions such as a "constant availability of calculators" starting in kindergarten, "extreme de-emphasis" of calculating with pencil and paper, and a reduced attention to "analytical and deductive methods."[25] None of the reform efforts of the 1980s remedied teachers' deficiencies in content knowledge, nor did they fortify an increasingly hollowed-out curriculum. Student performance had not improved by the end of the decade, and this failure was answered by more federal involvement at higher levels.

In 1989, President George H. W. Bush gathered a number of governors for a National Education Summit in Charlottesville, where they agreed on six national goals for education.[26] According to *Education Week*, "the real action took place in a room at the Boar's Head Inn, where three governors and a White House official, accompanied by their aides, hammered out an agreement on the document that was to be the summit's only tangible product."[27] Three governors setting policy for the nation!

The new initiative for national standards was labeled "America 2000." The Bush administration proceeded to fund model curriculum mandates in several subject areas and gave states money if their mandates mirrored the federal models. These mandates were given the PR-friendly label "standards," leading to the now-common phrases "standards-based education" and "standards-based reform." The mandates tell teachers what will appear on the annual tests that measure whether students have learned the prescribed material. The dominant strain of progressive educators regard these standards and tests as key to getting every school to offer every student the "right" curriculum at the "right" time and in the "right" manner.[28] Test-enforced mandates backed up with federal money are now the default structure of U.S. education.

In the 1992 presidential campaign, the three main candidates – the incumbent George H. W. Bush, Governor Bill Clinton, and Ross Perot – all endorsed national standards and tests in education.[29] The first two had played leading roles in the Charlottesville summit. When Clinton became president, "America 2000" morphed into "Goals 2000." Clinton's deputy education secretary, Marshall Smith, published a paper together with Jennifer O'Day of the American Institutes for Research calling for "systemic reform" of education that would include "a common content core." They called for states to align their curriculum standards and materials, tests, teacher training and professional development.[30] Funny how that sounds exactly like the Common Core of 2010. Indeed, Smith later served as an education adviser in the Obama administration.[31]

The centralized curriculum benchmarks were poised to go from recommended to mandatory when Congress passed the Goals 2000: Educate America Act in March 1994. The provisions of the new law included a National Education Standards and Improvement Council tasked with approving state standards.[32] But after Republicans took control of Congress in the 1994 elections – for the first time since federal education programs began – they gutted the council, charging that it smacked of a "national school board." The new Senate also passed a resolution by a vote of 99-1 denouncing proposed national history mandates that had been widely criticized as politically biased.[33] A revised set of history standards would later be released, and meanwhile the federal government was funding the writing of national standards in arts, English, science, foreign language, and civics.[34] Sandra Stotsky later described the English standards as an "abysmal failure" that "contained nothing resembling standards," a characterization that typifies the lot.[35]

Advocates of nationalizing education then went underground, working through private organizations instead of elected representatives. It wasn't a completely new strategy, though. After all, the "consensus-building process" around national education goals at the 1989 summit went on behind closed doors.[36] That conference was organized by the National Governors Association, which, again, is a private networking organization. NGA set about consolidating political and business support for national standards and tests.[37] It convened another summit in 1996, which gave birth to the nonprofit organization named Achieve, commissioned to "help states move toward a common standard."[38]

A Brookings Institution paper in 2000 (mentioned in Chapter 1) concluded that working through "a wide variety of nongovernmental national organizations" would be the most effective way to nationalize education policy, because doing it openly through the political process would stir up Americans' concerns about federal micromanagement of education.[39] In other words: We can't be honest about what we're doing, or people won't like it. Note how this strategy undermines Americans' right to government by consent. James Hunt Jr., former governor of North Carolina, helped drive this deceptive strategy after he left public office. Hunt's foundation took millions from the Gates Foundation to begin herding other governors into the coalition that would create Common Core.[40]

The chief architect of Common Core, David Coleman, has described how it emerged from the grasstops education initiatives of the 1980s and 1990s. "This movement of state-led work on higher standards had deep bipartisan roots, dating back to the Charlottesville summit in 1989," he said in a 2012 speech. "Building on that foundation, non-profits such as Achieve, the Hunt Institute, and the Alliance for Excellent Education had all been working with states for several years to achieve the foundations for common standards."[41]

Achieve recommended changes to state standards, tests, and graduation requirements, and it helped states compare their standards and bring them into alignment. Two of Common Core's five lead writers, Phil Daro and Susan Pimentel, worked for Achieve on these projects. The authors of the 2000 Brookings paper characterized Achieve as a private version of the national standards review board that Congress had axed. Apparently its work was not particularly effective, though, because Achieve later cited the low quality of state standards and tests – most of which it had directly influenced – to justify the creation of Common Core.

Federal involvement with curriculum mandates and tests deepened in 2001 with the passage of No Child Left Behind (NCLB), the most expensive and all-encompassing education law in U.S. history. As we know, it required states to establish curriculum mandates and test most of their students in reading and math, in exchange for federal education dollars. Every state quickly complied, despite estimates showing the high costs to taxpayers.[42] And much of that money is consumed by bureaucrats before the remainder trickles down to the classroom. In Florida, for example, only about *one-third* of the federal funding made its way to students.[43]

One of NCLB's many flaws, ironically, arose from a slight deference to law and custom. To reduce the appearance of federal meddling, NCLB allowed states to set curriculum and testing mandates at any level, while requiring that all children rate proficient on those tests by 2014. Not surprisingly, states typically set very low standards so as not to be penalized for falling short. Once again, promises by politicians to lift educational achievement failed.

"They know that No Child Left Behind has failed because it demanded that even underperforming students demonstrate progress, and schools did not do that," said Lil Tuttle. Still, she acknowledges that NCLB "did do what no federal program did: It did hold schools responsible for all of their students."

The central planners' answer to the failure of central planning was, as always, more central planning. Rather than reverse course and let state taxpayers put pressure on their lawmakers from the ground up, the central planners resolved to take even more freedom away from local communities and individuals. They would create national tests, with national curriculum mandates to match. Thus Common Core was born. As we know, the federal government used NCLB and Race to the Top grants to persuade states to get in line.

That's the federal way of running education, said Tuttle: "'We'll give you money if you'll do it our way.' The problem is, a good education is in the eye of the beholder, just like beauty. What is marvelous to the think tanks in D.C. and the educators and state school authors and textbook authors, they could dream up the very best system, but it wouldn't fit all children any better than the current one does." The leveling and standardization are especially harmful to the best students and to the struggling ones, as Tuttle observed. "If local education systems are fighting to meet federal guidelines so they can keep the money coming in, the non-average child is going to be the one falling through the cracks."

Diane Ravitch came to a similar conclusion in surveying all the progressive efforts at educational reform through the twentieth century:

What was sacrificed over the decades in which the schools were treated as vehicles for job training, social planning, political reform, social sorting, personality adjustment, and social efficiency was a clear definition of what schools can realistically and appropriately accomplish for children and for society. The century-long effort to diminish the intellectual purposes of the schools had harmful consequences, especially for children from disadvantaged backgrounds.[44]

Tuttle expects that Common Core, like "most grand education schemes handed down from dreamers," will prove to be "another costly exercise in futility and frustration and failure for students and ultimately the nation." Right now, public opinion shows a widespread sense of frustration and futility regarding the Common Core experiment. For instance, a poll of parents in 2016 found 32 percent saying the new standards had *decreased* how much their kids were learning in school, while 27 percent said the standards had made no difference.[45]

Early results from the major national tests indicate that student achievement has continued to decline since states phased in Common Core. The 2015 National Assessment of Educational Progress showed its first-ever nationwide decline, and also found that algebra enrollment in the eighth grade had dropped from 54 percent to 28 percent over a two-year period.[46] In 2016, the ACT showed a five-year decline in scores. ACT's leaders tried to brush off the decline by attributing it to the larger numbers of students taking the test (thus altering the demographics), yet every racial group except for Asian Americans showed declining scores over that time. This suggests that the bigger and more "diverse" pool of test takers is not what explains the downward trend.[47] (The SAT showed a similar decline between 2010 and 2015,[48] as it has since its inception; but its revamp in connection with Common Core, effective in spring 2016, resulted in noticeably inflated scores,[49] so it isn't yet possible to know if the downward trend is continuing.)

Common Core was supposed to be about accountability in education, but who will be held accountable for its failures? "When someone else sets the agenda," Tuttle said, "that ends the ability of anyone local to hold schools accountable for what they are learning. Teachers and schools will be looking to their masters, not parents." Yet those who imposed this disastrous scheme will not suffer any damage: "The paychecks keep coming, the doors stay open, everyone gets their benefits. Nobody pays a price when students go through the system and don't learn."

The Wheat Amid the Tares

The biblical book of Matthew records Jesus' parable of the tares: A man sows wheat in his field, but his enemies come and throw weed seeds onto the field while he sleeps. When the plants sprout, the man and his servants see weeds intermingled with the wheat. The servants ask,

> "Sir, did you not sow good seed in your field? How then does it have tares?" [The man] said to them, "An enemy has done this." The servants said to him, "Do you want us then to go and gather them up?" But he said, "No, lest while you gather up the tares you also uproot the wheat with them. Let both grow together until the harvest, and at the time of harvest I will say to the reapers, 'First gather together the tares and bind them in bundles to burn them, but gather the wheat into my barn.'"[50]

In our national culture today, Common Core is like weeds growing among the crops of knowledge and learning. Back when the weeds and wheat were young, it was hard to distinguish the two. But now that they have matured, it is easier. We can see more clearly that some approaches to education, although attractive, end up mentally and spiritually starving children and society, while others have proved over time to nourish young minds and cultivate civilization.

Today there are very good trends in education growing alongside the bad. Common Core has a bright silver lining: it has pushed many families to look for something better, or to build it themselves. While schools, teachers, parents, and children have been struggling beneath a one-size-fits-none curriculum and mandatory high-stakes testing, some exciting alternatives have been launched by people thinking differently about work, family, and culture. Technology now allows such likeminded people to interact across great distances.

For many families now, the only viable option is a local public school, which is why 85 percent of American children attend local public schools even though just 36 percent of adults say they would prefer it to other options for their children.[51] Poorer families cannot afford the same alternatives that many better-off families choose: to homeschool or send their children to private schools, or hire tutors, or move to better neighborhoods with superior public schools and less harried teachers. Many parents don't have the time to supplement their children's education in the evening. Often there is only one parent in the home. Many parents did not receive a good education themselves, so they cannot help their children with homework even if they do have the time.

But there is hope for their children. The frustration and suffering inflicted on American families by the nationalizing of the education system have spurred an opposite trend. While Common Core was rolling into schools, families and states were creating better options, rooted in individual responsibility and choice rather than coercive collectivism. From 2007 to 2012 (the latest data available from the National Center for Education Statistics), homeschooling increased by 17 percent.[52] Between 2009 and 2016, the number of private school choice programs nationwide grew from twenty-three to fifty-nine, and the number of students enrolled in such programs more than doubled.[53] A majority of states now offer choice programs, which give families control over some of the tax dollars allocated for their children's education, allowing them to pick among competing schools or education arrangements. In Arizona and Nevada, an innovative type of school choice program called "education savings accounts" lets parents spread their kids' education dollars among multiple options, including curriculum, private tutors, special-needs therapies, and extracurricular activities such as sports and band.

School choice frees families to vote with their feet regardless of their income level. It lets poor and middle-class families have a schooling arrangement they want, without having to move into another district with much pricier mortgages. They could freely choose Common Core-style education, or something completely different. School choice frees millions of Americans to fulfill their preferences regarding curriculum, testing, safety, culture, and so forth. It is not a panacea, but it does increase opportunities for everyone, particularly for the families who now have the fewest. That's why it isn't only conservatives who favor school choice; there is also a long history of progressive support for school vouchers, education savings accounts, and charter schools.[54] In fact, the latest edition of an annual poll tracking public opinion on school choice finds that a majority of Democrats support universal K-12 vouchers and an even higher percentage (along with majorities of Republicans) support tax-credit scholarships,[55] which give individuals and companies tax breaks for donating to K-12 scholarship funds.

One progressive who supports school choice today is Howard Fuller, a

Marquette University professor and civil rights activist who was in the crowd at King Solomon Baptist Church in Detroit in 1964 when Malcolm X gave his famous speech on "The Ballot or the Bullet." Fuller says it changed his life: "I see myself as a black man who has been engaged in struggle with the consistent theme of 'how do I help empower the poorest of my people.' I'm not just about black people, I'm about poor people, but my focus is on black people just because of the blood that runs in my veins."

Fuller sees a perfect confluence between his impulse to help "the least of these" and his vocal support for school choice. "Public education is the idea that we want the public to be educated, and we've come up with different systems to try and deliver on that promise," Fuller told me. He has made common cause with Republicans and other right-wingers on school choice for tactical reasons, just as some conservatives and progressives have done in opposition to Common Core. When he was superintendent of the Milwaukee Public Schools in the 1990s, he supported the Wisconsin legislature's decision to create the voucher program that is now the nation's oldest and applies to the entire state. Some on the left have tarred Fuller over his longtime support for school choice, in part because of its association with the political right. He thinks that's wrongheaded. Your interests may converge at points with those of people who don't share your worldview, he observed, so "you have to understand how to make temporary alliances to make change. Everyone has to decide what for them constitutes principle and for them constitutes strategy."

To Fuller, school choice is about leveling the playing field so all families can choose what their children learn in school and how they are taught. "For me it's a social justice issue, not about free markets," he said. School choice is a way of "trying to ensure that those families that have the least among us have some opportunity to choose the best environment for their children."

A comprehensive review of one hundred studies on school choice programs in 2016 found the research is clear that school choice improves the lives of children, and especially poor, minority children, far beyond the small positive effects of charter schools.[56] It shows that school choice programs have the widest reach and the greatest ability to benefit society when states do not impose testing mandates on participating private schools.[57] School choice also restores the natural connection between parents and their children, harnessing this bond for personal and societal good – unlike the kind of "reforms" that divide children from parents in order to control them and reshape society. Most of all, school choice fulfills the American founders' ideal of education that promotes the habits of self-government by empowering individuals to make their own decisions and bear the costs.

Andrew Kern, who advises classical schools across the country, observed that it requires an "almost superhuman" level of virtue to make wise decisions if you don't have to live with the consequences. Such virtue "hardly ever exists," he said. "We have a governing structure ... especially at the federal level, led by people who will never have to live with a single [negative] consequence of the decisions they make." Instead, "they ensure that they will benefit from the decision. They go to Washington and break Nevada, and they come out with millions and millions of dollars. So it is impossible for schools to succeed, because the people making the decisions don't have to live with the consequences."

The children of Bill Gates, like those of President Obama and Arne Duncan, attend Common Core-free schools, while Gates promotes something different for other people's kids. Naturally, this results in resentment and social friction. School choice for everyone defuses social conflict because it allows families and teachers who like Common Core – such as those in the Bensenville and Warren school districts – to keep it without forcing it upon people who have different ideas about what education should be. Today, the battle over curriculum is a zero-sum political game: for one heavily invested side to win, the other side must lose. School choice, on the other hand, is a win-win proposition.

The school choice movement is in direct conflict with the slow but steady centralization of American education, in which Common Core is only the latest step. Not surprisingly, Core-niks are attempting to use school voucher programs as a Trojan horse instead of a horse-borne knight in shining armor. They want to require private schools that accept vouchers to measure student progress with Common Core tests. To change metaphors, they're trying to convert an escape hatch into a net that catches families and flings them back into the system they were trying to leave. With apologies to Tolkien, the control-freaks want one standard to rule them all, and in the darkness bind them.

America's current education wars are a phase in a longer battle between two different views of children. The one side sees children as beings with minds that crave concrete knowledge and objective truth, which they can employ to govern themselves as free and responsible adults. The other side sees children as raw material for the elite to mold into cogs of a societal machine that the "best and brightest" continually tweak in a quest for perfection. The education wars are also part of a larger struggle between the American tradition of local self-governance and a highly centralized administrative state. Most fundamentally, the issue is whether we are free, self-determining citizens or merely subjects.

Americans have two options in the face of Common Core: We can demand that federal authorities let us manage our affairs locally and hold our own schools, teachers, and politicians accountable, or we can relapse into complacency and wait for another "education crisis" in about five years. Then the central planners will have more "solutions" for us. The cycle will never truly end, but parents do at least have power to rescue their children from schools that deform rather than cultivate their intellect and character. And parents ought to have far more power than they now do.

"The thing that is driving me," said Fuller, "is that I believe poor people need to have more control over their lives." So do we all. Lawmakers in both parties need to wake up and start serving their voters, not their campaign donors. Voters need to promote challengers to politicians who aren't getting the message. It's time for Americans once again to organize locally, vote locally, and educate locally. When only a tiny percentage of American kids get a Ridgeview education, oriented toward citizenship in a democratic republic, the nation's future is imperiled.

Let me conclude with the story of a sweet yet spirited woman who is proving that there's hope for our children and our country.

Christy's Search for Truth, Justice, and the American Way

One spring day in 2013, Christy Hooley walked to the podium in a satin-walled hotel room in Cheyenne, Wyoming. Her long earrings quivered as she looked out over the crowd of people waiting for her to speak at a public event to discuss Common Core, hosted by the Wyoming Liberty Group. Then she began telling her story.

Hooley had loved going to public school in Wyoming and always wanted to be a teacher. When she started teaching sixth graders, she found her work meaningful and exciting. Her first year was in Utah in 2008, and then she accepted a job offer that brought her back to Wyoming. She was disappointed to find that the state's academic expectations were lower than Utah's, so she was enthusiastic to hear about Common Core and expected it would help her students achieve more.

In July 2012, just before her fifth year of teaching, Hooley signed up for state-sponsored training to help teachers get up to speed on this new curriculum and testing project. She anticipated being "the voice for what Common Core is." At first she thought Common Core was better organized and required more from students than Wyoming's curriculum mandates. But she discovered that some Utah teachers opposed them on the grounds that they were infringing on teachers' autonomy in the classroom and eroding local control of education. "I was floored at that point," Hooley told me in an interview before the event. "I just saw this as something better for me as a teacher and for my students."

She started looking more deeply into Common Core so she could refute its opponents. Instead, she became one of them. Hooley first voiced her concerns with some close colleagues and emailed them links to source documents she had found. Then she brought up the topic with her boss in spring 2013.

The next day, one of the teachers she had emailed asked Hooley to express her thoughts on Common Core at a meeting among teachers in their grade. So she did. She noted that parents in Utah were pulling their kids from the trial tests, and that there were two sides to the matter. Her boss then told the group that they should stop talking about Common Core, either in person or by email, unless they were discussing how to put it into place. He followed up with an email reminding Hooley of the district's policy against using school resources to engage in politics.

Several colleagues privately thanked Hooley for the information, but said they were afraid to support her publicly "because some people who have done that have been known to be bumped around in positions." At that point, Hooley contacted the local representative of her teachers union to see what free-speech protection was available to her and her colleagues. The short answer: not much. Then Hooley saw the new teacher evaluations that came with Common Core, and she began to understand how it could be a means to control what and how she taught.

"I could not teach anymore if I had to be a hypocrite," Hooley told the audience in Cheyenne. Tearfully, with pauses to maintain her composure, she announced that she would no longer be teaching public school. The audience began standing up and applauding her.

That summer, Hooley opened a cottage school in her home, where she taught a small class of various ages. This effort quickly blossomed into a little private academy with three other teachers in its own facility outside Hooley's home. They use a classical approach, including the old McGuffey readers.

"It's amazing how much growth we have had in what is now the second year in our building," Hooley told me in 2015. "Watching my own children and our students learn to love learning because they are allowed to work at their own pace, level, and interest makes the sacrifice of our time and energy nothing."

Hooley's grassroots group, Wyoming Citizens Opposing Common Core, has grown into a parental-rights watchdog and school-choice advocacy organization – like Jenni White's in Oklahoma – because the members realize that Common Core is part of a broader agenda to separate parents from their children. "We understand how much more power parents have to change the direction of their child's education rather than just fighting a failing system," Hooley said. She has also joined the board of Citizens for Objective Public Education, a national parent-led advocacy organization.

Just two years earlier, Hooley was a dejected woman, stymied by a politically clogged school system. But she didn't stay down for long. She found a workaround, like generations of hardy Wyomingans and other Americans who never saw a problem they couldn't solve through ingenuity and elbow grease. So can you. Even if your elected representatives and local school officials ignore you, as they have your fellow citizens across the country, you and I are not helplessly stuck in a system that hurts our kids. We are not victims, but overcomers.

We can pick up our pens and keyboards to demand political redress and promote cultural remedies. We can refuse to let our kids take tests that perpetuate a failed system of education. We can show up at public meetings to voice our dissent for the record, and to support and inform our neighbors. We can even create better schools than those our government provides.

Common Core maintains its hold on our children only if we let it. No politician or bureaucrat can stop you from taking a part-time job to cover private tuition, or quitting a job to homeschool, or sitting every night with your children or grandchildren to read some classic books together, or starting a charter school like the parents who created Ridgeview, or whatever other solution you can think up to make a good life for your family. Over time, the choices you make, combined with the choices your fellow Americans make, have a substantial ripple effect over the country. The question is how much it matters to you. As Calvin Coolidge said: "Be ye lovers of freedom, and anxious for the fray."

RESOURCES FOR PARENTS
AND TEACHERS

Nᴇᴡs ᴀɴᴅ Uᴘᴅᴀᴛᴇs: The best site, bar none, for keeping track of developments on Common Core and its tests, student data privacy, and federal legislation about education is a national grassroots blog called Truth in American Education, at www.truthin americaneducation.com. The site is nonpartisan, and you can tell. They will also connect you to local groups for discussion and political butt-kicking.

Rᴇsᴇᴀʀᴄʜ: Two sites offer the best independent research on Common Core: the Pioneer Institute, at www.pioneer.org/common-core, and the Heartland Institute, at www.heartland.org/topics/education/common-core/index.html. Pioneer is the place to get big white papers; Heartland is the place to get booklets, talking points, and the like. Each does a lot more, but those are their specialties.

Fᴏʀ Pᴀʀᴇɴᴛs: The best place to start is the Core Knowledge Foundation's "What Your ___ Grader Needs to Know" series. Essentially every library has them. I also highly recommend Susan Wise Bauer's *The Well-Trained Mind*, and the Read-Aloud Revival (Google it), both of which have top-notch book recommendations. The latter is especially accessible and offers lots of podcasts and videos along with a superb kids' book-review site.

Ed Choice has the most comprehensive and accessible information about what school choice programs are available in your state and how they work, www.edchoice.org. GreatSchools.org offers reliable information about most public and private schools in the country. To learn which curriculum and tests are not aligned to Common Core, go to the Homeschool Resource Roadmap, at http://hsroadmap.org/common-core-project/. To start a classical charter school like Ridgeview, contact the Barney Charter School Initiative. The nationwide organization Classical Conversations will show you how to homeschool at a far higher level than you thought possible. (Disclosure: I tutor for them.)

General Information: Everyone interested in education should read E. D. Hirsch's *The Schools We Need (and Why We Don't Have Them)*, which contains an overview of the research from his best-selling book on cultural literacy. Then you should also read a critique by Neal McCluskey of the Cato Institute explaining why Hirsch's politics impede his curriculum preferences, at http://tinyurl.com/j77vkrs. To really get into the centuries-long conversation about what an educated person knows, and why, read Richard Gamble's *The Great Tradition*. For more digestible bits in a similar vein, my personal favorite is the blog of the CiRCE Institute: www.circeinstitute.org/blog.

ACKNOWLEDGMENTS

M Y DEAR HUSBAND and small children have sacrificed for four years while I spent thousands of long hours away from them – traveling frequently, working early mornings and late nights – to make this book possible. I don't know why they accept it, but I'm glad they do, and in the best of spirits.

The good people of the Heartland Institute wholeheartedly encouraged (and financed) my early plunge into a seemingly arcane topic that nobody knew about just six years ago but has since become a hot issue. Thank you all.

Thanks also to the Robert Novak Journalism Fellowship Program for having confidence in me and funding much of the reporting and research in this book.

My Federalist colleagues have also enthusiastically encouraged and developed my writing. Thanks for letting me learn in the fray with you. The same to Encounter Books, which took a chance on a young writer and sent me Carol Staswick, to whom I am grateful for excellent editing.

To all the mothers, fathers, grandparents, and citizen activists of all political orientations I have met and loved along the way, especially my friends at Truth in American Education and the Pioneer Institute: Your beautiful commitment to truth and freedom, for love of God, family, and country, gives me hope.

NOTES

PROLOGUE

1   Jim Stergios and Charles Chieppo, "Massachusetts Does It Better: How Washington Is Undermining the Bay State's Academic Standards," *Wall Street Journal*, April 3, 2010, http://www.wsj.com/articles/SB10001424052702303960604575157753524969156.

2   Common Core State Standards for English Language Arts: Introduction, p. 3, http://www.corestandards.org/assets/CCSSI_ELA%20Standards.pdf.

3   Terrence O. Moore, "Will Indiana Cut-and-Past Its Way to Common Core Serfdom?" Library of Law and Liberty, March 7, 2014, http://www.libertylawsite.org/2014/03/07/will-indiana-cut-and-paste-its-way-to-common-core-serfdom/.

4   Mark Bauerlein and Sandra Stotsky, "How Common Core's ELA Standards Place Language Readiness at Risk," Pioneer Institute White Paper no. 89, September 2012, p. 9, fig. 1, http://pioneerinstitute.org/download/how-common-cores-ela-standards-place-college-readiness-at-risk/.

5   Macey France, "Common Core–Approved Child Pornography," *Politichicks*, July 30, 2015, http://politichicks.com/2015/07/warning-graphic-common-core-approved-child-pornography/.

6   Donna Garner, "Tenth Grade Class Reads Erotic Novel Recommended by Common Core Proponents," Education Action Group Foundation, EAGnews.org, September 11, 2013, http://eagnews.org/10th-grade-class-reads-erotic-novel-recommended-by-common-core-proponents/.

7   Common Core State Standards for Mathematics: Grade 6: Number System, standard 1 (6.NS.1), p. 42, http://www.corestandards.org/wp-content/uploads/Math_Standards.pdf.

8   Marina Ratner, "Making Math Education Even Worse," *Wall Street Journal*, August 5, 2014, http://www.wsj.com/articles/marina-ratner-making-math-education-even-worse-1407283282.

9   Heather Crossin at Common Core Forum sponsored by the Civitas Institute and the Heritage Foundation in Raleigh, North Carolina, September 19, 2013 (video posted October 10, 2013), https://www.youtube.com/watch?v=fr2no9xwrog.

10   Illinois Loop, Mathematics – Specific Math Programs: UCSMP "Everyday Mathematics" (a.k.a. "Chicago Math"), IllinoisLoop.org, http://www.illinoisloop.org/mathprograms.html#chicagomath.

217

11   Jeremy C. Fox, "Mass. Students Are Again Tops in National Testing," *Boston Globe*, October 28, 2015, https://www.bostonglobe.com/metro/2015/10/27/mass-again-tops-national-test-student-achievement/8RrxW2veaCO6nGxJHxsUEO/story.html.

12   Ze'ev Wurman, "Reassess Common Core and Consider Reversing Direction," *Breitbart*, December 25, 2015, http://www.breitbart.com/big-government/2015/12/25/re-assess-common-core-and-consider-reversing-direction/.

13   Neal McCluskey, "The Common Core Is in Retreat," Cato Institute, October 12, 2015, http://www.cato.org/blog/common-core-retreat.

CHAPTER 1 – ORIGINS

1   Diane Ravitch, "Teaching in an Age of Injustice," *Diane Ravitch's Blog*, January 23, 2013, http://dianeravitch.net/2013/01/23/teaching-in-an-age-of-injustice/.

2   See Sandra Stotsky, *The Death and Resurrection of a Coherent Literature Curriculum: What Secondary English Teachers Can Do* (Lanham, Md.: Rowman & Littlefield, 2012), p. 163.

3   The full title of the English standards is: "Common Core State Standards for English Language Arts and Literacy in History/Social Studies, Science and Technical Subjects," http://www.corestandards.org/assets/CCSSI_ELA%20Standards.pdf.

4   Common Core State Standards for English Language Arts: Introduction: Key Design Considerations, p. 5, http://www.corestandards.org/ELA-Literacy/introduction/key-design-consideration/.

5   Mark Bauerlein and Sandra Stotsky, "How Common Core's ELA Standards Place Language Readiness at Risk," Pioneer Institute White Paper no. 89, September 2012, p. 4, http://pioneerinst.wpengine.com/download/how-common-cores-ela-standards-place-college-readiness-at-risk/.

6   On the question of Gladwell's factual accuracy, see Alexis Sobel Fitts, "The Gladwellian 'Debate,'" *Columbia Journalism Review*, October 10, 2013, http://www.cjr.org/the_observatory/the_gladwellian_debate.php.

7   Anthony Esolen, Jamie Highfill, and Sandra Stotsky, "'The Dying of the Light': How Common Core Damages Poetry Instruction," Pioneer Institute White Paper no. 113, April 2014, pp. 20–21, http://pioneerinst.wpengine.com/download/the-dying-of-the-light-how-common-core-damages-poetry-instruction/.

8   Common Core State Standards for English Language Arts: Appendix A, p. 8, fig. 3, http://www.corestandards.org/assets/Appendix_A.pdf.

9   Blaine Greteman, "Federal Bureaucrats Declare 'Hunger Games' More Complex than 'The Grapes of Wrath': The Common Core's Absurd New Reading Guidelines," *New Republic*, October 29, 2013, http://www.newrepublic.com/article/115393/common-core-standards-make-mockery-novels-complexity.

10   Lyndsey Layton, "Common Core State Standards in English Spark War over Words," *Washington Post*, December 2, 2012, http://www.washingtonpost.com/local/education/common-core-state-standards-in-english-spark-war-over-words/2012/12/02/4a9701bo-38e1-11e2-8a97-363bof9a0ab3_story.html.

11   Nancy Carlsson-Paige, Geralyn Bywater McLaughlin, and Joan Wolfsheimer Almon, "Reading Instruction in Kindergarten: Little to Gain and Much to Lose," Defending the Early Years and Alliance for Childhood, January 2015, https://deyproject.files.wordpress.com/2015/01/readinginkindergarten_online-1.pdf.

12   Mark Bertin, "When Will We Ever Learn: Dissecting the Common Core State Standards with Dr. Louisa Moats," *Huffington Post*, January 22, 2014, http://www.huffingtonpost.com/mark-bertin-md/when-will-we-ever-learn_b_4588033.html.

13   Common Core State Standards Initiative, "Myths vs. Facts," http://www.corestandards.org/about-the-standards/myths-vs-facts/.

14   Arne Duncan, "Duncan Pushes Back on Attacks on Common Core Standards," Remarks at the American Society of News Editors Annual Convention, Washington, D.C., June 25, 2013, U.S. Department of Education, http://www.ed.gov/news/speeches/duncan-pushes-back-attacks-common-core-standards.

15   See Sandra Stotsky, ed., *What's at Stake in the K–12 Standards Wars: A Primer for Educational Policy Makers* (New York: Peter Lang Publishing, 2000); and Williamson Evers, "Implementing Standards and Testing," in *What Lies Ahead for America's Children and Their Schools*, ed. Chester Finn Jr. and Richard Sousa (Stanford, Calif.: Hoover Institution Press, 2014), available at http://www.hoover.org/research/what-lies-ahead-americas-children-and-their-schools.

16   Robert S. Eitel and Kent D. Talbert, "The Road to a National Curriculum: The Legal Aspects of the Common Core Standards, Race to the Top, and Conditional Waivers," Pioneer Institute White Paper no. 81, February 2012, p. 1, http://pioneerinstitute.org/download/the-road-to-a-national-curriculum/.

17   William J. Bushaw and Valerie J. Calderon, "Try It Again, Sam," 46th Annual PDK/Gallup Poll of the Public's Attitudes toward the Public Schools, p. 18, Table 17, September 2014, http://pdkintl.org/noindex/PDK_Poll46_2014.pdf.

18   William J. Bushaw and Valerie J. Calderon, "Testing Doesn't Measure Up for Americans," 47th Annual PDK/Gallup Poll of the Public's Attitudes toward the Public Schools, September 2015, p. 30, http://pdkpoll2015.pdkintl.org/wp-content/uploads/2015/10/pdkpoll47_2015.pdf.

19   Ibid., p. 14.

20   Robert B. Schwartz and Marian A. Robinson, "Goals 2000 and the Standards Movement," Brookings Papers on Education Policy, 2000, pp. 173–206, available at http://muse.jhu.edu/journals/brookings_papers_on_education_policy/v2000/2000.1schwartz.html. Thanks to grassroots researcher Erin Tuttle for sending me this paper.

21   Ibid., p. 204.

22   These are the former governors listed in an advisory group that first specifically called for the Common Core to be created; the group was convened under the auspices of the three organizations that went on to do so. See the report by the National Governors Association, the Council of Chief State School Officers, and Achieve, Inc., "Benchmarking for Success: Ensuring Students Receive a World-Class Education," NGA Center for Best Practices, 2008, p. 3, http://www.nga.org/files/live/sites/NGA/files/pdf/0812BENCHMARKING.PDF.

23   Lyndsey Layton, "How Bill Gates Pulled Off the Swift Common Core Revolution," *Washington Post*, June 7, 2014, http://www.washingtonpost.com/politics/how-bill-gates-pulled-off-the-swift-common-core-revolution/2014/06/07/a830e32e-ec34-11e3-9f5c-9075d5508f0a_story.html.

24   Walton Family Foundation tax return for 2011, http://www.guidestar.org/FinDocuments/2011/133/441/2011-133441466-08bac74b-F.pdf.

25   Broad Foundation, Combined Financial Statements and Supplemental Information, December 31, 2010 and 2009, p. 2, http://www.broadfoundation.org/asset/101-2009-10financialstatement.pdf.

26   Bill and Melinda Gates Foundation tax return for 2010, http://www.guidestar.org/FinDocuments/2010/562/618/2010-562618866-07bd0cb7-F.pdf.

27   Author's calculations from Gates Foundation grants database, available in a detailed spreadsheet here: https://docs.google.com/spreadsheets/d/16U6R490jgBYvCtxvhdfiEqfcOskqeaCVq6IoqSeFWUY/edit?usp=sharing.

28   Sarah Reckhow, "Gates Shifts Strategy and Schools Get Smaller Share," Scholastic: Administrators, February 5, 2013, http://scholasticadministrator.typepad.com/thisweekineducation/2013/02/shifting-strategies-at-gates-who-wins.html.

29   Sarah Reckhow and Megan Tompkins-Stange, "'Singing from the Same Hymnbook': Education Policy Advocacy at Gates and Broad," paper delivered at the American Enterprise Institute conference "Is the 'New' Education Philanthropy Good for Schools? Examining Foundation-Funded School Reform," February 5, 2015, p. 10, http://www.aei.org/wp-content/uploads/2015/01/Reckhow-Tompkins-Stange.pdf.

30   Ibid., and two other papers presented at the same conference: Jay P. Greene, "Buckets into Another Sea," http://www.aei.org/wp-content/uploads/2015/01/Greene.pdf; and Jeffrey W. Snyder, "How Old and New Education Foundation Granting Differ," http://www.aei.org/publication/old-new-education-foundation-granting-differ/.

31   Sam Dillon, "Behind Grass-Roots School Advocacy, Bill Gates," *New York Times*, May 21, 2011, http://www.nytimes.com/2011/05/22/education/22gates.html?_r=0.

32   Reckhow and Tompkins-Stange, "'Singing from the Same Hymnbook,'" p. 2.

33   Ibid., p. 26.

34   See Mary Grabar's eyewitness account of the Georgia hearing, "The 'Show' of Support for Common Core in Georgia," *PJ Media*, March 26, 2014, https://pjmedia.com/blog/the-show-of-support-for-common-core-in-georgia/2/; then cross-reference names of Common Core proponents with the Gates Foundation grants database at http://www.gatesfoundation.org/How-We-Work/Quick-Links/Grants-Database#q/k=georgia, which includes several Georgia school districts, the Georgia Department of Education, and the Georgia Chamber of Commerce as grant recipients.

35   Reckhow and Tompkins-Stange, "'Singing from the Same Hymnbook,'" pp. 11-12.

36   Ibid., p. 29.

37   Michael Q. McShane and Jenn Hatfield, "The Backlash against 'Reform' Philanthropy," paper delivered at the American Enterprise Institute conference "Is the 'New' Education Philanthropy Good for Schools?" February 5, 2015, p. 14, http://www.aei.org/wp-content/uploads/2015/01/McShane-Hatfield.pdf. Disclosure: I was interviewed for the nonquantitative part of this study.

38 Gates Foundation grants database, search term "Editorial Projects in Education," the name of *Education Week*'s foundation repository for grant funds, accessed August 5, 2016, http://www.gatesfoundation.org/How-We-Work/Quick-Links/Grants-Database# q/k=%22editorial%20projects%20in%20education%22.

39 Ibid., search term "Education Writers Association," http://www.gatesfoundation.org/ How-We-Work/Quick-Links/Grants-Database#q/k=%22education%20writers%20asso ciation%22. The staff of the Education Writers Association, the national professional organization for education journalism, kicked me out of its email list-serv explicitly because I reported on behalf of a libertarian nonprofit organization, although EWA allowed list-serv access to writers from the overtly political *Huffington Post* and other nonprofit news outlets such as *Chalkbeat*.

40 Ibid., search term "EdSource," http://www.gatesfoundation.org/How-We-Work/Quick-Links/Grants-Database#q/k=edsource.

41 Ibid., search term "Chalkbeat," http://www.gatesfoundation.org/How-We-Work/Quick-Links/Grants-Database/Grants/2014/03/OPP1099534.

42 *Hechinger Report*, "Supporters," accessed August 5, 2016, http://hechingerreport.org/ supporters/.

43 Gates Foundation grants database, search term "The Atlantic," accessed August 5, 2016, http://www.gatesfoundation.org/How-We-Work/Quick-Links/Grants-Database/ Grants/2015/11/OPP1140915.

44 Bill and Melinda Gates Foundation tax return for 2013, http://www.guidestar.org/Fin Documents/2013/562/618/2013-562618866-0b03e8ad-F.pdf.

45 Reckhow and Tompkins-Stange, "'Singing from the Same Hymnbook,'" p. 6.

46 Layton, "How Bill Gates Pulled Off the Swift Common Core Revolution."

47 Clay Holtzman, "Growing D.C. Presence for Gates Foundation," *Puget Sound Business Journal*, May 17, 2009, http://www.bizjournals.com/seattle/stories/2009/05/18/story2. html?page=all; Joy Pullmann, "Education Policies Led by Gates, Not States?" *Heartlander* (Heartland Institute), February 11, 2013, http://news.heartland.org/newspaper-article/2013/02/11/education-policies-led-gates-not-states; Stephanie Simon and Erin Mershon, "Gates Masters D.C. – and the World," *Politico*, February 4, 2014, http:// www.politico.com/story/2014/02/bill-gates-microsoft-policy-washington-103136.html.

48 Reckhow and Tompkins-Stange, "'Singing from the Same Hymnbook,'" p. 14.

49 Information from the Gates Foundation grants database, available at http://www.gates foundation.org/How-We-Work/Quick-Links/Grants-Database. The figure includes two grants to the Chicago Community Foundation that funded the same project as the foundation's grants to Chicago Public Schools directly – restructuring Chicago's high schools: http://www.gatesfoundation.org/How-We-Work/Quick-Links/Grants-Database/ Grants/2001/09/OPP13129, and http://www.gatesfoundation.org/How-We-Work/Quick-Links/Grants-Database/Grants/2003/04/OPP27824.

50 Reckhow and Tompkins-Stange, "'Singing from the Same Hymnbook,'" p. 14.

51 Simon and Mershon, "Gates Masters D.C. - and the World."

52 Ibid.

53 National Governors Association, Council of Chief State School Officers, and Achieve, Inc., "Benchmarking for Success: Ensuring U.S. Students Receive a World-Class Edu-

cation," NGA Center for Best Practices, 2008, pp. 6-7, 37, https://www.scribd.com/full screen/24346614?access_key=key-eilzpsp2m9bnmylmgsk&allow_share=true&escape =false&view_mode=scroll.

54   Ibid., p. 26.

55   Patrick Murphy and Elliot Regenstein, with Keith McNamara, "Putting a Price Tag on the Common Core: How Much Will Smart Implementation Cost?" Thomas B. Fordham Institute, May 2012, p. 27, http://www.edexcellencemedia.net/publications/2012/20120530-Putting-A-Price-Tag-on-the-Common-Core/20120530-Putting-a-Price-Tag-on-the-Common-Core-FINAL.pdf.

56   AccountabilityWorks, "National Cost of Aligning States and Localities to the Common Core Standards," Pioneer Institute and American Principles Project White Paper no. 82, February 2012, p. 2, http://pioneerinstitute.org/download/national-cost-of-aligning-states-and-localities-to-the-common-core-standards/.

57   Jason Hart, "Governor Kasich Lies about Obamacare, Common Core, on WTAM 1100," *Media Trackers*, May 5, 2014, http://mediatrackers.org/ohio/2014/05/05/kasich-lies-about-obamacare-common-core-wtam-1100.

58   Dane Linn, "Governors and the Common Core," paper prepared for the American Enterprise Institute conference "Common Core Meets the Reform Agenda," March 25, 2013, http://www.aei.org/publication/governors-and-the-common-core/.

59   Mal Leary, "LePage Pulls Out of National Governors Association," *Bangor Daily News*, September 30, 2002, http://bangordailynews.com/2012/09/30/politics/lepage-pulls-out-of-national-governors-association/?ref=mostReadBoxNews.

60   National Governors Association and National Governors Association Center for Best Practices, Consolidated Financial Report, June 30, 2014, p. 6, http://www.nga.org/files/live/sites/NGA/files/pdf/14NGAFINANCIALREPORT.PDF.

61   Ibid., p. 6.

62   National Governors Association and National Governors Association Center for Best Practices, Consolidated Financial Report, June 30, 2011, p. 6, http://www.nga.org/files/live/sites/NGA/files/pdf/11NGAFINANCIALREPORT.PDF.

63   Council of Chief State School Officers, Financial Statements Years Ended June 30, 2014 and 2013, p. 6, http://www.ccsso.org/Documents/2015/CCSSOFinancialStatementsYE 2014.pdf.

64   Council of Chief State School Officers, Financial Statements Years Ended June 30, 2011 and 2010, p. 8, http://www.ccsso.org/Documents/2011/FY11%20Audited%20Financials. pdf.

65   Council of Chief State School Officers, Financial Statements Years Ended June 30, 2014 and 2013, p. 22.

66   Council of Chief State School Officers, Meetings and Events, http://www.ccsso.org/News_and_Events/Meetings_and_Events.html.

67   Achieve, Inc., "Who We Are," http://www.achieve.org/.

68   Achieve, Inc. tax return for 2012, http://www.guidestar.org/FinDocuments/2013/522/o 06/2013-522006429-0a1eb949-9.pdf.

69   Ibid.

70 Council of Chief State School Officers tax return for 2011, http://www.guidestar.org/FinDocuments/2012/530/198/2012-530198090-08f56a08-9.pdf.

71 National Governors Association Center for Best Practices tax return for 2010, http://www.guidestar.org/FinDocuments/2011/237/391/2011-237391796-08582ffa-9.pdf.

72 Linn, "Governors and the Common Core," p. 2.

73 Council of Chief State School Officers and National Governors Association Center for Best Practices, Common Core Standards Memorandum of Agreement, May 7, 2009, http://www.freedomkentucky.org/images/c/c6/2009_CCSS_Commitment_MOA_from_Open_Recs_Request.pdf.

74 National Conference of State Legislatures, "Common Core State Standards," May 1, 2014, http://www.ncsl.org/research/education/common-core-state-standards.aspx.

75 National Association of State School Boards, "About Us," http://www.nasbe.org/about-us/state-boards-of-education/.

76 National Governors Association, "Governors Explore Strategies to Make the United States a Global Leader in Education," Press Release, June 10, 2008, original link at http://www.nga.org/cms/home/news-room/news-releases/page_2008/col2-content/main-content-list/title_governors-explore-strategies-to-make-the-united-states-a-global-leader-in-education.html; the page has since been deleted, but is available on the Internet Archive in its initial form at https://web.archive.org/web/20130624123931/http://www.nga.org/cms/home/news-room/news-releases/page_2008/col2-content/main-content-list/title_governors-explore-strategies-to-make-the-united-states-a-global-leader-in-education.html.

77 National Governors Association, "Top State Education Policy Organizations Form Expert Advisory Group on International Benchmarking," Press Release, September 8, 2008, http://www.nga.org/cms/home/news-room/news-releases/page_2008/col2-content/main-content-list/title_top-state-education-policy-organizations-form-expert-advisory-group-on-international-benchmarking.html.

78 Linn, "Governors and the Common Core," p. 7.

79 National Governors Association, "Forty-Nine States and Territories Join Common Core Standards Initiative," Press Release, June 1, 2009, http://www.nga.org/cms/home/news-room/news-releases/page_2009/col2-content/main-content-list/title_forty-nine-states-and-territories-join-common-core-standards-initiative.html.

80 James B. Hunt, Jr. Institute for Educational Leadership and Policy, and NGA Center for Best Practices, "Perfecting the Formula: Effective Strategies = Educational Success," A Report from the 2009 Governors Symposium, June 14-15, 2009, p. ii, http://www.hunt-institute.org/wp-content/uploads/2015/04/GES_Report_09_Final.pdf.

81 Arne Duncan, Remarks to the 2009 Governors Education Symposium, June 14, 2009, Cary, North Carolina, pp. 1-2, http://www.hunt-institute.org/wp-content/uploads/2015/04/GES_Remarks-Duncan.doc.pdf.

82 Commission on No Child Left Behind, *Beyond NCLB: Fulfilling the Promise to Our Nation's Children* (Washington, D.C.: Aspen Institute, 2007), http://www.aucd.org/docs/Aspen Commission on NCLB.pdf.

83 National Governors Association, "Common Core State Standards Development Work

Group and Feedback Group Announced," Press Release, July 1, 2009, http://www.nga.
org/cms/home/news-room/news-releases/page_2009/col2-content/main-content-list/
title_common-core-state-standards-development-work-group-and-feedback-group-
announced.html.

84 National Governors Association, "Common Core State Standards Initiative Validation
Committee Announced," Press Release, September 24, 2009, archived at http://web.
archive.org/web/20111219030455/http://www.nga.org/cms/home/news-room/news-
releases/page_2009/col2-content/main-content-list/title_common-core-state-standards-
initiative-validation-committee-announced.html.

85 Linn, "Governors and the Common Core," p. 9.

86 National Governors Association Center for Best Practices and Council of Chief State
School Officers, "Reaching Higher: The Common Core State Standards Validation
Committee," Common Core State Standards Initiative, June 2010, http://www.corestan
dards.org/assets/CommonCoreReport_6.10.pdf.

87 William J. Bennett, "The Conservative Case for Common Core," Wall Street Journal,
September 10, 2014, http://www.wsj.com/articles/william-j-bennett-the-conservative-
case-for-common-core-1410390435. See also, Bill Bennett, "The Common Core: Setting
the Record Straight," Forbes, February 20, 2015, http://www.forbes.com/sites/realspin/
2015/02/20/the-common-core-setting-the-record-straight/.

88 "Jeb Bush Speaks Out: Talking Education Policy with Florida's Former Governor," Education Next, November 12, 2014, http://educationnext.org/jeb-bush-speaks-interview/.

89 Council of Chief State School Officers and National Governors Association Center for
Best Practices, Common Core Standards Memorandum of Agreement, May 7, 2009.

90 Caitlin Emma, "Jindal Sues over Common Core," Politico, August 27, 2014, p. 2, http://
politi.co/1p8fJpF.

91 U.S. Department of Education, 34 CFR Subtitle B, Chapter II, Race to the Top Fund,
Federal Register, vol. 74, no. 221 (November 18, 2009), p. 59689, http://www.gpo.gov/
fdsys/pkg/FR-2009-11-18/pdf/E9-27426.pdf.

92 Jane Robbins, "Feds Confess Truth about Common Core," The Pulse 2016, September
14, 2015, http://thepulse2016.com/jane-robbins/2015/09/14/feds-confess-truth-about-
common-core/.

93 Layton, "How Bill Gates Pulled Off the Swift Common Core Revolution."

94 U.S. Department of Education, 34 CFR Subtitle B, Chapter II, Race to the Top Fund.

95 Layton, "How Bill Gates Pulled Off the Swift Common Core Revolution."

96 U.S. Department of Education, Race to the Top Fund: States' Applications, Scores and
Comment for Phase 1, http://www2.ed.gov/programs/racetothetop/phase1-applications
/index.html.

97 Layton, "How Bill Gates Pulled Off the Swift Common Core Revolution."

98 Holtzman, "Growing D.C. Presence for Gates Foundation."

99 U.S. Department of Education, Race to the Top Fund: Phase Two Resources, http://
www2.ed.gov/programs/racetothetop/phase2-resources.html.

100 U.S. Department of Education, Race to the Top Fund: States' Applications for Phase 2,
http://www2.ed.gov/programs/racetothetop/phase2-applications/index.html.

101 Author's calculations using data from these two sources: Mark Lavenia, "The Common Core State Standards Initiative: An Event History Analysis of State Adoption of Common K-12 Academic Standards," Florida State University, 2010, p. 4, http://diginole.lib. fsu.edu/islandora/object/fsu%3A254160; and Catherine Gewertz, "Common-Standards Watch: New Mexico Makes 40," *Education Week*, October 20, 2010, http://blogs. edweek.org/edweek/curriculum/2010/10/common-standards_watch_new_mex.html? r=1657793449.

102 Tennessee State Board of Education, Meeting Minutes, July 30, 2010, p. 6, archived at https://web.archive.org/web/20110518001243/http://www.state.tn.us/sbe/October2010 pdfs/July%202010%20Minutes.pdf.

103 Connecticut State Board of Education, Meeting Minutes, July 7, 2010, VI.A, Adoption of Common Core Standards, p. 4, http://www.sde.ct.gov/sde/lib/sde/pdf/board/min utes2010/minutes_SBE_070710.pdf.

104 Emmeline Zhao, "Common Core Copyright: What Does It Really Mean? 5 Questions with Chris Minnich," *Real Clear Education*, October 8, 2014, http://www.realclearedu cation.com/articles/2014/10/08/common_core_copyright_1112.html.

105 Eitel and Talbert, "The Road to a National Curriculum: The Legal Aspects of the Common Core Standards, Race to the Top, and Conditional Waivers," p. 23.

106 U.S. Department of Education, Laws and Guidance, Elementary and Secondary Education: ESEA Flexibility, http://www.ed.gov/esea/flexibility/documents/esea-flexibility. doc.

107 U.S. Department of Education, ESEA Flexibility, http://www2.ed.gov/policy/elsec/ guid/esea-flexibility/index.html.

108 U.S. Department of Education, "U.S. Secretary of Education Duncan Announces Winners of Competition to Improve Student Assessments," Press Release, September 2, 2010, http://www.ed.gov/news/press-releases/us-secretary-education-duncan-announ ces-winners-competition-improve-student-asse.

109 Cooperative Agreement between U.S. Department of Education and the Smarter Balanced Assessment Consortium and the State of Washington (fiscal agent), January 7, 2011, p. 5, http://www2.ed.gov/programs/racetothetop-assessment/sbac-cooperative-agreement.pdf.

110 Catherine Gewertz, "Common-Assessment Groups to Undergo New Federal Review Process," *Education Week*, April 1, 2013, http://blogs.edweek.org/edweek/curriculum/ 2013/04/common_assessment_groups_to_undergo_new_federal_review_process.html.

111 Cooperative Agreement between U.S. Department of Education and the Smarter Balanced Assessment Consortium and the State of Washington (fiscal agent), January 7, 2011, p. 10.

112 Washington State, on behalf of the SMARTER Balanced Assessment Consortium, Race to the Top Assessment Program Application for New Grants, June 10, 2010, p. 6, archived at https://web.archive.org/web/20121105183632/http://www.smarterbalanced. org/wordpress/wp-content/uploads/2011/12/Smarter-Balanced-RttT-Application.pdf.

113 Ibid., p. 35.

114 Ibid., pp. 111-12.

115 Ibid., p. 143.

116 PARCC, Race to the Top Assessment Program Application for New Grants, U.S. Department of Education, May 28, 2010, p. 39, http://www2.ed.gov/programs/racetothetop-assessment/rtta2010parcc.pdf.

117 Ibid., p. 57.

118 Ibid., p. 216.

119 Joanne Weiss, "Competing Principles: Race to the Top, a $4 Billion US Education Reform Effort, Produced Valuable Lessons on Designing a Competition-Based Program," *Stanford Social Innovation Review*, Fall 2015, archived at https://web.archive.org/web/20150911050843/http://ssir.org/articles/entry/competing_principles#sthash.lncob-NMm.dpuf.

120 Testimony of Michael Cohen, President of Achieve, before the Michigan House of Representatives Subcommittee on Common Core State Standards, July 16, 2013, p. 11, http://www.achieve.org/files/MCohenCommonCoreTestimony071613.pdf.

121 Chris Edwards, "Federal Aid-to-State Programs Top 1,100," *Cato Institute, Tax and Budget Bulletin* no. 63 (February 2011), http://object.cato.org/sites/cato.org/files/pubs/pdf/tbb_63.pdf.

122 U.S. Department of Education, Race to the Top Fund: States' Applications, Scores and Comment for Phase 1.

123 I included the word "standards" to reduce statistical noise from the use of "common core" for unrelated subjects.

124 Michael Q. McShane and Frederick M. Hess, "Flying under the Radar? Analyzing Common Core Media Coverage," Education Outlook, American Enterprise Institute, March 2014, http://www.aei.org/wp-content/uploads/2014/03/-flying-under-the-radar-analyzing-common-core-media-coverage_140948155793.pdf.

125 William J. Bushaw and Shane J. Lopez, "Which Way Do We Go?" 45th Annual PDK/Gallup Poll on the Public's Attitudes toward the Public Schools, September 2013, Table 4, http://pdkintl.org/noindex/2013_PDKGallup.pdf.

126 McShane and Hess, "Flying under the Radar," p. 6.

CHAPTER 2 – EXPERIENCE

1 Global Report Card, District vs. International Educational Achievement: Indiana: Marion: Warren Township, http://globalreportcard.org/map.html?state=indiana&district=Warren+Township.

2 MSD Warren Township, 2012 Reports, http://mpcms.blob.core.windows.net/0975b797-d19b-4bf5-a32f-b341aca3a157/docs/6a26914b-2e45-4a0a-83af-06dbcf5688a9/2012-annual-performance-report.pdf.

3 Metropolitan School District of Warren Township, Indianapolis, Indiana, Race to the Top, Application for Funding, p. 12 & passim, http://mpcms.blob.core.windows.net/0975b797-d19b-4bf5-a32f-b341aca3a157/docs/96b504fe-5ad3-4080-9cbe-1e075e190edd/msd-warren-in-rttt-application-10.26.12.pdf.

4   Remarks by the President in State of the Union Address, Office of the Press Secretary, The White House, January 24, 2012, https://www.whitehouse.gov/the-press-office/2012/01/24/remarks-president-state-union-address.

5   Remarks by the President in State of the Union Address, Office of the Press Secretary, The White House, January 25, 2011, https://www.whitehouse.gov/the-press-office/2011/01/25/remarks-president-state-union-address.

6   Remarks by the President in State of the Union Address, Office of the Press Secretary, The White House, February 12, 2013, https://www.whitehouse.gov/the-press-office/2013/02/12/remarks-president-state-union-address.

7   "Primary Sources: America's Teachers on Teaching in an Era of Change," Common Core State Standards Preview, Scholastic and the Bill and Melinda Gates Foundation, http://www.scholastic.com/primarysources/2013preview/PrimarySourcesCCSS.pdf.

8   Emmanuel Felton, "More Teachers Are Souring on Common Core, Finds One Survey," *Hechinger Report*, October 3, 2014, http://hechingerreport.org/teachers-souring-common-core-finds-one-survey/.

9   Common Core State Standards for Mathematics, http://www.corestandards.org/assets/CCSSI_Math%20Standards.pdf.

10   Common Core State Standards for Mathematics, Grade 1: Introduction, http://www.corestandards.org/Math/Content/1/introduction.

11   Valerie Strauss, "Louis C.K.: Common Core Makes My Kids Cry," *Washington Post*, April 28, 2014, http://www.washingtonpost.com/blogs/answer-sheet/wp/2014/04/28/louis-c-k-common-core-makes-my-kids-cry/.

12   Fred Dews, "Brookings Scholar Explains Infamous 'Common Core' Math Problem," Brookings Institution Blogs, May 1, 2014, http://www.brookings.edu/blogs/brookings-now/posts/2014/05/brookings-scholar-explains-infamous-common-core-math-problem.

13   Common Core State Standards for English Language Arts: Writing: Grade 9–10, standard 6, http://www.corestandards.org/ELA-Literacy/W/9-10/6/.

14   Metropolitan School District of Warren Township, Race to the Top, Application for Funding, p. 17.

15   Timothy Shanahan, with Ann Duffett, "Common Core in the Schools: A First Look at Reading Assignments," Thomas B. Fordham Institute, October 2013, p. 35, http://www.edexcellence.net/sites/default/files/publication/pdfs/20131023-Common-Core-in-the-Schools-a-First-Look-at-Reading-Assignments.pdf.

16   Description of *To Kill a Mockingbird* by Harper Lee on Scholastic's Book Wizard, http://www.scholastic.com/teachers/book/kill-mockingbird.

17   Common Core State Standards for English Language Arts: College and Career Readiness Anchor Standards for Language, http://www.corestandards.org/ELA-Literacy/CCRA/L/#CCSS.ELA-Literacy.CCRA.L.5.

18   Math Common Core PD, no. 2, 7th Grade Math Lesson, BlendSpace, https://www.blendspace.com/lessons/g6bAmQtptC9qcg/math-common-core-pd.

19   See E.D. Hirsch Jr., *The Schools We Need, and Why We Don't Have Them* (New York: Anchor Books, 2010).

20   Sheila Byrd Carmichael et al., "Indiana: English Language Arts," *The State of State*

Standards – and the Common Core – in 2010, Thomas B. Fordham Institute, July 21, 2010, pp. 119–24, http://edexcellencemedia.net/publications/2010/201007_state_education_standards_common_standards/Indiana.pdf.

21 Indiana Department of Education, "Indiana Academic Standards," accessed August 12, 2016, http://www.doe.in.gov/standards.

22 See, for example, this July 2014 presentation by the Warren Township superintendent, Dena Cushenberry, "Opening Day," http://az480170.vo.msecnd.net/0975b797-d19b-4bf5-a32f-b341aca3a157/docs/e5120193-e6eb-486d-81c2-44d1fb599ad9/opening-day-presentation-7.24.14-rev.pdf. See also the district's "Professional Development," http://www.warren.k12.in.us/staff-professional-development, and its "College and Career Ready Standards," http://www.warren.k12.in.us/c-ccr, both of which cite Common Core resources.

23 Shaina Cavazos, "Some Townships Show ISTEP Gains Despite Challenges of Growing Poverty," *Chalkbeat*, August 5, 2014, http://www.chalkbeat.org/posts/in/2014/08/05/township-schools-credit-istep-gains-to-new-programs-teacher-efforts/#.V64YRPkrKYk.

24 Sterling Public Schools, Illinois Race to the Top Phase 3 Preliminary Allocation for Participating LEAs, March 2, 2012, http://www.sterlingpublicschools.org/index.php/race-to-the-top/18-preliminary-allocation-for-participating-leas/file.

25 State of Illinois, Race to the Top Application for Phase 3 Funding, December 16, 2011, http://www2.ed.gov/programs/racetothetop/phase3-applications/illinois-2.pdf.

26 Bensenville Elementary School District 2, "Preparing Students for a World of Opportunity," Report to the Community, 2013, http://issuu.com/bsd2publications/docs/2013_annual_report.

27 Description of *Pop's Bridge* by Eve Bunting on Scholastic's Book Wizard, http://www.scholastic.com/teachers/book/pops-bridge.

28 Description of *Grandfather's Journey* by Allen Say on Scholastic's Book Wizard, http://www.scholastic.com/teachers/book/grandfathers-journey.

29 Common Core State Standards for English Language Arts: Reading: Literature: Grade 8, http://www.corestandards.org/ELA-Literacy/RL/8/#CCSS.ELA-Literacy.RL.8.4.

30 Description of *Bud, Not Buddy* by Christopher Paul Curtis on Scholastic's Book Wizard, http://www.scholastic.com/teachers/book/bud-not-buddy.

31 PARCC, ELA Model Frameworks, Grades 3–11, http://www.parcconline.org/mcf/english-language-artsliteracy/structure-model-content-frameworks-elaliteracy.

32 David Coleman, "Close Reading of a Text: MLK 'Letter from Birmingham Jail,'" Common Core Video Series, EngageNY, New York State Department of Education, December 5, 2012, https://www.engageny.org/resource/middle-school-ela-curriculum-video-close-reading-of-a-text-mlk-letter-from-birmingham-jail.

33 "David Coleman on Common Core Assessments," video, with summary by Elfrieda H. Hiebert, TextProject, July 2, 2103, http://www.textproject.org/library/professional-development/virtual-institute-on-assessment-and-the-common-core/david-coleman-on-common-core-assessments/.

34 E. D. Hirsch Jr., *Cultural Literacy: What Every American Needs to Know* (New York: Vintage Books, 1988).

35 Core Knowledge Foundation, CKLA Research Basis and Pilot Program, http://www.coreknowledge.org/ckla-research-basis.

36 E. D. Hirsch Jr., "Why I'm For the Common Core: Teacher Bashing and Common Core Bashing Are Both Uncalled For," *Huffington Post*, August 27, 2013, http://www.huffingtonpost.com/e-d-hirsch-jr/why-im-for-the-common-cor_b_3809618.html. Thanks to Neal McCluskey of the Cato Institute for noticing Hirsch's self-contradiction: "Common Core Confusion: Blame Supporters," Cato Institute, February 26, 2015, http://www.cato.org/publications/commentary/common-core-confusion-blame-supporters.

37 Common Core State Standards for English Language Arts, Appendix B: Text Exemplars and Sample Performance Tasks, p. 6, http://www.corestandards.org/assets/Appendix_B.pdf.

38 Robert Pondiscio, "There Are No Shortcuts: Mending the Rift between Content Knowledge and Deeper Learning," in *Knowledge at the Core: Don Hirsch, Core Knowledge, and the Future of the Common Core*, ed. Chester E. Finn Jr. and Michael J. Petrilli (Washington, D.C.: Thomas B. Fordham Institute, 2014), pp. 48–62, http://edexcellence.net/publications/knowledge-at-the-core-don-hirsch-core-knowledge-and-the-future-of-the-common-core.

39 National Civic Literacy Board, "Enlightened Citizenship: How Civic Knowledge Trumps a College Degree in Promoting Active Civic Engagement," Intercollegiate Studies Institute, February 2011, http://www.americancivicliteracy.org/report/pdf/02-22-11/civic_literacy_report_11.pdf.

40 Robert Pondiscio, "A Missed Opportunity for Common Core," Thomas B. Fordham Institute, July 2, 2014, http://edexcellence.net/articles/a-missed-opportunity-for-common-core.

41 "Teachers' Views on the Common Core State Standards One Year Later," 2014 Common Core Update, *Primary Sources*, 3rd ed., Scholastic and the Bill and Melinda Gates Foundation, http://www.scholastic.com/primarysources/teachers-on-the-common-core.htm.

42 Michael B. Henderson, Paul E. Peterson, and Martin R. West, "The 2015 EdNext Poll on School Reform," *Education Next*, Winter 2016, http://educationnext.org/2015-ednext-poll-school-reform-opt-out-common-core-unions/.

43 Moriah Balingit and Donna St. George, "Is It Becoming Too Hard to Fail? Schools Are Shifting toward No-Zero Grading Policies," *Washington Post*, July 5, 2016, https://www.washingtonpost.com/local/education/is-it-becoming-too-hard-to-fail-schools-are-shifting-toward-no-zero-grading-policies/2016/07/05/3c464f5e-3cb0-11e6-80bc-d0671ifd2125_story.html.

CHAPTER 3 – CONTROL

1 Arne Duncan, "Beyond the Bubble Tests: The Next Generation of Assessments," Secretary Arne Duncan's Remarks to State Leaders at Achieve's American Diploma Project Leadership Team Meeting, September 2, 2010, http://www.ed.gov/news/speeches/

beyond-bubble-tests-next-generation-assessments-secretary-arne-duncans-remarks-state-leaders-achieves-american-diploma-project-leadership-team-meeting.

2   Ashley Jochim and Patrick McGuinn, "The Politics of the Common Core Assessments," *Education Next*, Fall 2016, http://educationnext.org/the-politics-of-common-core-assessments-parcc-smarter-balanced/.

3   Kyle Olson, "Union Prez: We're Flying the 'Common Core' Plane As We're Building It," *Town Hall*, June 27, 2013, http://townhall.com/columnists/kyleolson/2013/06/27/union-prez-were-flying-the-common-core-plane-as-were-building-it-n1627318.

4   Liz Bowie, "Teachers Complain about Access to New Curriculum," *Baltimore Sun*, September 23, 2013, http://articles.baltimoresun.com/2013-09-23/news/bs-md-co-common-core-20130918_1_elementary-teachers-curriculum-school-system.

5   StateImpact Ohio, "OFT President Says Teachers Are Still Adjusting to the Common Core," IdeaStream, October 21, 2013, https://stateimpact.npr.org/ohio/2013/10/21/oft-president-says-teachers-are-still-adjusting-to-the-common-core/.

6   Diane Stark Rentner and Nancy Kober, "Common Core State Standards in 2014: Curriculum and Professional Development at the District Level," Center on Education Policy, October 29, 2014, pp. 2, 10, http://www.cep-dc.org/displayDocument.cfm?DocumentID=441.

7   Ashley Bateman, "Feds May Raise Phone Taxes to Fund Common Core Test-Taking," *Heartlander* (Heartland Institute), July 13, 2013, http://news.heartland.org/newspaper-article/2013/07/13/feds-may-raise-phone-taxes-fund-common-core-test-taking.

8   Diane Stark Rentner and Nancy Kober, "Common Core State Standards in 2014: District Implementation of Consortia-Developed Assessments," Center on Education Policy, October 30, 2014, p. 2, http://cep-dc.org/displayDocument.cfm?DocumentID=442%20.

9   Bateman, "Feds May Raise Phone Taxes to Fund Common Core Test-Taking."

10 Dian Schaffhauser, "E-Rate Reform at Hand as FCC Pledges $2 Billion More for Wireless Broadband," *THE Journal*, February 4, 2014, http://thejournal.com/articles/2014/02/04/e-rate-reform-at-hand-at-fcc-pledges-2-billion-more-for-wireless-broadband.aspx.

11 AccountabilityWorks, "National Cost of Aligning States and Localities to the Common Core Standards," Pioneer Institute and American Principles Project White Paper no. 82, February 2012, http://pioneerinstitute.org/download/national-cost-of-aligning-states-and-localities-to-the-common-core-standards/.

12 Schaffhauser, "E-Rate Reform at Hand as FCC Pledges $2 Billion More for Wireless Broadband."

13 Jane Robbins, "E-Rate Is Another Failed Big Government Program, Why Not Double Down?" *The Pulse 2016*, September 2, 2016, http://thepulse2016.com/jane-robbins/2016/09/02/e-rate-is-another-failed-big-government-program-why-not-double-down/.

14 Bob Schaeffer, "Computerized School Exam Problems in Two-Thirds of States," FairTest, April 13, 2016, http://www.fairtest.org/computerized-school-exam-problems-twothirds-states.

15 Bob Schaeffer, "Computerized Testing Problems – Chronology," FairTest, June 14, 2016, http://fairtest.org/computerized-testing-problems-chronology.

16 Duncan, "Beyond the Bubble Tests."

17 American Psychological Association, "Standards for Educational and Psychological Testing," http://www.apa.org/science/programs/testing/standards.aspx; American Psychological Association, "Appropriate Use of High-Stakes Testing in Our Nation's Schools," http://www.apa.org/pubs/info/brochures/testing.aspx.

18 Valerie Strauss, "Alice in PARCCland: Does 'Validity Study' Really Prove the Common Core Test Is Valid?" *Washington Post*, May 27, 2016, https://www.washingtonpost.com/news/answer-sheet/wp/2016/05/27/alice-in-parccland-does-validity-study-really-prove-the-common-core-test-is-valid/.

19 "Dr. Gary Thompson's $100,000 Reward for SAGE Common Core Validity Test Reports," Common Core: Education without Representation, March 24, 2015, https://whatiscommoncore.wordpress.com/2015/03/24/dr-gary-thompsons-100000-reward-for-sage-common-core-test-validity-reports/.

20 Leslie Harris O'Hanlon, "Schools Test-Drive Common Core," Digital Directions, *Education Week*, July 11, 2013, http://www.edweek.org/dd/articles/2013/06/12/03commoncore.h06.html.

21 Mercedes Schneider, "Smarter Balanced: Lacking Smarts; Precariously Balanced," *Deutsch29*, November 21, 2014, https://deutsch29.wordpress.com/2014/11/21/smarter-balanced-lacking-smarts-precariously-balanced/.

22 Ibid.

23 Valerie Strauss, "Bill Gates: 'It would be great if our education stuff worked but…',", *Washington Post*, September 27, 2013, https://www.washingtonpost.com/news/answer-sheet/wp/2013/09/27/bill-gates-it-would-be-great-if-our-education-stuff-worked-but/.

24 Anne Gassel, "SBAC Tests Show No Validity or Reliability," Missouri Education Watchdog, February 6, 2015, http://missourieducationwatchdog.com/sbac-tests-show-no-validity-or-reliability/.

25 Mercedes Schneider, "PARCC Technical Advisor Says PARCC Is an 'Evolving Enterprise,'" *Deutsch29*, May 26, 2015, https://deutsch29.wordpress.com/2015/05/26/parcc-technical-advisor-says-parcc-is-an-evolving-enterprise/.

26 Katharine Beals, "Math Problems of the Week: Common Core–Inspired Explanations Requirements," *Out in Left Field* blog, June 23, 2016, http://oilf.blogspot.com/2016/06/math-problems-of-week-common-core_23.html.

27 Katharine Beals, "Math Problems of the Week: Common Core–Inspired Open-Ended Test Questions," *Out in Left Field* blog, May 20, 2016, http://oilf.blogspot.com/2016/05/math-problems-of-week-common-core_20.html.

28 Wayne Bishop, "Does Common Core Add Up for California's Math Students?" *San Gabriel Valley Tribune*, September 2, 2016, http://www.sgvtribune.com/opinion/20160902/does-common-core-add-up-for-californias-math-students-guest-commentary.

29 Leonard Medlock, "EdSurge Talks Common Core Assessments with SmarterBalanced's Tony Alpert," *EdSurge*, December 18, 2012, https://www.edsurge.com/n/2012-12-18-edsurge-talks-common-core-assessment-with-smarterbalanced-s-tony-alpert.

30 Catherine Gewertz, "Testing Group Scales Back Performance Items," *Education Week*, November 30, 2012, http://www.edweek.org/ew/articles/2012/11/30/13tests.h32.html.

31 Mark McQuillan, Richard P. Phelps, and Sandra Stotsky, "How PARCC's False Rigor Stunts the Academic Growth of All Students," Pioneer Institute White Paper no. 35,

October 2016, p. 18, http://www.uaedreform.org/wp-content/uploads/How-PARCCs-False-Rigor-Stunts-the-Academic-Growth-of-All-Students.pdf.

32   Sandra Stotsky, "Testing Limits," *Academic Questions*, August 1, 2016, pp. 9, 10.

33   Lisa Hansel, "Reading Test Developers Call Knowledge a Source of Bias," Core Knowledge Blog, October 1, 2014, http://blog.coreknowledge.org/2014/10/01/reading-test-developers-call-knowledge-a-source-of-bias/.

34   Catherine Gewertz, "U.S. Ed. Dept. Issues Guidance on 'Double-Testing' Flexibility," *Education Week*, September 17, 2013, http://blogs.edweek.org/edweek/curriculum/2013/09/us_ed_department_issues_guidan.html.

35   Michele McNeil, "Common Core Field Tests Gain Foothold in States," *Education Week*, March 4, 2014, http://www.edweek.org/ew/articles/2014/03/05/23waiver.h33.html.

36   John Fensterwald, "What's Next for Standardized Testing in California?" *EdSource*, October 22, 2013, https://edsource.org/2013/whats-next-for-standardized-testing-in-california/40454.

37   Motoko Rich, "States Given a Reprieve on Ratings of Teachers," *New York Times*, August 21, 2014, http://www.nytimes.com/2014/08/22/education/education-secretary-allows-reprieve-on-test-based-teacher-ratings.html?_r=0.

38   Cooperative Agreement between the U.S. Department of Education and the Partnership for Assessment of Readiness of [*sic*] College and Careers, January 7, 2011, p. 10, http://www2.ed.gov/programs/racetothetop-assessment/parcc-cooperative-agreement.pdf; Cooperative Agreement between the U.S. Department of Education and the Smarter Balanced Assessment Consortium and the State of Washington (fiscal agent), January 7, 2011, p. 10, http://www2.ed.gov/programs/racetothetop-assessment/sbac-cooperative-agreement.pdf.

39   Will Estrada and Katie Tipton, "The Dawning Database: Does the Common Core Lead to National Data Collection?" HSLDA, September 10, 2013, http://www.hslda.org/docs/news/2013/201309100.asp?src=CR.

40   Emmett McGroarty, Joy Pullmann, and Jane Robbins, "Cogs in the Machine: Big Data, Common Core, and National Testing," Pioneer Institute White Paper no. 114, May 2014, http://pioneerinstitute.org/download/cogs-in-the-machine-big-data-common-core-and-national-testing/.

41   National Education Data Model, "Religious Affiliation," National Center for Education Statistics, http://nces.ed.gov/forum/datamodel/eiebrowser/techview.aspx?instance=religiousAffiliation; and "Bus Route," http://nces.ed.gov/forum/datamodel/eiebrowser/techview.aspx?instance=busRoute; both accessed September 10, 2016.

42   Joy Pullmann, "Education Department Helps Leak Students' Personal Data," *Heartlander* (Heartland Institute), March 23, 2013, http://news.heartland.org/editorial/2013/03/23/education-department-helps-leak-students-personal-data.

43   Mary Madden, "Privacy and Cybersecurity: Key Findings from Pew Research," Pew Research, January 16, 2015, http://www.pewresearch.org/key-data-points/privacy/.

44   Victor Nava, "Protect Students from Corporate Data-Mining in the Classroom," *National Review Online*, June 30, 2015, http://www2.nationalreview.com/article/420506/protect-students-corporate-data-mining-classroom-victor-nava.

45   U.S. Department of Education, "College- and Career-Ready Standards," http://www.ed.gov/k-12reforms/standards.

46   Estrada and Tipton, "The Dawning Database."

47   Cooperative Agreement between the U.S. Department of Education and the Partnership for Assessment of Readiness of [sic] College and Careers, January 7, 2011, pp. 191, 192, http://www2.ed.gov/programs/racetothetop-assessment/parcc-cooperative-agreement.pdf.

48   Ibid., p. 223.

49   Washington State, on behalf of the SMARTER Balanced Assessment Consortium, Race to the Top Assessment Program Application for New Grants, June 10, 2010, p. 100, archived at https://web.archive.org/web/20121105183632/http://www.smarterbalanced.org/wordpress/wp-content/uploads/2011/12/Smarter-Balanced-RttT-Application.pdf.

50   Ibid., p. 142.

51   Michael Farris, "My Conversation with the Leader of the Common Core," HSLDA, July 29, 2013, http://www.hslda.org/docs/news/2013/201307290.asp.

52   McGroarty, Pullmann, and Robbins, "Cogs in the Machine," pp. 20–21, 44.

53   Joshua Bleiberg and Darrell M. West, "Using Standards to Make Big Data Analytics Work," TechTank, Brookings Institution Blogs, March 7, 2014, http://www.brookings.edu/blogs/techtank/posts/2014/03/06-common-core-standards-big-data-bleiberg-west.

54   Shawn Bay speaking at Education Datapalooza 2012, The White House, https://www.youtube.com/watch?t=604&v=9RIgKRNzC9U.

55   Nicole Shechtman et al., *Promoting Grit, Tenacity, and Perseverance: Critical Factors for Success in the 21st Century*, Office of Educational Technology, U.S. Department of Education, February 2013, pp. v, 6, http://pgbovine.net/OET-Draft-Grit-Report-2-17-13.pdf.

56   The Gordon Commission, "A Statement Concerning Public Policy," p. 13, http://www.edweek.org/media/gordonpublicpolicy.pdf.

57   Washington State, on behalf of the SMARTER Balanced Assessment Consortium, Race to the Top Assessment Program Application for New Grants, p. 45.

58   Ibid., p. 88n.

59   ACT, "Engage Teacher Edition User's Guide," August 2012, p. 2, archived at https://web.archive.org/web/20150907211022/http://www.act.org/engage/pdf/teacher_user_guide.pdf.

60   Valerie Strauss, "U.S. Government to Collect Data on 'Grit' Level of Students," *Washington Post*, July 11, 2015, http://www.washingtonpost.com/blogs/answer-sheet/wp/2015/07/11/u-s-government-to-collect-data-on-grit-levels-of-students/.

61   Sarah Sparks, "'Nation's Report Card' to Gather Data on Grit, Mindset," *Education Week*, June 2, 2015, http://www.edweek.org/ew/articles/2015/06/03/nations-report-card-to-gather-data-on.html.

62   Joy Pullmann, "Tennessee to Create 'Safe Spaces' in K–12 Schools," *The Federalist*, August 8, 2016, http://thefederalist.com/2016/08/08/tennessee-to-create-safe-spaces-in-k-12-schools/.

63   Michelle Malkin, "Look Who's Data-Mining Your Toddler," October 9, 2014, http://michellemalkin.com/2014/10/09/look-whos-data-mining-your-toddlers/.

64 Shechtman et al., *Promoting Grit, Tenacity, and Perseverance*, p. 44.

65 McGroarty, Pullmann, and Robbins, "Cogs in the Machine," pp. 24–25.

66 Privacy Rights Clearinghouse, Chronology of Data Breaches, http://www.privacy rights.org/data-breach/new.

67 Karen Gray, "Dad Told Seeing State's Records on His Kids Will Cost Him $10 Grand," *Nevada Journal*, April 24, 2014, http://nevadajournal.com/2014/04/24/dad-told-seeing-states-records-his-kids-will-cost-him-10-grand/.

68 Paul E. Peterson and Martin R. West, "Public Supports Testing, Opposes Opt-Out, Opposes Federal Intervention," *Education Next*, July 28, 2015, http://educationnext.org/public-supports-testing-opposes-opt-opposes-federal-intervention/.

69 Paul DiPerna, *2015 Schooling in America Survey: Perspectives on School Choice, Common Core, and Standardized Testing*, Polling Paper no. 24, Friedman Foundation for Educational Choice, June 2015, pp. 58, 60–61, http://www.edchoice.org/wp-content/uploads/2015/07/SIA-Poll-Full-Report-WEB-6-29-15.pdf.

70 Joan Richardson et al., "Why School? Americans Speak Out on Education Goals, Standards, Priorities, and Funding," 48th Annual PDK Poll of the Public's Attitudes toward the Public Schools, September 2016, p. 22, http://pdkpoll2015.pdkintl.org/wp-content/uploads/2016/08/pdkpoll48_2016.pdf.

71 U.S. Department of Education, ESEA Flexibility, update June 7, 2012, pp. 2–3, http://www2.ed.gov/policy/eseaflex/approved-requests/flexrequest.doc.

72 Andy Smarick, "The Disappointing but Completely Predictable Results from SIG," Thomas B. Fordham Institute, November 19, 2012, http://edexcellence.net/commentary/education-gadfly-daily/flypaper/2012/the-disappointing-but-completely-predictable-results-from-SIG.html.

73 Valerie Strauss, "High-Stakes Testing Protests Spreading," *Washington Post*, May 30, 2012, https://www.washingtonpost.com/blogs/answer-sheet/post/high-stakes-testing-protests-spreading/2012/05/30/gJQA6OQXoU_blog.html; Massachusetts Statement against High-Stakes Standardized Testing, http://matestingstatement.wordpress.com/statement/.

74 Craig S. Semon, "Tantasqua Says Parents Can Opt Children Out of PARCC Tests," *Telegram* (Worcester, Mass.), March 18, 2014, http://www.telegram.com/article/20140318/NEWS/303189839/1160/SPECIALSECTIONS04&source=rss?flv=1.

75 Scott O'Connell, "Education Official: Students Can't Be Forced to Take PARCC," *Medway*, March 20, 2014, http://medway.wickedlocal.com/article/20140320/NEWS/140329703.

76 Dale R. Erquiaga, Superintendent of Public Instruction, Guidance Memorandum #13–02, U.S. Department of Education, November 1, 2013, https://docs.google.com/file/d/0B6tD9ZDQMNs2azZDOHNCc1FIRGc/edit.

77 Oren Pizmony-Levy and Nancy Green Saraisky, "Who Opts Out and Why?" Teachers College Columbia University, August 2016, p. 5, https://www.tc.columbia.edu/media/news/docs/Opt_Out_National-Survey----FINAL-FULL-REPORT.pdf.

78 Lolly Bowean, "Parents Blast CPS for Questioning Students about Not Taking State Tests," *Chicago Tribune*, March 26, 2014, http://articles.chicagotribune.com/2014-03-26/

news/chi-parents-blast-cps-for-questioning-students-about-not-taking-state-tests-2014
0326_1_cps-officials-isat-chicago-teachers-union.

79 Susan Greene, "Opting Out: Skipping State Testing Gains Momentum, Including among the Children of Teachers," *Colorado Independent*, March 24, 2014, http://www.coloradoindependent.com/146615/opting-out.

80 Anthony Cody, "Chicago Children Who Opt Out Face Pressure," Living in Dialogue, *Education Week* Teacher Blogs, March 9, 2014, http://blogs.edweek.org/teachers/living-in-dialogue/2014/03/chicago_children_who_opt_out_f.html.

81 Nicholas Garcia, "Denver Releases New Opt-Out Guidance for Schools after Parent Conflict," *Chalkbeat*, Colorado, March 13, 2014, http://co.chalkbeat.org/2014/03/13/denver-to-release-new-opt-out-guidance-after-parent-conflict/.

82 Diane Brooks, "These Seattle Teachers Boycotted Standardized Testing – and Sparked a Nationwide Movement," *Truthout*, March 18, 2014, http://www.truth-out.org/news/item/22539-these-seattle-teachers-boycotted-standardized-testing-and-sparked-a-nationwide-movement.

83 Joey Garrison, "More Nashville Parents Opt Kids Out of Testing," *Tennessean*, March 25, 2014, http://www.tennessean.com/story/news/education/2014/03/24/nashville-parents-opt-kids-testing/6850305/.

84 Nick McCrea, "Testing Opt-Out Movement, Common Core Pushback Hit Maine Legislature," *Bangor Daily News*, May 11, 2015, http://bangordailynews.com/2015/05/11/news/state/testing-opt-out-movement-common-core-pushback-hit-maine-legislature/.

85 Erin Richards, "As Wisconsin's New Badger Exam Rolls Out, Parents Opting Kids Out," *Milwaukee Journal-Sentinel*, April 20, 2015, http://archive.jsonline.com/news/education/as-wisconsins-new-badger-exam-rolls-out-parents-opting-kids-out-b99483487z1-3007 15501.html.

86 Leslie Brody, "Opt-Outs Persist as Exams Begin across New York," *Wall Street Journal*, April 5, 2016, http://www.wsj.com/articles/opt-outs-persist-as-exams-begin-across-new-york-1459903965.

87 Pizmony-Levy and Saraisky, "Who Opts Out and Why?" p. 6.

88 Elizabeth A. Harris, "20% of New York State Students Opted Out of Standardized Tests This Year," *New York Times*, August 12, 2015, http://www.nytimes.com/2015/08/13/nyregion/new-york-state-students-standardized-tests.html?_r=0.

89 Kate Taylor, "New York Schools with Many Opting Out of Tests May Be Penalized," *New York Times*, August 13, 2015, http://www.nytimes.com/2015/08/14/nyregion/new-york-schools-with-many-opting-out-of-tests-may-be-penalized.html.

90 Stephanie Aragon, Julie Rowland, and Micah Anne Wixom, "Assessment Opt-Out Policies: State Responses to Parent Pushback," Education Trends, Education Commission of the States, February 2015, http://www.ecs.org/clearinghouse/01/17/68/11768.pdf.

91 Patrick Wall, "As Opt-Out Numbers Grow, Arne Duncan Says Feds May Have to Step In," *Chalkbeat*, New York, April 21, 2015, http://ny.chalkbeat.org/2015/04/21/as-opt-out-numbers-grow-arne-duncan-says-feds-may-have-to-step-in/; "A Conversation with Sec. Arne Duncan," EWA National Seminar, Chicago, April 21, 2015, http://www.ewa.org/video/conversation-sec-arne-duncan.

92 Valerie Strauss, "New Rules, Old Fight: Critics Say U.S. Proposals on Implementing Education Law Are Heavy Handed," *Washington Post*, May 26, 2016, https://www.washingtonpost.com/news/answer-sheet/wp/2016/05/26/new-rules-old-fight-critics-say-u-s-proposals-on-implementing-education-law-are-heavy-handed/.

93 U.S. Department of Education, Elementary and Secondary Education Act of 1965, As Amended by the Every Student Succeeds Act, Accountability and State Plans, Proposed Rule, Section 200.15, *Federal Register*, vol. 81, no. 104 (May 31, 2016), p. 34548, https://www.federalregister.gov/articles/2016/05/31/2016-12451/elementary-and-secondary-education-act-of-1965-as-amended-by-the-every-student-succeeds#h-28.

94 Shane Vander Hart, "More Parents Indicate They Will Refuse the Test," *Truth in American Education* blog, July 11, 2016, http://truthinamericaneducation.com/common-core-assessments/parents-indicate-will-refuse-test/.

95 Chad Aldeman, "Politicians Couldn't Agree on a 'Common' Yardstick for Schools. Statisticians Created One Anyway," *Education Next*, September 16, 2015, http://educationnext.org/politicians-couldnt-agree-on-a-common-yardstick-for-schools-statisticians-created-one-anyway/.

96 National Assessment of Educational Progress, "Mapping State Proficiency Standards," National Center for Educational Statistics, July 1, 2016, http://nces.ed.gov/nationsreportcard/studies/statemapping/.

97 Peter Behuniak, "Maintaining the Validity of the National Assessment of Educational Progress in a Common Core Based Environment," National Center for Education Statistics, August 2015, p. 2, http://www.air.org/sites/default/files/Validity-NAEP-Common-Core-Environment-March-2015.pdf.

98 Julie Rowland Woods, "State Summative Assessments: 2015–16 School Year," 50-State Review, Education Commission of the States, November 2015, http://www.ecs.org/ec-content/uploads/12141.pdf. This table lists Massachusetts as a member of PARCC, which it left in November 2015.

99 Mercedes Schneider, "In Attempting to Save Itself, PARCC Now Offers 'Testing Options,'" *Deutsch29*, November 12, 2015, https://deutsch29.wordpress.com/2015/11/12/in-attempting-to-save-itself-parcc-now-offers-testing-options/.

100 Author's calculation using K–12 population data from the National Center for Education Statistics and the data on consortia participants in Woods, "State Summative Assessments: 2015–16 School Year."

101 Paul E. Peterson and Matthew Ackerman, "States Raise Proficiency Standards in Math and Reading," *Education Next*, Summer 2015, http://educationnext.org/states-raise-proficiency-standards-math-reading/; Joy Resmovits, "States Still Differ Dramatically in Their Academic Expectations, Study Finds," *Huffington Post*, July 9, 2015, http://www.huffingtonpost.com/2015/07/09/mapping-the-naep_n_7757414.html.

102 Gautham Nagesh, "Education Secretary Says Schools Have Been Lying to Children and Parents," *The Hill*, August 29, 2010, http://thehill.com/blogs/blog-briefing-room/news/116255-duncan-says-schools-have-been-lying-to-children-parents.

103 Laura Moser, "Ohio Kids Are Doing Better at Common Core Tests (but Only Because Ohio Defines 'Better' Creatively)," *Slate*, October 8, 2015, http://www.slate.com/blogs/schooled/2015/10/08/ohio_s_creative_common_core_definitions_are_undermining_

the_national_education.html; Emma Brown, "Another State Redefines 'Proficiency' on Common Core Tests, Inflating Performance," *Washington Post*, October 12, 2015, https://www.washingtonpost.com/news/education/wp/2015/10/12/another-state-redefines-proficiency-on-common-core-tests-inflating-performance/.

104 Motoko Rich, "Test Scores under Common Core Show That 'Proficient' Varies by State," *New York Times*, October 6, 2015, http://www.nytimes.com/2015/10/07/us/test-scores-under-common-core-show-that-proficient-varies-by-state.html.

105 Duncan, "Beyond the Bubble Tests."

106 Diane Rado, "State Superintendent Letter Warns Schools to Brace for PARCC Results," *Chicago Tribune*, September 14, 2015, http://www.chicagotribune.com/ct-parcc-results-letter-met-20150914-story.html.

107 John Mooney, "NJ Education Department Gears Up for Release of PARCC Test Scores," *NJSpotlight*, October 9, 2015, http://www.njspotlight.com/stories/15/10/08/nj-education-department-gears-up-for-release-of-parcc-test-scores/.

108 Ellen Ciurczak, "Where Are Those State Test Scores?" *Hattiesburg American*, September 26, 2015, http://www.hattiesburgamerican.com/story/news/education/2015/09/26/test-scores/72907032/.

109 Richard Chang, "Company Fails to Return Test Scores for 200,000 Nevada Students," *THE Journal*, August 19, 2016, https://thejournal.com/articles/2016/08/19/company-fails-to-return-test-scores-for-200000-nevada-students.aspx.

110 Ann Marie Awad, "Year Two of Common Core Tests Still Not Enough to See Trends in Colorado," KUNC, August 11, 2016, http://www.kunc.org/post/year-two-common-core-tests-still-not-enough-see-trends-colorado#stream/0.

111 Lori Higgins and Kristi Tanner, "Why Michigan M-STEP Results Are Cause for Concern," *Detroit Free Press*, August 30, 2016, http://www.freep.com/story/news/education/2016/08/30/mstep-michigan-exam-results-released/89541644/.

112 Duncan, "Beyond the Bubble Tests."

113 Marissa Horn, "State School Board to Release New PARCC Exam Results in Late Fall with Lower Scores Expected," *MarylandReporter.com*, September 22, 2015, http://marylandreporter.com/2015/09/22/state-school-board-to-release-new-parcc-exam-results-in-late-fall-with-lower-scores-expected/.

114 Bonnie Bolden, "Scuffle for PARCC Data Continues," *News Star*/KLFY, October 9, 2015, http://klfy.com/2015/10/09/scuffle-for-parcc-data-continues/.

115 Duncan, "Beyond the Bubble Tests."

116 Arne Duncan, "After Ten Years, It's Time for a New NCLB," Op-Ed, *Washington Post*, January 8, 2012, http://www.ed.gov/blog/2012/01/after-10-years-it%E2%80%99s-time-for-a-new-nclb/.

117 Partnership for Assessment of Readiness for College and Careers, "States Working Together to Build the Next Generation of Assessments: Key Messages," http://www.achieve.org/files/PARCC-KeyMessages-Final.pdf.

118 Remarks by Bill Gates to the National Conference of State Legislatures, July 21, 2009, Bill and Melinda Gates Foundation, http://www.gatesfoundation.org/media-center/speeches/2009/07/bill-gates-national-conference-of-state-legislatures-ncsl.

CHAPTER 4 – BACKLASH

1 Sheila Byrd Carmichael et al., *The State of State Standards – and the Common Core – in 2010*, Thomas B. Fordham Institute, July 2010, p. 6, http://edex.s3-us-west-2.amazon aws.com/publication/pdfs/SOSSandCC2010_FullReportFINAL_8.pdf.

2 Author's calculations using Fordham ELA ratings and National Center for Education Statistics enrollment data for fall 2010 from Table 203.20, "Enrollment in public elementary and secondary schools, by region, state, and jurisdiction," *Digest of Education Statistics*, 2013, https://nces.ed.gov/programs/digest/d13/tables/dt13_203.20.asp.

3 Jim Stergios, "Don't Count Your Chickens before Elections: Tony Bennett's Defeat in Indiana," *Schoolhouse Blog*, Pioneer Institute, November 8, 2012, http://pioneerinstitute. org/blog/dont-count-your-chickens-before-elections-tony-bennetts-defeat-in-indiana/.

4 Rick Hess, "How Sec. Duncan Helped the Teachers Unions Take Out Tony Bennett," Rick Hess Straight Up, *Education Week*, November 7, 2012, http://blogs.edweek.org/ edweek/rick_hess_straight_up/2012/11/how_sec_duncan_helped_the_teachers_uni ons_take_out_tony_bennett.html.

5 Andrew Rotherham, "Morning After," *Eduwonk*, November 7, 2012, http://www.edu-wonk.com/2012/11/morning-after.html.

6 National Conference of State Legislatures, 2016 Legislative Overview: Career and College Readiness Standards Legislation, http://www.ccrslegislation.info/.

7 Valerie Strauss, "Arne Duncan: 'White Suburban Moms' Upset That Common Core Shows Their Kids Aren't 'Brilliant,'" *Washington Post*, November 16, 2013, https://www. washingtonpost.com/blogs/answer-sheet/wp/2013/11/16/arne-duncan-white-surburban-moms-upset-that-common-core-shows-their-kids-arent-brilliant/.

8 Motoko Rich, "Bill to Alter Bush-Era Education Law Gives States More Room," *New York Times*, June 4, 2013, http://www.nytimes.com/2013/06/05/education/harkin-schools-legislation.html?_r=0.

9 Arne Duncan, "Duncan Pushes Back on Attacks on Common Core Standards," Remarks at the American Society of News Editors Annual Convention, Washington, D.C., June 25, 2013, U.S. Department of Education, http://www.ed.gov/news/speeches/ duncan-pushes-back-attacks-common-core-standards.

10 Stephanie Simon, "Navigating the Wild World of Ed Tech – LAUSD's John Deasy to Step Down? – Duncan, Hess Clash on Common Core," Morning Education, *Politico*, October 25, 2013, http://www.politico.com/tipsheets/morning-education/2013/10/navi gating-the-wild-world-of-ed-tech-lausds-john-deasy-to-step-down-duncan-hess-clash-on-common-core-012023. Full video here: https://www.youtube.com/watch?v=kyjZ_ A2faWU.

11 Alyson Klein, "What Do Common Core and the Fiscal Fight Have in Common?" Politics K-12, *Education Week*, October 21, 2013, http://blogs.edweek.org/edweek/campaign-k-12/2013/10/what_do_common_core_and_the_fi.html.

12 Lyndsey Layton, "Common Core State Standards in English Spark War over Words," *Washington Post*, December 2, 2012, https://www.washingtonpost.com/local/education/ common-core-state-standards-in-english-spark-war-over-words/2012/12/02/4a9701b0-38e1-11e2-8a97-363b0f9a0ab3_story.html.

13   Diane Ravitch, "Why I Cannot Support the Common Core Standards," *Diane Ravitch's Blog*, February 26, 2013, http://dianeravitch.net/2013/02/26/why-i-cannot-support-the-common-core-standards/.

14   List of University of Chicago Laboratory Schools People, Wikipedia, https://en.wikipedia.org/wiki/List_of_University_of_Chicago_Laboratory_Schools_people.

15   Chicago Lab administers standardized tests in a few grade levels, but they are not the same tests the state uses: "Assessment and Standardized Testing," University of Chicago Laboratory Schools website, accessed September 2, 2016, https://www.ucls.uchicago.edu/program/assessment-standardized-testing.

16   Jay Mathews, "What Our Most Famous Private School Is Hiding," *Washington Post*, May 11, 2014, https://www.washingtonpost.com/local/education/what-our-most-famous-private-school-is-hiding/2014/05/11/41bbe350-d6e0-11e3-8a78-8fe50322a72c_story.html?tid=a_inl.

17   Valerie Strauss, "Open Letter to Arne Duncan from Chicago Teachers," *Washington Post*, February 15, 2013, https://www.washingtonpost.com/blogs/answer-sheet/wp/2013/02/15/open-letter-to-arne-duncan-from-chicago-teachers/.

18   Bill Ayers, "An Open Letter to President Obama," *GOOD Magazine*, November 8, 2012, http://magazine.good.is/articles/an-open-letter-to-president-obama-from-bill-ayers.

19   Jim Siegel, "Common Core Foe in Ohio House Runs into Opposition," *Columbus Dispatch*, October 10, 2013, www.dispatch.com/content/stories/local/2013/10/10/common-core-foe-runs-into-opposition.html.

20   Bryan Ekvall, "Common Bore: WI Democrats Question Education Standards Hearings," Wisconsin WatchDog, October 4, 2013, http://watchdog.org/109293/wr-common-bore/.

21   Brian Smith, "Michigan's Common Core Vote Delayed a Day as New Resolution Introduced in House," *MLive*, September 25, 2013, http://www.mlive.com/education/index.ssf/2013/09/common_core_vote_delayed_as_ne.html.

22   Jack Markell, "The Tea Party Is Wrong on the Common Core Curriculum," *Washington Post*, June 9, 2013, www.washingtonpost.com/opinions/the-tea-party-is-wrong-on-the-common-core-curriculum/2013/06/09/b7c85ae4-ceba-11e2-8845-d970ccb04497_story.html.

23   Grace Tatter, "Haslam Says the Future of Common Core Now Rests with Educators, not Elected Officials," *Chalkbeat*, Tennessee, November 15, 2015, http://tn.chalkbeat.org/2015/11/05/haslam-says-the-future-of-common-core-now-rests-with-educators-not-elected-officials/#.Vj5DSberTBQ.

24   Frederick M. Hess and Kelsey Hamilton, "The Real Deal with Public Opinion and the Common Core," American Enterprise Institute, October 19, 2015, https://www.aei.org/publication/the-real-deal-with-public-opinion-and-the-common-core/.

25   "NY Parents React in Fury to Common Core and Testing; Commissioner John King Disengages," New York Public School Parents, October 12, 2013, http://nycpublicschoolparents.blogspot.com/2013/10/commission-john-king-disengages-from.html.

26   Anthony Cody, "Parents Voice Concerns about Common Core: NY Dept of Ed Cancels Further Hearings," Living in Dialogue, *Education Week*, October 12, 2013, http://blogs.edweek.org/teachers/living-in-dialogue/2013/10/parents_voice_concerns_about_c.html.

27   Ron Matus, "Jeb Bush to Common Core Critics: Drop the Conspiracy Theories," *redefineED*, October 17, 2013, http://www.redefinedonline.org/2013/10/jeb-bush-common-core-critics-drop-conspiracy-theories/.

28   Ibid.

29   "Senate President Gaetz Follows Bush Playbook and Mocks Citizen Concerns on Federal Interference with Standards and Tests," Florida Stop Common Core Coalition, November 2013, http://www.flstopcccoalition.org/news/2013-11/senate-president-gaetz-follows-bush-playbook-mocks-citizen-concerns-federal-interference-with-standards-tests.htm.

30   "Parent Arrested from Common Core Meeting in Baltimore County, MD," video posted September 20, 2013, https://www.youtube.com/watch?v=XEQmUnisDEM.

31   Richard P. Phelps and R. James Milgram, "The Revenge of K-12: How Common Core and the New SAT Lower College Standards in the U.S.," Social Science Research Network, September 6, 2014, http://papers.ssrn.com/sol3/papers.cfm?abstract_id=2519889.

32   "Exclusive Video: School Supers Have Parent Arrested from Common Core Meeting," *Examiner*, September 20, 2013, http://www.examiner.com/article/exclusive-video-school-supers-have-parent-arrested-from-common-core-meeting.

33   Liz Bowie, "Charges Dropped against Maryland Parent Who Spoke against Common Core Standards," *Baltimore Sun*, September 23, 2013, http://articles.baltimoresun.com/2013-09-23/news/bs-md-arrest-small-20130923_1_common-core-standards-police-officer-new-standards.

34   "Raw Video: Man Arrested at Gilford School Board Meeting," posted May 5, 2014, https://www.youtube.com/watch?time_continue=80&v=OsbS9JD7Pvw.

35   Neal McCluskey, "Cutting Federal Aid for K-12 Education," Downsizing the Federal Government, April 21, 2016, http://www.downsizinggovernment.org/education/k-12-education-subsidies#_edn41.

36   Idaho State Department of Education, "Department, Idahoans for Excellence in Education Partner to Launch Awareness Campaign," Press Release, January 13, 2014, http://origin.library.constantcontact.com/download/get/file/1110622789246-65/CORE+STANDARDS+MEDIA+CAMPAIGN+PRESS+RELEASE.pdf.

37   Alex Leary, "Jeb Bush's Common Core Problem Strikes at Heart of His Foundation," *Tampa Bay Times*, May 30, 2014, http://www.tampabay.com/news/politics/stateroundup/jeb-bushs-common-core-problem-strikes-at-heart-of-his-foundation/2182256.

38   Connecticut State Department of Education, Request for Proposals: Academic Office Support in the Area of Communication of the Common Core Standards in Connecticut, November 19, 2013, http://www.sde.ct.gov/sde/lib/sde/pdf/rfp/rfp14sde0011rfp_academic_office_common_core_state_standards_communications_111913.pdf.

39   Christopher Keating and Kathleen Megan, "Malloy's Decision to Slow Down Education Reform: Was It Politically Motivated?" *Hartford Courant*, January 29, 2014, http://www.courant.com/news/politics/hc-malloy-teachers-election-0130-20140129,0,6114252.story.

40   Arizona Public Engagement Task Force, "Arizona's Common Core Standards Communications Toolkit," September 5, 2012, http://www.azed.gov/azcommoncore/files/2012/09/az-common-core-standards-commuinications-toolkit.pdf.

41 Cathryn Cremo, "Campaign to Defend Standards in Arizona Schools," *AZ Central*, January 27, 2014, http://www.azcentral.com/news/politics/articles/20140123arizona-campaign-defend-standards-schools.html.

42 Sandra Stotsky, "Wanted: Internationally Benchmarked Standards in English, Mathematics, and Science," Pioneer Institute, May 8, 2013, http://pioneerinstitute.org/news/wanted-internationally-benchmarked-standards-in-english-mathematics-and-science/.

43 Michael J. Petrilli and Brandon L. Wright, "America's Mediocre Test Scores: Education Crisis or Poverty Crisis?" *Education Next*, Winter 2016, http://educationnext.org/americas-mediocre-test-scores-education-poverty-crisis/.

44 State of Nevada, Common Core State Standards Steering Committee, Final Report to the Governor, December 23, 2013, http://www.nevada.edu/ir/Documents/CCSS_Initiatives/Steering_Committee_Report_Final.pdf.

45 Nevada Department of Education, "Nevada Academic Content Standards: Communications Action Plan," CCSS Appendix D, November 2013, p. 2, archived at https://web.archive.org/web/20150907084907/http://www.nevada.edu/ir/Documents/CCSS_Initiatives/CCSS_Appendices.pdf.

46 Steven Miller and Kyle Gillis, "Government Paying Union Employees Millions a Year to Perform Union Work," *Nevada Journal*, February 9, 2012, http://nevadajournal.com/2012/02/09/governments-paying-union-employees-millions-year-perform-union-work/.

47 PARCC, Race to the Top Assessment Program Application for New Grants, U.S. Department of Education, May 28, 2010, pp. 311, 313, http://www2.ed.gov/programs/racetothetop-assessment/rtta2010parcc.pdf.

48 Smarter Balanced, Race to the Top Assessment Program Application for New Grants, U.S. Department of Education, June 15, 2010, p. 143, http://www2.ed.gov/programs/racetothetop-assessment/rtta2010smarterbalanced.pdf.

49 State of Washington, Office of Superintendent of Public Instruction, Request for Proposals, Smarter Balanced RFP no. 21, p. 12, http://www.k12.wa.us/RFP/pubdocs/SBAC-RFP21-2013/SBACRFP21StandardSettingFINAL3-103013.pdf.

50 PARCC, "Frequently Asked Questions: PARCC Educator Leader Cadres," February 2012, p. 2, archived at https://web.archive.org/web/20120413115718/http://www.azed.gov/standards-development-assessment/files/2012/02/parcc-elc-faq_020912.pdf.

51 National Math and Science Initiative, *Transforming Math and Science Education*, Annual Report 2012, http://nms.org/Portals/0/Docs/2012 Annual Report.pdf.

52 National Math and Science Initiative, Funders/Donors, http://nms.org/AboutNMSI/FundersDonors.aspx.

53 "NMSI Awarded $4.3 Million Contract to Lead PARCC Educator Leader Cadres," PR Newswire, June 18, 2012, http://www.prnewswire.com/news-releases/nmsi-awarded-43-million-contract-to-lead-parcc-educator-leader-cadres-159403165.html.

54 PARCC, "Frequently Asked Questions: PARCC Educator Leader Cadres," p. 1.

55 Ibid.

56 "PARCC Educator Leader Cadres Roles," PARCC, June 2012, archived at https://web.archive.org/web/20141014230313/http://education.ohio.gov/getattachment/Topics/Testing/Next-Generation-Assessments/Ohio%E2%80%99s-Educator-Leader-Cadre-Team/ELC-Roles.pdf.aspx.

57   Partnership for Assessment of Readiness for College and Careers, *Race to the Top Assessment*, Year Two Report, U.S. Department of Education, May 2013, pp. 13, 16, 28, http://www2.ed.gov/programs/racetothetop-assessment/reports/parcc-year-2.pdf.

58   PARCC, "Engaging Teacher Voices: How Your State Can Leverage PARCC's Educator Leader Cadres to Build and Maintain Support for Key Reforms," January 2014, https://currikicdn.s3-us-west-2.amazonaws.com/resourcefiles/55c312212bd0a.pdf.

59   Smarter Balanced Assessment Consortium, *Race to the Top Assessment*, Year Two Report, U.S. Department of Education, May 2013, p. 23, http://www2.ed.gov/programs/racetothetop-assessment/reports/sbac-year-2.pdf.

60   State of Washington, Office of Superintendent of Public Instruction, Request for Proposals, Smarter Balanced RFP no. 21, p. 5.

61   Ibid., p. 21.

62   Helios Education Foundation, "College and Career Readiness," Annual Report 2014, http://annualreport.helios.org/2014/community-impact/college-career-readiness/.

63   The Weiss Associates LLC website still lists the Schusterman Family Foundation as a client and says that Weiss "Support[s] the grantmaking done by the Schusterman Foundation on common core implementation, collaborate[s] with other funders on these issues, and actively share[s] knowledge and expertise to maximize impact." Website accessed September 8, 2016, http://weissassociates.net/schusterman.

64   Education Strategy Group, "Matt Gandal, Founder and President," webpage accessed September 3, 2016, http://www.edstrategy.org/#!matt-gandal/i6qn9.

65   Rick Wagner, "LIFT, Which Includes Kingsport and Sullivan School Leaders, Urges Moving Forward with Common Core in Tennessee," *Kingsport Times-News*, March 18, 2014, http://e-edition.timesnews.net/article/9074591/lift-which-includes-kingsport-and-sullivan-school-leaders-urges-moving-forward-with-common-core-in-tennessee.

66   Douglas N. Harris and Tim R. Sass, "Teacher Training, Teacher Quality, and Student Achievement," Heartland Institute Policy Document, March 7, 2008, https://www.heartland.org/policy-documents/teacher-training-teacher-quality-and-student-achievement; Marcus A. Winters, "Let a Thousand Teachers Bloom," *Weekly Standard*, March 19, 2012, http://www.weeklystandard.com/articles/let-thousand-teachers-bloom_633428.html.

67   Drew H. Gotimer, "Teacher Quality in a Changing Policy Landscape," Heartland Institute Policy Document, December 10, 2007, http://news.heartland.org/policy-documents/teacher-quality-changing-policy-landscape.

68   Matthew C. Makel and Jonathan A. Plucker, "Facts Are More Important than Novelty: Replication in the Education Sciences," *Educational Researcher*, vol. 20, no. 10 (2014), p. 1, http://edr.sagepub.com/content/early/2014/07/23/0013189X14545513.full.pdf+html?ijkey=w5mrNxPVD8zSg&keytype=ref&siteid=spedr.

69   Indiana State Board of Education, Standards Evaluation Process and Team Selection Methodology, http://www.in.gov/sboe/files/XI_F_Standards_Evaluation_Process_Update.pdf.

70   Heather Crossin, "Indiana Common Core Review: A Stacked Deck?" Hoosiers Against Common Core, February 12, 2014, http://hoosiersagainstcommoncore.com/indiana-common-core-review-stacked-deck/.

71   Common Core State Standards for English Language Arts: Reading: Literature: Grade 2,

standard 9 (RL.2.9). With thanks to Terrence O. Moore for his analysis in *The Story-Killers: A Common-Sense Case Against the Common Core* (CreateSpace Independent Publishing Platform, 2013), p. 67.

72 Sandra Stotsky and Ze'ev Wurman, "Common Core's Standards Still Don't Make the Grade: Why Massachusetts and California Must Regain Control over Their Academic Destinies," Pioneer Institute White Paper no. 65, July 2010, p. 7, http://pioneerinsti tute.org/download/common-cores-standards-still-dont-make-the-grade/.

73 Ibid, p. 8.

74 Ibid, p. 10.

75 Kathleen Porter-Magee, "When 1 + 1 = 0: Why the New Indiana Draft Standards Don't Make the Grade," Thomas B. Fordham Institute, February 27, 2014, http://www.edex cellence.net/commentary/education-gadfly-daily/common-core-watch/when-1-1-0-why-the-new-indiana-draft-standards.

76 Erin Tuttle, "Side by Side Comparison of Indiana's 'New' K-12 Math Standards," Hoosiers Against Common Core, March 6, 2014, http://hoosiersagainstcommoncore.com/side-side-comparison-indianas-new-k-12-math-standards/.

77 Indiana Chamber, "New Draft K-12 Standards Are Good Starting Point, but Areas of Concern Exist," Press Release, February 25, 2014, http://www.indianachamber.com/index.php/media-center/press-releases/2885-new-draft-k-12-standards-are-good-starting-point-but-areas-of-concern-exist.

78 Terrence O. Moore, "Will Indiana Cut-and-Past Its Way to Common Core Serfdom?" Library of Law and Liberty, March 7, 2014, http://www.libertylawsite.org/2014/03/07/will-indiana-cut-and-paste-its-way-to-common-core-serfdom/.

79 Indiana Education Roundtable, "Partners," archived at https://web.archive.org/web/20110314233628/http://www.in.gov/edroundtable/2329.htm.

80 Elle Moxley, "Indiana Education Officials Release Final Draft of Proposed Academic Standards," StateImpact Indiana, April 15, 2014, http://indianapublicmedia.org/state impact/2014/04/15/indiana-education-officials-release-final-draft-proposed-academic-standards/.

81 J. E. Funk, "Three Common Core Executive Orders Change Little," *Heartlander* (Heartland Institute), October 16, 2013, http://news.heartland.org/newspaper-article/2013/10/21/three-common-core-executive-orders-change-little.

82 "FL DOE Officials Continue Plans to Implement Common Core Even Before Comment Period Ends," Florida Stop Common Core Coalition, November 2013, http://www.flstopcccoalition.org/news/2013-11/fl-doe-officials-continue-plans-implement-common-core-even-before-comment-period-ends.htm.

83 John Huppenthal, "Why Common Core Needs a New Name," *AZCentral*, September 23, 2013, http://archive.azcentral.com/opinions/articles/20130923common-core-needs-new-name-huppenthal.html.

84 State Names for Common Core Standards, *Washington Post*, http://apps.washington post.com/g/documents/local/state-names-for-common-core-standards/1228/.

85 Nate Robson, "Experts: State's Draft of Education Standards Has Many Flaws," Oklahoma Watch, October 6, 2015, http://oklahomawatch.org/2015/10/06/top-education-standards-for-oklahoma-just-talk-says-expert/.

86   Andrew Ujifusa, "Traction Limited in Rolling Back Common Core," *Education Week*, April 21, 2015, http://www.edweek.org/ew/articles/2015/04/22/traction-limited-in-rolling-back-common-core.html.

CHAPTER 5 – DISILLUSIONMENT

1   Kathryn M. Doherty and Sandi Jacobs, *State of the States 2015: Evaluating Teaching, Leading, and Learning*, National Council on Teacher Quality, November 2015, p. 2, http://www.nctq.org/dmsView/StateofStates2015.

2   Tim Walker, "NEA Survey: Nearly Half of Teachers Consider Leaving Profession Due to Standardized Testing," *NEA Today*, November 2, 2014, http://neatoday.org/2014/11/02/nea-survey-nearly-half-of-teachers-consider-leaving-profession-due-to-standardized-testing-2/.

3   Ulrich Boser and Robert Hanna, "In the Quest to Improve Schools, Have Teachers Been Stripped of Their Autonomy?" Center for American Progress, January 21, 2014, http://www.americanprogress.org/issues/education/report/2014/01/21/81062/in-the-quest-to-improve-schools-have-teachers-been-stripped-of-their-autonomy/.

4   Emmanuel Felton, "More Teachers Are Souring on Common Core, Finds One Survey," *Hechinger Report*, October 3, 2014, http://hechingerreport.org/teachers-souring-common-core-finds-one-survey/.

5   Barbara Hollingsworth, "Poll: Only 40% of Teachers Support Common Core," CNS News, August 18, 2015, http://www.cnsnews.com/news/article/barbara-hollingsworth/poll-only-40-teachers-support-common-core.

6   Paul E. Peterson et al., "Ten-Year Trends in Public Opinion from the EdNext Poll: Common Core and Vouchers Down, but Many Other Reforms Still Popular," *Education Next*, Winter 2017, http://educationnext.org/ten-year-trends-in-public-opinion-from-ednext-poll-2016-survey/.

7   Jason Richwine and Andrew G. Biggs, "Assessing the Compensation of Public-School Teachers," Heritage Foundation Center for Data Analysis, Report no. 11–03 on Education, November 11, 2011, http://www.heritage.org/research/reports/2011/10/assessing-the-compensation-of-public-school-teachers,

8   Nat Malkus, "On Declining Teacher Autonomy: It's for Real," *AEIdeas*, American Enterprise Institute blog, December 8, 2015, http://www.aei.org/publication/on-declining-teacher-autonomy-its-for-real/.

9   National Center for Education Statistics, School and Staffing Survey, 2012–13, Table 7, http://nces.ed.gov/surveys/sass/tables/TFS1213_2014077_fin_007.asp.

10 National Center for Education Statistics, State Education Data Profiles, 2013–14, http://nces.ed.gov/programs/stateprofiles/sresult.asp?mode=short&s1=36.

11 New York State Education Department, "State Education Department Releases Spring 2016 Grades 3–8 ELA and Math Assessment Results," July 29, 2016, http://www.nysed.gov/news/2016/state-education-department-releases-spring-2016-grades-3-8-ela-and-math-assessment-results.

12 Steve Farkas and Ann Duffett, *Cracks in the Ivory Tower? The Views of Education Professors*

ca. 2010, Thomas B. Fordham Institute, September 2010, p. 9, http://edex.s3-us-west-2.
amazonaws.com/publication/pdfs/Cracks%20In%20The%20Ivory%20Tower%20-%20
Sept%202010_8.pdf.

13 Diane Ravitch, *Left Back: A Century of Failed School Reforms* (New York: Simon & Schuster, 2000), p. 337.

14 Ibid., p. 340.

15 Ibid., p. 414.

16 See E. D. Hirsch, *The Schools We Need, and Why We Don't Have Them* (New York: Anchor Books, 2010); and Sandra Stotsky, *An Empty Curriculum: The Need to Reform Teacher Licensing Regulation and Tests* (Lanham, Md.: Rowman & Littlefield, 2015).

17 E. D. Hirsch Jr., *Why Knowledge Matters: Rescuing Our Children from Failed Education Theories* (Cambridge, Mass.: Harvard Education Press, 2016), especially Chapter 2 and Appendix I.

18 Michael Q. McShane, "If Teachers Are More Risk-Averse than Other Professionals, What Does That Mean for Education Reform?" American Enterprise Institute, October 21, 2014, http://www.aei.org/publication/teachers-risk-averse-professionals-mean-education-reform/.

19 Brad McQueen, "AZ Dept. of Education to Anti–Common Core Teacher: 'What a F*cktard'!" *Arizona Daily Independent,* June 30, 2014, https://arizonadailyindependent.com/2014/06/30/az-dept-of-education-to-anti-common-core-teacher-what-a-fcktard/.

20 Starlee Coleman, "Ariz. Department of Education Retaliates against Tucson Teacher Opposed to Common Core," Goldwater Institute, December 2, 2014, http://goldwater institute.org/en/work/topics/constitutional-rights/free-speech/ariz-department-of-education-retaliates-against-tu/.

CHAPTER 6 — ALTERNATIVES

1 Gene Edward Veith Jr. and Andrew Kern, *Classical Education: The Movement Sweeping America* (Capital Research Center, 2001), https://www.circeinstitute.org/store/books/classical-education-movement-sweeping-america-new-edition.

2 William Gonch, "Being Part of a People: Ridgeview Classical Schools and Civic Education," AEI Program on American Citizenship, Policy Brief no. 16, February 2014, p. 2, http://www.aei.org/wp-content/uploads/2014/02/-citizenship-policy-brief-no-16-february-2014_131324367600.pdf.

3 E. D. Hirsch Jr., *Why Knowledge Matters: Rescuing Our Children from Failed Education Theories* (Cambridge, Mass.: Harvard Education Press, 2016), p. 103.

4 Sandra Stotsky, *An Empty Curriculum: The Need to Reform Teacher Licensing Regulation and Tests* (Lanham, Md.: Rowman & Littlefield, 2015).

5 Raj Chetty, John Friedman, and Jonah Rockoff, "Measuring the Impacts of Teachers II: Teacher Value-Added and Student Outcomes in Adulthood," National Bureau of Economic Research, Working Paper 19424, September 2013, pp. 1–2, http://www.nber.org/papers/w19424.pdf.

6 Tom Loveless, "How Well Are American Students Learning?" The 2012 Brown Center

Report on American Education, Brookings Institution, February 2012, http://www.brookings.edu/~/media/newsletters/0216_brown_education_loveless.pdf; Eric Hanushek, "Is the Common Core Just a Distraction?" *Education Next*, May 9, 2012, http://educationnext.org/is-the-common-core-just-a-distraction/; Jay P. Greene, "One Size Fits None," *Arkansas Democrat-Gazette*, April 11, 2010: http://jaypgreene.com/2010/04/11/sandy-and-jay-on-national-standards/.

7   Luman Strong, *A Psychonometric Study of the Teacher Work-Autonomy Scale with a Sample of U.S. Teachers*, Doctoral Dissertation, Lehigh University, November 2011 (published 2012), http://preserve.lehigh.edu/cgi/viewcontent.cgi?article=2092&context=etd.

8   National Alliance for Public Charter Schools, data for Colorado, 2014–15, http://www.publiccharters.org/get-the-facts/law-database/states/CO.

9   Frederick Hess and Olivia Meeks, "School Boards Circa 2010: Governance in the Accountability Era," National School Boards Association, Thomas B. Fordham Institute, and Iowa School Boards Foundation, 2010, pp. 13, 21, http://files.eric.ed.gov/fulltext/ED515849.pdf.

10   Frederick M. Hess and Max C. Eden, "The Most Interesting School District in America?" *National Review*, September 17, 2013, http://www.nationalreview.com/article/358627/most-interesting-school-district-america-frederick-m-hess-max-c-eden.

11   "Interactive Map: The Best and Worst School Districts in America (and How They Rate against the World)," *The Atlantic*, http://www.theatlantic.com/misc/global-report-card.

12   Ibid.

13   U.S. Small Business Administration, Office of Advocacy, from data provided by the U.S. Census Bureau, Business Dynamics Statistics, "Establishments and employment by employment size of firm," author's calculations from cells B39 and M39, accessed September 5, 2016, https://www.sba.gov/sites/default/files/files/bds_firmsize.xlsx.

14   Todd Engdahl, "Douglas County School Board Resolution Opposes Common Core," *Chalkbeat*, Colorado, July 17, 2013, http://co.chalkbeat.org/2013/07/17/douglas-county-school-board-resolution-opposes-common-core/#.VdZG2flViko.

15   Colorado House Bill 1202 (2014), LegiScan, http://legiscan.com/CO/text/HB1202/2014.

16   Todd Engdahl, "Colorado Hustles to Roll Out New Testing Plan," *Chalkbeat*, Colorado, June 23, 2015, http://co.chalkbeat.org/2015/06/23/colorado-hustles-to-roll-out-new-testing-plan/#.VdZDdPlViko.

17   Rocky Heights Middle School Lip Dub, video posted May 29, 2013, https://www.youtube.com/watch?v=MsdHPDeHtlE.

18   Mark Keierleber, "Inside New Hampshire's Innovative Push to Change the Way We Test Students," *The 74*, August 10, 2015, https://www.the74million.org/article/inside-new-hampshires-innovative-push-to-change-the-way-we-test-students.

19   On this subject, see Thomas J. Kane, Douglas E. Rockoff, and Thomas O. Staiger, "What Does Certification Tell Us about Teacher Effectiveness? Evidence from New York City," NBER Working Paper no. 12155, National Bureau of Economic Research, April 2006, http://www.nber.org/papers/w12155.

20   Chris Neal, "Common Core Spurs Increase in Homeschooling in North Carolina," *Heartlander* (Heartland Institute), November 6, 2014, http://news.heartland.org/newspaper-article/2014/11/06/common-core-spurs-increase-homeschooling-north-carolina.

21 Swapna Venugopal Ramaswamy, "Out of the Classroom: Parents Explore Home-Schooling," *USA Today*, November 9, 2014, http://www.usatoday.com/story/news/nation/2014/11/09/parents-explore-home-schooling/18771967/.

22 "Home Schooling Up 9.6 Percent in State," July 19, 2015, *Herald Tribune*, http://www.heraldtribune.com/article/20150719/ARTICLE/150719667?tc=ar.

23 Patrick Anderson, "Common Core: Math Standards Prompt Parents to Push Back," *Argus Leader* (Sioux Falls), November 9, 2014, http://www.argusleader.com/story/news/education/2014/11/08/math-standards-prompt-parents-push-back/18748943/.

24 Perry Chiaramonte, "Opposition to Common Core Spurs Jump in Homeschooling," Fox News, November 30, 2014, http://www.foxnews.com/us/2014/11/30/opposition-to-common-core-spurs-jump-in-homeschooling/.

CHAPTER 7 – REBOOT

1 Robert Holland, *Not with My Child You Don't: A Citizen's Guide to Eradicating OBE and Restoring Education* (Richmond, Va.: Chesapeake Capital Services, 1995).

2 Continental Congress, "An Ordinance for the Governance of the Territory of the United States North West of the River Ohio," July 13, 1787, *Journals of the Continental Congress*, vol. 32, p. 334, U.S. Library of Congress, https://memory.loc.gov/cgi-bin/am page?collId=lljc&fileName=032/lljc032.db&recNum=343. The other elements of the "organic laws" as designated by the 43rd Congress (1873-1875) are the Declaration of Independence, the Articles of Confederation, and the Constitution of the United States.

3 John Dewey, "The Influence of Darwin on Philosophy," 1910, available at https://www.brocku.ca/MeadProject/Dewey/Dewey_1910b/Dewey_1910_01.html.

4 Diane Ravitch, *Left Back: A Century of Failed School Reforms* (New York: Simon & Schuster, 2000), p. 459.

5 Ibid., p. 335.

6 Ibid., pp. 163-64.

7 Ibid., p. 165.

8 Ibid., p. 97.

9 Ibid., p. 164.

10 Dana Goldstein, "Bill de Blasio's Pre-K Crusade," *The Atlantic*, September 7, 2016, http://www.theatlantic.com/education/archive/2016/09/bill-de-blasios-prek-crusade/498830/.

11 Williamson M. Evers, "Implementing Standards and Testing," in *What Lies Ahead for America's Children and Their Schools*, ed. Chester E. Finn Jr. and Richard Sousa (Stanford, Calif.: Hoover Institution Press, 2014), p. 89, available at http://www.hoover.org/sites/default/files/research/docs/finnsousa_whatliesahead_final_ch6.pdf.

12 Gene Edward Veith Jr. and Andrew Kern, *Classical Education: The Movement Sweeping America* (Capital Research Center, 2015), pp. 2-3.

13 See E. D. Hirsch, *The Schools We Need, and Why We Don't Have Them* (New York: Anchor Books, 2010).

14 William Schmidt, Richard Houang, Sharif Shakrani, "International Lessons about

National Standards," Thomas B. Fordham Institute, August 2009, p. 5, http://files.eric.ed.gov/fulltext/ED506947.pdf.

15   Hirsch's seminal work on this is *Cultural Literacy: What Every American Needs to Know* (New York: Vintage Books, 1988), but he also outlines and updates the argument in *Why Knowledge Matters: Rescuing Our Children from Failed Education Theories* (Cambridge, Mass.: Harvard Education Press, 2016).

16   Diane Ravitch, *National Standards in American Education: A Citizen's Guide* (Brookings Institution, 1995), p. 40. Ravitch declared her support for national curriculum mandates in this book.

17   National Science Foundation, "A Timeline of NSF History," http://www.nsf.gov/about/history/overview-50.jsp#1950s.

18   Robert S. Eitel and Kent D. Talbert, "The Road to a National Curriculum: The Legal Aspects of the Common Core Standards, Race to the Top, and Conditional Waivers," Pioneer Institute White Paper no. 81, February 2012, p. 1, http://pioneerinstitute.org/download/the-road-to-a-national-curriculum/.

19   Evers, "Implementing Standards and Testing," pp. 89–90.

20   Michael McKeown, David Klein, and Chris Patterson, "The National Science Foundation Systemic Initiatives: How a Small Amount of Federal Money Promotes Ill-Designed Mathematics and Science Programs in K–12 and Undermines Local Control of Education," in *What's at Stake in the K–12 Standards Wars*, ed. Sandra Stotsky (New York: Peter Lang Publishing, 2000), p. 317.

21   Evers, "Implementing Standards and Testing," pp. 87–88.

22   U.S. Department of Education, "A Nation at Risk," April 1983, https://www2.ed.gov/pubs/NatAtRisk/risk.html.

23   Paul E. Peterson et al., "Ten-Year Trends in Public Opinion from the EdNext Poll: Common Core and Vouchers Down, but Many Other Reforms Still Popular," *Education Next*, Winter 2017, http://educationnext.org/ten-year-trends-in-public-opinion-from-ednext-poll-2016-survey/.

24   FairTest Examiner, "New Evidence Strengthens Claim that Testing Narrows Curriculum," FairTest, October 2007, http://www.fairtest.org/new-evidence-strengthens-claim-testing-narrows-cur/.

25   Evers, "Implementing Standards and Testing," p. 90.

26   Robert B. Schwartz and Marian A. Robinson, "Goals 2000 and the Standards Movement," Brookings Papers on Education Policy, 2000, p. 198, http://muse.jhu.edu/journals/brookings_papers_on_education_policy/v2000/2000.1schwartz.html.

27   Julie A. Miller, "Small Group's Inside Role in Goals-Setting Provides Clue to Education Policymaking," *Education Week*, March 14, 1990, http://www.edweek.org/ew/articles/1990/03/14/09300021.h09.html.

28   These efforts to implement "standards-based reform" are recounted in detail by Ravitch in *Left Back*, and by Hirsch in *The Schools We Need*. For a more concise account of progressive dominance in American education, see Heather Mac Donald, "Why Johnny's Teacher Can't Teach," *City Journal*, Spring 1998, http://www.city-journal.org/html/8_2_a1.html.

29 Schwartz and Robinson, "Goals 2000 and the Standards Movement," p. 198.

30 Evers, "Implementing Standards and Testing," p. 89.

31 Ibid.

32 Boyce Brown, "Standards-Based Education Reform in the United States since 'A Nation at Risk,'" University of Hawaii College of Education, June 1, 2009, p. 9, http://www.hawaii.edu/hepc/pdf/Reports/FINAL-History_of_Standards-Based_Education_Reform.pdf.

33 "Are We There Yet? Business, Politics, and the Long (Unfinished) Road to National Standards," Frontline, PBS, http://www.pbs.org/wgbh/pages/frontline/shows/schools/standards/bp.html.

34 Brown, "Standards-Based Education Reform in the United States since 'A Nation at Risk,'" p. 11.

35 Sandra Stotsky, "The State of Literary Study in National and State English Language Arts Standards: Why It Matters, and What Can Be Done about It," in What's at Stake in the K-12 Standards Wars, ed. Stotsky, p. 242.

36 Schwartz and Robinson, "Goals 2000 and the Standards Movement," p. 198.

37 "Are We There Yet? Business, Politics, and the Long (Unfinished) Road to National Standards."

38 Schwartz and Robinson, "Goals 2000 and the Standards Movement," p. 203.

39 Ibid., p. 206.

40 Emmett McGroarty and Jane Robbins, "Controlling Education from the Top: Why Common Core Is Bad for America," Pioneer Institute and American Principles Project White Paper no. 87, May 2012, p. 3, http://americanprinciplesproject.org/wp-content/uploads/Controlling-Education-From-the-Top-2013.pdf.

41 Remarks by President David Coleman at the College Board National Forum, Miami, October 24, 2012, https://web.archive.org/web/20121119041503/http://press.college-board.org/releases/2012/remarks-president-david-coleman-college-board-national-forum.

42 Dan Lips and Evan Feinberg, "The Administrative Burden of No Child Left Behind," Heritage Foundation, March 23, 2007, http://www.heritage.org/research/reports/2007/03/the-administrative-burden-of-no-child-left-behind.

43 Jennifer A. Marshall, Testimony before the House Education Subcommittee on Early Childhood, Elementary and Secondary Education, United States House of Representatives, March 15, 2011, pp. 3-4, http://edworkforce.house.gov/uploadedfiles/03.15.11_marshall.pdf.

44 Ravitch, Left Back, p. 459.

45 Joan Richardson et al., "Why School? Americans Speak Out on Education Goals, Standards, Priorities, and Funding," 48th Annual PDK Poll of the Public's Attitudes toward the Public Schools, September 2016, p. 22, http://pdkpoll2015.pdkintl.org/wp-content/uploads/2016/08/pdkpoll48_2016.pdf.

46 Ze'ev Wurman, "Re-Assess Common Core and Consider Reversing Direction," Breitbart, December 25, 2015, http://www.breitbart.com/big-government/2015/12/25/re-assess-common-core-and-consider-reversing-direction/.

47 Scott Jaschik, "ACT Scores Drop as More Take Test," *Inside Higher Ed*, August 24, 2016, https://www.insidehighered.com/news/2016/08/24/average-act-scores-drop-more-people-take-test.

48 Caralee J. Adams, "2015 SAT, ACT Scores Suggest Many Students Aren't College-Ready," *Education Week*, September 9, 2015, http://www.edweek.org/ew/articles/2015/09/09/2015-sat-act-scores-suggest-many-students.html.

49 Nick Anderson, "Why Your New SAT Score Is Not as Strong as You Think It Is," *Washington Post*, May 11, 2016, https://www.washingtonpost.com/news/grade-point/wp/2016/05/11/why-your-new-sat-score-is-not-as-strong-as-you-think-it-is/.

50 Matthew 13:24–30, King James Version.

51 Paul diPerna, 2015 *Schooling in America Survey: Perspectives on School Choice, Common Core, and Standardized Testing*, Friedman Foundation for Educational Choice, Polling Paper no. 24, June 2015, p. 23, http://www.edchoice.org/wp-content/uploads/2015/07/SIA-Poll-Full-Report-WEB-6-29-15.pdf#page=10.

52 Author's calculations using data from Table 206.10, *Digest of Education Statistics, 2014*, 50th Edition, National Center for Education Statistics and U.S. Department of Education (April 2016), p. 130, http://nces.ed.gov/pubs2016/2016006.pdf.

53 Friedman Foundation for Educational Choice, *The ABCs of School Choice: The Comprehensive Guide to Every Private School Choice Program in America*, 2016 Edition, p. 4, http://www.edchoice.org/wp-content/uploads/2016/02/2016-ABCs-WEB-2.pdf.

54 See Howard Fuller's *No Struggle, No Progress: A Warrior's Life from Black Power to Education Reform* (Milwaukee: Marquette University Press, 2014), and the corresponding series on the left's support for school choice at the *redefinED* blog: https://www.redefinedonline.org/common-ground/.

55 Peterson et al., "Ten-Year Trends in Public Opinion from the EdNext Poll," http://educationnext.org/ten-year-trends-in-public-opinion-from-ednext-poll-2016-survey/.

56 Greg Forster, "A Win-Win Solution: The Empirical Evidence on School Choice," 4th Edition, Friedman Foundation for Educational Choice, May 2016, pp. 1–2, http://www.edchoice.org/wp-content/uploads/2016/05/A-Win-Win-Solution-The-Empirical-Evidence-on-School-Choice.pdf.

57 Brian Kisida, Patrick J. Wolf, and Evan Rhinesmith, "Views from Private Schools: Attitudes about School Choice Programs in Three States," American Enterprise Institute, January 2015, pp. 14–19, https://www.aei.org/wp-content/uploads/2015/01/Views-from-Private-Schools-7.pdf; Jay P. Greene, "Does Regulation Protect Kids and Improve Outcomes from Choice?" *Jay P. Greene's Blog*, October 5, 2015, http://jaypgreene.com/2015/10/05/does-regulation-protect-kids-and-improves-outcomes-from-choice/.

INDEX

Index

Index

A NOTE ON THE TYPE

THE EDUCATION INVASION *has been set in Mentor, a family of types designed by Michael Harvey for Monotype. An accomplished designer of typefaces, Harvey began his career as a lettercarver, working as an assistant to Reynolds Stone in the late 1950s. He designed his first dustjackets in 1957, moving on to create his first type, Zephyr, in 1964, at which time he also began teaching lettering arts. Awarded an MBE for services to art in 2001, Harvey remained a prolific designer and continued to carve inscriptional lettering until his death in 2013. With their meticulous drawing and strong calligraphic underpinnings, the Mentor types attest to Harvey's close study of the work of Eric Gill and Hermann Zapf, yet the stylish letterforms - especially those of the vibrant italic - reveal the designer's singular and deeply personl approach to the art of letter design.*

DESIGN AND COMPOSITION BY CARL W. SCARBROUGH